MW00439662

The Negritude Moment

Cinquantenaire du 1er Congrès international des écrivains et artistes noirs
50th Anniversary of the 1st International Congress of Black Writers and Artists
1956-2006

THE NEGRITUDE MOMENT

Explorations in Francophone African
and Caribbean Literature and Thought

F. ABIOLA IRELE

AFRICA WORLD PRESS

TRENTON | LONDON | CAPE TOWN | NAIROBI | ADDIS ABABA | ASMARA | IBADAN | NEW DELHI

AFRICA WORLD PRESS
541 West Ingham Avenue | Suite B
Trenton, New Jersey 08638

Copyright © 2011 F. Abiola Irele
First Printing 2011

All rights reserved. No part of this publication may be reproduced, stored in a retrieval system or transmitted in any form or by any means electronic, mechanical, photocopying, recording or otherwise without the prior written permission of the publisher.

Book and cover design: Saverance Publishing Services

Library of Congress Cataloging-in-Publication Data

Irele, Abiola.
  The negritude moment : explorations in francophone African and Caribbean literature and thought / F. Abiola Irele.
    p. cm.
  Includes bibliographical references and index.
    ISBN 1-59221-797-4 (hard cover : alk. paper) -- ISBN 1-59221-798-2 (pbk. : alk. paper) 1. Negritude (Literary movement)--Africa, French-speaking. 2. Negritude (Literary movement)--Caribbean area. 3. African literature (French)--Black authors--History and criticism. 4. Caribbean literature (French)--Black authors--History and criticism. 5. Blacks--Africa, French-speaking--Intellectual life. 6. Blacks--Caribbean area--Intellectual life. 7. Blacks in literature. I. Title.
  PQ3980.5.I74 2010
                       840.9'896--dc22

Ils ont prévalu leurs yeux intacts au plus fragile
de l'image impardonnable
de la vision mémorable du monde à bâtir
de la fraternité qui ne saurait manquer de venir
quoique malhabile

They have preserved their eyes intact beyond the
most fragile shade of the unpardonable image
for the memorable vision of a world to build
for the fraternity that cannot fail to come
albeit unsteady.

AIMÉ CÉSAIRE, « VAMPIRE LIMINAIRE »

In memory of Francis Jaiyeola Irele

An exemplary father

TABLE OF CONTENTS

INTRODUCTION

Some years ago, Paul Johnson, the English liberal turned conservative, noted with evident relish that colonialism was back.[1] One might retort that the anti-colonial response is back too. The case of Negritude is perhaps the most evident sign of this dialectic of contemporary history. Indeed, the concept of Negritude has never, it seems, been more relevant than in this our postcolonial age. From being a theme of marginal interest in the academy, Negritude has been looming ever larger within the space of contemporary critical thought and discourse. This has happened largely through the considerable interest the work of Frantz Fanon has generated, as attested by the numerous studies devoted to him in recent years. There is something of a paradox involved here, for despite his testimony of the impact of Aimé Césaire on the moral condition and growth of consciousness in the French Caribbean, and the evidence in all his work of the enduring influence of Césaire on his own thought and sensibility, Fanon himself maintained an ironic distance towards Negritude, especially in its formulation by Léopold Sédar Senghor. But it is undeniable that the dynamics involved in the collective response to the peculiar circumstances of the Black historical experience and the racial awakening represented by Negritude provided the original impulse to the tremendous effort of reflection on the Black condition to which Fanon's work bears witness. What we might call the-Black-existence-in-history thus forms the determining context of Fanon's work and remained the constant reference of his thought, even as this widened to embrace other issues that were not immediately focused on the Black/ White dialectic.

It is in this connection, in which the Negritude movement served as a necessary background to any consideration of Fanon's work, that the concept has come to assume a new prominence and thus acquired a certain importance for postcolonial theory and criticism. There is indeed a real sense in which the focus on Fanon lent a strong current to postcolonial discourse, despite the ambivalent character of his relation to the Negritude movement.[2] And as a recently completed study by Donna Jones demonstrates, this current has led to the recognition of the vital relation between the structure of thought that informs its expressive modes and one of the most influential directions of modern thought.[3]

Recent events in France related to immigration and the problematic situation of the Black community in that country have also facilitated the growth of a new Black racial consciousness and thus reinforced the intellectual trend evoked above. As is well known, the steady influx of Africans and Arabs into France since the end of the colonial period, leading to the growth of substantial immigrant communities all over the country, has posed a major challenge to the conception held by the French of their national identity. It has given rise not merely to an interrogative process on the question but also to a new form of French nationalism, animated notably by Jean-Marie Le Pen, whose conservative and right wing position on many questions, in particular the racial composition of the French nation, reflects a political and ideological response to the immigrant presence.[4]

In these circumstances, the re-emergence of race as an issue in French life and politics has, as it were. lent a new lease of life to Negritude as an idea and as an attitude on the part of a younger generation of Francophone Blacks. It explains the renewed attention to the French colonial legacy that has been the object of debate in France for a time, and has continued to haunt Francophone literature and artistic production. The imaginative reconstruction of the immigrant experience in works such as Daniel Biyaoula's *L'Impasse,* and Alain Mabanckou's *Bleu-blanc-rouge* has drawn attention to the climate of social tension and racial apprehension with which Blacks have had to contend as a condition of their French sojourn.[5] It is indeed significant that the French colonial adventure itself has come under close scrutiny in films such as Ousmane Sembene's *Tyaroye*, Jean-Marie Teno's *Afrique, je te plumerai*, *La bataille d'Alger* (directed by Gillo Pontecorvo),[6] and Rachid Bouchareb's *Les Indigènes*.[7] These works provide evidence of a deep sensitiveness to the question of France's relations with its ex-colonies occasioned by the dilemmas that have attended the phenomenon of post colonial immigration.

These dilemmas form the background to the reappraisal of Negritude that can be discerned at this time in the work of the new generation of Francophone African and Black intellectuals. Where hitherto the association of Negritude with an essentialist conception of race caused it to be viewed with disfavour and suspicion—and even a certain hostility—by radical Black intellectuals, whose commitment to the cause of colonial emancipation took precedence over any form of racial or ethnic allegiance, there is apparent in the postcolonial context a new understanding of the concept of race in its relation to culture upon which the Negritude assertion was grounded. There is even more a disposition toward a fuller appreciation of the necessity for this assertion: of the acute sense felt by the older generation of the essential fragility of their place within the colonial scheme of things, and the urge to reclaim their cultural and spiritual inheritance as a means of liberation. As Wole Soyinka has remarked, the return to origins constitutes here a gesture of "racial retrieval" that forms part of a process of self-knowledge.

The essays collected here are concerned with this earlier phase of Negritude: with the moment of its emergence as a movement and its elaboration as a concept. The first two, written up from a lecture delivered at the University of Dar-es-Salaam and published in the Cambridge *Journal of Modern African Studies* in 1965 and 1966, were intended to provide general information to Anglophone readers who desired to find out about the movement and the personalities involved with it. The reach of these two essays was extended by their inclusion in the Bobbs-Merril Reprint series and their reproduction in a number of collective volumes, thus justifying my intention in writing them. These essays along with subsequent ones offer both a historical account of Negritude as a movement, and a discussion of some of the issues related to the Black experience that came to be forcefully raised in the course of its elaboration as a concept by various Francophone writers and intellectuals. The chapter entitled "The Negritude Debate" in particular considers the controversies it has generated in both Anglophone and Francophone Africa. I have also included a critical essay on the imagery of Aimé Césaire's poetry as an illustration of his exceptional powers of vision and expression, and a review essay on philosophy in postcolonial Africa which places the movement in its wider context of discourse in contemporary Africa.

The focus in these essays on the historical and sociological context of Francophone literature and thought has meant that the analytical tools available to me at the time they were written were derived largely from the sociology that was prevalent in the nineteen fifties and sixties, but I hope it will be apparent that my discussion anticipates questions relating to the Black Diaspora, Double consciousness, hybridity, the subaltern condition, and other issues that have fed into postcolonial discourse. I have endeavored in this regard to bring the bibliography up to date; thus, apart from works cited, I've added recent titles with a bearing on Francophone literature and thought, to which, as movement and concept, Negritude remains central.

Finally, it is only proper for me to avow that the idea for this volume originated with my publisher, Kassahun Checole; but for his persistence, I would not have proceeded to bring these essays together as a collection. Laurie Calhoun deserves thanks for sustained editorial work on the volume, and Ruthmarie Mitsch for previewing the essay on Aimé Césaire.

NOTES

1. Paul Johnson, 1993.

2. See Said, 1979 and 1994; Eze, 2001; Bernasconi, 2001.

3. Donna Jones, 2010.

4. The potential for conflict inherent in this situation became evident in the drama of what became known as "L'affaire des sans-papiers de Saint-Bernard," so named after the church in Paris that was occupied in the summer of 1996 by African immigrants reacting to what was perceived as harassment by French authorities. The situation was to deteroriate, as the resentment engendered by an ambient racism fuelled the series of race riots by young immigrants that shook France in 2005 and caught the attention of the world.

5. These problems are discussed in Gueye, 2001, Moudileno, 2006, and Papa Ndiaye, 2008. For a personal testimony of the hostility that Blacks are likely to encounter in France, see Diawara. 1998.

6. The screenplay was by Pontecorvo and Franco Salinas; the concept was Saadi Yacef's who approached Pontecorvo and the film took shape in a collaborative process.

7. To this list we might add Raoul Peck's *Lumumba*, though its immediate focus is on Belgian colonialism.

SOURCES

"Negritude or Black Cultural Nationalism." *Journal of Modern African Studies*, Cambridge, Vol. 3, No. 3, 1965, 321-48.

"Negritude: Literature and Ideology." *Journal of Modern African Studies*, Cambridge, Vol. 3, No. 4, 1965, 499-526.

"Negritude Revisited." *Odu: A Journal of West African Studies.* New Series, No. 5, April 1971.

"The Negritude Debate," in Albert Gérard (ed.) *European Language Writing in Sub-Saharan Africa* Vol 1. Budapest, 1986: Akademiai Kiado, pp. 379-93.

"Contemporary Thought in French-speaking Africa," in Richard Bjornson and Isaac Mowoe (eds.), *Africa and the West* Westport, CT.: Greenwood Press, 1986. 121-58.

"Essential Landscape: Image and Symbol in the Poetry of Aimé Césaire." *African Literature Today* Vol. 16 (Special Number on Poetry). James Currey Publishers, London, 1989, pp. 142-57.

"In Search of Camara Laye." *Textual Ownership in Francophone Africa*. Special Number, *Research in African Literatures*. Ed. by Alec Hargreaves. Vol 37, No 1. Spring, 2006. 110-27.

Addendum: "Philosophy and the Postcolonial Condition in Africa." *Research in African Literatures*, Vol. 35, No. 4, Winter, 2004, 160-70.

Editorial Note

As can be seen from the dates of publication, the essays reprinted in this volume span some forty years. The conventions of academic writing have changed during this period. It used to be normal practice to refer to "Man" as a universal category and therefore to employ the masculine pronoun exclusively for this term taken as its antecedent. Similarly, the word "Negro" was regularly employed to designate the Black race. I'm aware that such usage is no longer acceptable. However, it would be too time-consuming and too costly to revise the essays in order to conform to current usage. Readers will also observe that the note format is different for the various chapters. This is due to the different house styles of the journals in which they first appeared. As this does not appear to be an inconvenience, I have not deemed it necessary to make the note format uniform throughout the volume.

I ought to add finally that all translations are mine except where indicated otherwise.

CHAPTER ONE
NEGRITUDE OR BLACK
CULTURAL NATIONALISM

It is well known that nationalist movements are generally accompanied by parallel movements of ideas that make it possible for its leaders to mold a new image of the dominated people. And, as Thomas Hodgkin has shown, the need for African political movements to "justify themselves" and "to construct ideologies" has been particularly strong.[1] Nationalist movements were to a large extent founded upon emotional impulses, which imparted a distinctive tone to the intellectual clamour that went with them, and which continued to have a clear resonance after independence.

In order to understand certain aspects of African nationalism and its carry-overs, it is important to consider the fact that colonial rule was not only a political and economic affair, but that it also imposed a specific social framework for the African's experience of the world and of himself. Political domination created areas of contact between Africans and Europeans all over the continent under conditions that constantly underscored racial and cultural differences. The colonial relationship thus involved the total cultural situation, and nationalist movements were in fact efforts at cultural as well as purely political autonomy. "Although they have an economic political basis, they involve the question of a common racial and cultural heritage," observes Franklin Frazier.[2] It is in this sense that one can speak of "cultural nationalism" as a distinctive part of the liberation movements.

The only really significant expression of cultural nationalism associated with Africa—apart from small-scale local movements—is the concept of Negritude, which was developed by French-speaking Negro intellectuals. Because of its extra-African connections and implications, and because of its vigorous organization as a movement, it has developed far beyond the concept of the "African personality," which long remained more or less a catchword or simple ideological slogan,[3] whereas Negritude tended more toward a comprehensive worldview.

However, I take Negritude to mean not the philosophical idea of a Negro essence, which appears to me not only abstract but quite untenable—Léopold Sédar Senghor himself moved far away from this point of view—but rather a historical phenomenon, a social and cultural movement closely related to African nationalism. Negritude has aroused considerable controversy and inspired reactions ranging from enthusiastic partisanship to outright hostility. Nonetheless, it has been acknowledged as an important historical phenomenon, and it is as such that it may most conveniently be examined and its significance fully appreciated.

ANTECEDENTS

Negritude in fact appears as the culmination of the complete range of reactions provoked by the impact of Western civilization on the African, and of the whole complex of social and psychological factors that have formed Black people's collective experience of Western domination. Its roots thus lie deep down in the total historical experience of the Black man's contact with the White.

THE COLONIAL SITUATION

It is hardly an exaggeration to say that the advent of the European in Africa turned out to be a shattering experience for the African in more than a metaphorical sense. Although the early phase of contact was marked by an ambiguously calm relationship, the European presence in Africa developed gradually into a situation of conflict, first through the slave trade, and later with the establishment of colonial rule. African history since the arrival of the White man presents examples of violent reactions to this situation, and resistance movements—like those of Peter Lobengula in Southern Africa, and Samory Touré in what is now Guinea—form an essential part of the stock of symbols that have nourished the nationalistic strain of Negritude.

But the main interest of the historical origins of the movement lies in the *indirect* forms of resistance provoked by the colonial situation. As Georges Balandier has pointed out, the establishment of colonial rule in Africa brought with it a drastic reordering of African societies and human relations. The fact of domination, and all that this meant in the arbitrary political and social reorganization of the African communities, along with the misunderstandings that naturally followed, created "a state of latent crisis." Colonial rule also substituted new poles of reference for social organization and individual life, which were often in conflict with the established traditional pattern, and thus created a society which, in Balandier's words, "appeared to possess an essentially non-authentic character."[4] In other words, colonial rule created a state of cultural fluctuation in varying degrees all over Africa, with immense potential for tension at every level of collective and individual experience.

It is against this background that certain popular movements in Africa represent a search for new values, an attempt at readjustment; perhaps the most striking of these indirect reactions to the colonial situation have been religious. It is an objective fact that the Christian missionary was an important agent in cultural change, and his role in the introduction of new values, both voluntary and involuntary, was by no means negligible.[5] Neither is it necessary to belabor the point that Christianity was largely identified with colonial rule, as part of the cultural baggage of the colonizer.

In this light, the separatist churches in colonial Africa have been recognized as symptoms of cultural malaise and as indications of cultural readjustment.[6] But their real significance appears in their links with nationalist feeling. Again, Balandier's analysis affords an insight into the problem.[7] The main fact that takes precedence over all others is that of *domination*. Taking a cue from Gabriel d'Arboussier, who attributes to European influence "the oppression of the cultural stock" of the indigenous African—thus a double politicoeconomic and sociocultural domination—Balandier has pointed out how the separatist movements, particularly that of Simeon Kibangi in the ex-Belgian Congo, represented "a total response to a situation felt to be creative of internal 'crisis' and propitious for the maintenance of (a state of) alienation." The two main characteristics of these movements, as analyzed by Balandier, appear to be their political radicalism—a direct consequence of their schismatic attitude in religious matters, sometimes assuming the proportion of an aggressive racialism—and their syncretic messianism. On the one hand, we have a negative gesture of refusal, a denial of an imposed world order attributed to the colonizer, and the wish for a cultural *differentiation*, which gives rise to a nascent political awareness, or "nationalist consciousness in the raw state." [8] On the other hand, we have a recasting of foreign and indigenous elements into a new cultural structure, which offers new possibilities of self-expression.

These popular religious movements did not, of course, always transform into political movements. In many cases, they helped their adherents escape from the pressures of a difficult situation; indeed, some of these movements also represented forms of cultural regression.[9] But they throw into relief the cultural and psychological problems involved in the colonial situation, for the African was in most cases drawn into the cultural world of the European, but constrained to a secondary position. While he was refused acceptance as an equal by the colonizers, his life and values had come to be ruled by the norms imposed or sanctioned by the latter. He thus lived with the European in a state of symbiosis, but marked by ambiguity. The result has been described by Bronislaw Malinowski:

> Since Africans cannot share the ideals, interests, and full benefits of co-operative activities with the Whites, they naturally fall back on their own system of belief, value and sentiment. To be a mere carbon copy is not satisfactory as a substitute for all the African had initially to give up…. The African thus is forced at least spiritually to recross the first line and to reaffirm many of the tribal values abandoned at the first crossing.[10]

A particularly dramatic example of this "spiritual recrossing of the line" was the so-called Mau-Mau revolt. This largely Kikuyu nationalist rebellion was buttressed by a resort to tradition, particularly the oath, designed to counter the influence of European cultural incursion. That this was effective in its psychological purpose can be judged from this testimony of a former Mau-Mau detainee: "Afterwards in the maize, I felt exalted with a new spirit of power and strength. All my previous life seemed empty and meaningless. Even my education, of which I was so proud, appeared trivial beside this splendid and terrible force that had been given me. *I had been born again*" (emphasis added).[11]

The same instinctive falling back on tradition in the face of political domination formed a regular feature in African societies, especially among educated Africans. In the Congo, the Abako started out as a movement of cultural regroupment for the Bakongo, and the Egbe Omo Oduduwa served the same purpose for the Yoruba in Western Nigeria and was later to give birth to the Action Group, a political party founded by Obafemi Awolowo.

In short, colonial rule was felt as a shock that reverberated right down to the foundations of African society: a truly traumatic experience that could not but provoke a reaction. This has taken many forms, from makeshift individual adjustments to organized collective movements. The messianic movements presented in bold relief certain traits which were to figure in the more sophisticated reaction to colonial rule, Negritude. In other words, Negritude had a popular precedent in Africa; it can be seen as an articulation by the educated elite of sentiments that were felt and confusedly expressed by humbler folk. Balandier has, not without cause, called Negritude "the literary replica of African messianisms."[12] Nonetheless, popular movements in Africa furnish an indication of the historical and cultural origins of Negritude, although it was to receive its immediate inspiration, as well as most of its distinctive characteristics, from Black people in America.

THE BLACK DIASPORA

The starting point of Negro history in America is slavery, a reality which has determined to a large extent the nature of the global experience of Black people in the New World. The drastic character of this experience needs no underlining. What is important for our present concern is the general pattern of the Negro's reaction to his condition in America.

In the first place, this reaction took the form of organized movements of violent resistance. The history of the Negro in America has known some heroic moments, the most celebrated of which was the successful revolution under Toussaint Louverture, which gave birth in 1804 to the first Negro republic, Haiti.[13] The example itself is of direct relevance here, since Toussaint has also become a symbol in the literature, and Aimé Césaire has hailed Haiti as the cradle of the revolutionary spirit of Negritude.[14] The heroic dimensions and the universal import of these resistance movements were not lost upon the slaves themselves, as shown by the proclamation of another group of slaves—who revolted in Guadeloupe under Louis Delgrès—and which begins thus: "To the entire world, the last cry of innocence and of despair," and ends: "And you, posterity, grant a tear to our misfortunes, and we shall die content."[15] This lyrical note adopted by the desperate slaves in commenting upon their situation was to reappear in a more extended form in Negro spirituals.

Negro spirituals represent the earliest examples of Black people's indirect defense, through an art form, against the conditions of contact with the White man. The spiritual appears in this light as a direct ancestor of the Negritude poem. For the Negro slave not only offered observations on his lot, but also created a whole mechanism of defense through lyrical symbols. As Langston Hughes has pointed out, some of the spirituals, such as "Steal Away," were disguised songs of resistance.[16] Furthermore, they contain the first form of Negro religious expression: elements taken from the dominating culture of the White master were adapted to the Negro's temperament as well as reinterpreted to apply to his situation. Thus, an analogy between the history of the Jews of the Old Testament and that of the Negro slaves was struck in spirituals like "Go Down, Moses," forms in which the Negro slave's sentiment of exile found an appropriate and socially acceptable expression. This analogy survived slavery and has been developed into the idea of a Black *diaspora*, both in the popular imagination and in the intellectual movements among Black people in the Americas.

The New World Negro's sense of Africa varies considerably according to the area and the social class in which he lives, but it is undeniable that it has functioned as a potent factor of Black diaspora awareness.[17] Furthermore, the marked racial distinction of the Negro, living as a minority group in White-dominated societies, has created a differentiation of the Black population in the Americas, producing Negro subcultures throughout the continent. At one extreme lies the largely spontaneous religious syncretism of the Negro in Latin America, notably in Brazil with the *candomblé*, and in Haiti with *vodun*. At the other extreme lies the urban subculture of the Negro in the northern United States, created by the failure to complete the process of integration of the Black population. In between can be cited examples like Afro-Cuban music (the *son*, and the *rhumba*) and the "Nancy" Tales of the British West Indies.[18] Whatever the particular significance that these varied forms of Negro subculture were to have in the social context of the countries in which they are found, they kept alive in varying measures a sense of Africa, and even a myth of Africa as original, home, to which the Haitian writer Jacques Roumain has given expression in his poem "Guinea":

> It's the long road to Guinea
> No bright welcome will be made for you

In the dark land of dark men:
Under a smoky sky pierced by the cry of birds,
Around the eye of the river
The eyelashes of the trees open on a decaying light
There, there awaits you beside the water
    a quiet village,
And the hut of your fathers, and the hard ancestral
    stone where your head will rest at last.[19]

In general, it is probably safe to suppose that the presence in America of Negro subcultures composed in part of African elements, and the complementary existence of a myth of Africa among Black people, would never have assumed any kind of active significance without the impact of certain social factors. The most important of these was without doubt the caste system which followed emancipation in the United States.[20] This had the effect of stratifying U.S. society by forcing the Negro into a distinct social organization, to the extent that Booker T. Washington was able to remark that the Negro had become "a nation within a nation." Racial discrimination, which gravely limited the Negroes' opportunity for social advancement, and the various humiliations to which they were exposed, created a discontent which gave rise to various political movements. A "nationalist tradition" thus developed among Black people in the United States, which was to have a cultural parallel.[21]

The race problem, and its immediate effects on life in the United States, has made the entire Negro population conscious of its ethnic identity, and has rendered its leaders and intellectuals sensitive to the historical implications. For the caste system was maintained through an elaborate cultural myth governed mainly by the idea of the biological inferiority of the Black man.[22] It has often been argued that racial prejudice developed out of attempts to rationalize the slave trade. There is no doubt, however, that the arguments for Black inferiority were based upon an evaluation of the Negro's African origins. Melville Herskovits describes how "the myth of the Negro past" conditioned the life of the Negro in the United States:

> For though it has often been pointed out that the skin colour of the Negro makes him an all too visible mark for prejudice, it is not so well-realized that the accepted opinion of the nature of the Negro's cultural heritage is what makes him the only element in the peopling of the United States that has no operative past except in bondage.[23]

The extension of colonial conquest in Africa all through the nineteenth and the early years of the twentieth century lent weight to the idea of African and, by extension, Negro inferiority, giving rise to the imperialist ideologies embodied in Kipling's well-known slogan "the white man's burden." Greater still was the effect of these events upon the Negro population in the United States, deprived of any discernible historical tradition.

This is the background that gives a profound meaning to popular movements such as those inspired by Noble Drew Ali and Marcus Garvey. The cultural position of the Black man in the United States, though possessing its own specific characteristics, nonetheless offered certain resemblances to that of his African counterpart. He too lived in a symbiotic relationship with the White man and was likewise held in a subordinate position by the caste system. At the same time, he was, even more than the African, governed by the secondary institutions imposed or sanctioned by the Whites, especially in the fields of religion and social morality. The result resembles that observed in the case of the African, for, as Udosen Essien-Udom has remarked, "Negroes have sought to strike out for themselves in those areas of activity in which the resistance of the white society is marginal."[24] The Negro wish for independent expression found a ready springboard in those elements of Negro subculture which segregation had helped to mold into something of a definite structure, particularly the separatist religious movements.

The role of Noble Drew Ali and Marcus Garvey was to capitalize upon this latter aspect of the Negro's situation and to endow it with a historic sense derived from what had up till then remained largely a rudimentary, atavistic instinct—namely, the Negro's sense of his African origin. Garvey's "Back to Africa" movement, in particular, differed from those of others before him in that it was presented not as an escape from America, but as a national return to an original home, as a positive rather than a negative gesture. For Garvey appreciated the psychological needs of his adherents, realizing that what they hankered after was not merely political freedom but also, and more fundamentally, "freedom from contempt."[25]

Garvey's mythical revaluation of Africa had the precise function of abolishing the world order created by the White man *in the mind of the Negro*.[26] The prophetic character of Garvey's movement offered a striking similarity to African messianism. Its visionary nature, springing in part from the historic dimensions of his conception, and in part from his remoteness from Africa itself, necessarily informed his movement with a strong millenary strain, and his last directions to his followers from his Atlanta jail were characteristic:

> Look for me in the whirlwind or storm, look for me all around you, for with God's grace, I shall come and bring with me countless millions of Black slaves who have died in America and the West Indies and the millions in Africa to aid you in the fight for Liberty, Freedom, and Life.[27]

Garvey's contribution to Black awakening was twofold. He helped to crystallize the ambiguous and troubled race feeling of his followers into a definite racial consciousness that verged on racialism. He was also among the first to create a *mystique*, based on a revaluation of the African cultural heritage, as a source of inspiration to the Blacks in America and in the world.[28]

For in the early years of the twentieth century, the Black man's worth was low indeed, not only in the eyes of his White overlord, but (and as a consequence) also in his own eyes. He occupied the lowest rung of the racial hierarchy established by Western civilization. As Césaire has observed, referring to the San Domingo revolution, this was not merely a hierarchy, but even "an ontology: at the top, the white man—Being, in the full sense of the term—at the bottom, the black man...the thing, as much as to say, a nothing."[29] This was a situation which Black intellectuals were to combat with all their strength, a counteroffensive that was to infuse a passionate vigor into their movements.

PRECEDENTS

The Black population in the Western hemisphere occupied a definite cultural position, to say the least, and in the United States this position was manifestly uncomfortable. While living in the White man's society, the Black man retained an awareness of his racial differences and in some cases was forced to organize his life on a racial basis. Thus, distinctive Black currents appeared in the "mainstream" of the majority culture in some American societies.

Where this process was not accentuated by the caste system, it was often helped on by the class system which grew out of slavery. Usually the Black man, the former slave, became the peasant or the unskilled worker, and the Negro subcultures also became identified in some American societies with a definite social classification, especially in the southern United States.[30] But this combination was implicit in other areas, such as Brazil and Cuba.

Thus, even where there were no fullblown nationalist movements based on clear social grievances, there were minor manifestations of ethnic feeling. These were kept to a minimum in Brazil, for example, where racial issues were almost unknown, due to the favorable traditions that had been built up during the slave period and the consequently unproblematic racial assimilation of the population.[31] Ethnic feelings were manifested in popular and cultural movements, which were partly dictated by economic and social factors, and partly by the reaction of Black people to Brazilians' "aesthetic prejudice," as it has been called, against the Black color, distinct from racial prejudice against Black people.[32]

These movements combined a revaluation of the Black population and their subculture together with social protest. They culminated in the literature of the so-called "cannibalistic" school, which was animated mainly by radical White writers and whose misguided literary primitivism was a reaction against Christian and middle-class values. This accounts for the fact that the Negro and the native Indian were often glorified on the basis of White stereotypical conceptions of their respective cultural heritages.

Afro-Cubanism

It was in Cuba that the Negro and his subculture were to have a preponderant influence on intellectual movements. From the beginning, an antislavery tradition had put the Negro at the center of Cuban literary and ideological interests, a position that was to be reinforced by the writings which accompanied the Cuban independence struggle.[33] The ideological stand of the Cuban revolutionaries against slavery—particularly in the work of José Martí—although part of a general mood of dissent directed against the Spanish colonizer, had the effect of affirming the Negro subculture as an integral part of the distinctive national heritage of Cuba, and eventually gave rise, in the years 1920–1940 to what has been called the "Afro-Cuban school" or *Negrismo*.

As in Brazil, *Negrismo* was essentially an affair of White writers, and it, too, had its share of primitivism. The Negro was seen mainly as a stereotype, and, in many cases, the poetry he inspired was no compliment to him or to his African origins.[34] But there was a positive side to *Negrismo*, which had to do, in the first place, with the technical revolution achieved by some of the poets who turned to Africanisms in Cuba and worked them into their poetry to arrive at a striking originality of idiom. This was true, in particular, of their integration into their verses of the rhythms of Afro-Cuban music.[35] But more than this, some of the Cuban writers and intellectuals were to achieve a real sympathy with theNegro and his culture. In this, the Cubans were helped by the presence in their midst of the Black writer Nicolas Guillén, for whom, as G. R. Courthauld has observed, "the Negro theme is not just a fashion, a subject for literature, but the living heart of his creative activity.[36]

Guillén introduced an element of racial and social protest into Afro-Cubanism, along with its formal modes. His long poem "West Indies Ltd.," written in 1934, combines the stylistic devices of *Negrismo* and a radical tone that prefigures in many ways another classic of Black literature, Aimé Césaire's *Cahier d'un retour au pays natal*, the first version of which was published three years later. In other poems, such as "The Name" and "Ballad of the Two Grandfathers," Guillén evokes the memory of his African ancestry and of the slave trade, although he invariably ends by reconciling this with his Spanish ancestry in a common cause and experience:

> Black anguish and White anguish
> Both of the same measure.
> Shouting, dreaming, weeping, singing,
> Dreaming, weeping, singing. Weeping, singing,
> Singing.[37]

Guillén's work offers no indication of any serious internal conflict arising out of his Negro connections, and its militant character is clearly due more to social than to racial reasons. And although the intellectuals of the Afro-Cuban movement concerned themselves seriously with the situation of the Negro, the political aims of their movement were vague, and their championship of the Black cause was conceived rather in a liberal spirit. A nationalist strain and a distinct racial consciousness were thus absent in Afro-Cubanism.

The Negro Renaissance in the United States

A completely different picture emerges from a consideration of the situation in the United States. Two factors were to play a determining role in this respect: the problematic situation of the Negro in U.S. society, and the fact that what can rightly be called Negro literature in the United States was the work of Negroes themselves.[38]

The social situation of the Negro in the United States made of him an essentially divided individual, a man with a double awareness of himself. This split in the Negro's consciousness, a direct result of racial prejudice, went hand in hand with the other psychological effects of discrimination upon his social life to create a permanent state of mental conflict. He felt a double alienation: by and in society, and also from himself.

Thus, even when a Negro was assimilated to the culture of the White majority, he was rejected by society, and remained what Robert E. Park has called the "marginal man" burdened with conflicting ethnic and national loyalties.[39] Here is the problem which is at the bottom of the extreme racial consciousness of the Negro intellectual in the United States, and which appears notably in the "New Negro Movement," variously called the "Negro Renaissance" or "The Harlem Renaissance," which sprang up in the wake of the intense racial agitation that occurred after the First World War.

The outstanding figure in Negro intellectual life in the United States during this period was W. E. B. Du Bois. He was the first to analyze with clarity the ambiguous social position of the Negro in the United States. In *The Souls of Black Folk*, which first appeared in 1903, the conflict in the Negro's mind was set out in these pathetic yet vigorous terms:

> It is a peculiar sensation, this double consciousness, this sense of always looking at one's self through the eyes of others, measuring one's soul by the tape of a world that looks on in amused contempt and pity. One ever feels his two-ness—an American, a Negro: two souls, two thoughts, two unreconciled strivings, two warring ideals, in one dark body, whose dogged strength alone keeps it from being torn asunder.[40]

This sentiment of alienation furnished the incentive that led Du Bois to a passionate analysis of the distinctive aspects of Negro life and history in the United States from their very beginnings, and induced him, in his consideration of the religious life of the Negro communities and of the spirituals, to see them as continuations of the Negro's African heritage. This was a position that he was to develop in another book, *Black Folk Then and Now* (1939), which was, in the words of Herskovits, an effort "to comprehend the entire picture of the Negro, African and New World, in its historical and functional setting."[41] Thus, at the same time as Garvey, but on a different plane, Du Bois began to develop the racial ethos which informed his political activities as the founder and moving spirit of Pan-Africanism.[42] His Pan-Negro cultural ideal is well summed up in the following extract:

> We are Americans, not only by birth and by citizenship, but by our political ideals, our language, our religion. Further than that, our Americanism does not go. At that point, we are Negroes, members of a vast historic race that from the very dawn of creation has slept, but half awakening in the dark forest of its African hinterland. We are the first fruits of this new nation, the harbinger of that black tomorrow which is yet to soften the whiteness of the Teutonic today. We are the people whose subtle sense of song has given America its only American music, its only American fairy tales, its only touch of pathos and humor amid its mad money-making plutocracy. As such, it is our duty to conserve our physical powers, our intellectual endowments, our spiritual ideals; as a race, we must strive by race-organization, by race solidarity, by race unity to the realization of that broader humanity which freely recognizes differences in men, but sternly deprecates inequality in their opportunities of development.[43]

Du Bois gives voice here to certain sentiments which his Negro compatriots were the first to echo, although we have come to associate them with Léopold Sédar Senghor. The cultivation of a Negro identity, culturally as well as socially and politically, and the expression of a total racial solidarity based not only on a common social experience but also on a common spiritual feeling, came to dominate the literature of the American Negro. The apologetic tones and veiled revolt that had characterized Negro writing before then gave way to a new revolutionary accent. Claude McKay, Countee Cullen, Langston Hughes, Sterling Brown, and others established a radical and militant tone, and Negro poetry became "characteristically the poetry of rebellion and self assertion"[44]:

I oppose all laws of state and country,
All creeds of church and social orders,
All conventionalities of society and system
Which cross the path of the light of Freedom
Or obscure the reign of the Right.[45]

This new Negro poetry was only part of a cultural revival which included a new type of Negro novel of protest, culminating in Richard Wright's *Native Son* (1940), and in which jazz and the blues had an important function: to differentiate the Negro and to give him the sense of a distinct cultural heritage. The theme of Africa as the distant home of the Black man came to acquire a new importance. In the circumstances, these poets could not avoid the pitfalls of exoticism, but the theme came to carry a strong emotional weight of personal involvement, as this passage from Cullen's poem "Heritage" illustrates:

What is Africa to me:
Copper sun or scarlet sea
Jungle star or jungle track,
Strong bronzed men, or regal black
Women from whose loins I sprang
When the birds of Eden sang?
One three centuries removed
From the scenes his fathers loved,
Spicy grove, cinnamon tree,
What is Africa to me?[46]

Garvey's movement and Du Bois's ideas had begun to give the Negro a pride in his race and origins, and the poets were beginning to affirm this in tones that soon acquired a mystical character, as can be observed in Langston Hughes's poem "The Negro Speaks of Rivers":

I've known rivers:
I've known rivers ancient as the world and
older than the flow of human blood in human veins
My soul has grown deep like the rivers.
I bathed in the Euphrates when dawns were young
I built my hut near the Congo and it lulled me to sleep

I looked upon the Nile, and raised my pyramids above it
I heard the ringing of the Mississippi when Abe Lincoln
went down to New Orleans
And I've seen its muddy bosom turn all golden at sunset
I've known rivers
Ancient, dusky rivers
My soul has grown deep like the rivers.[47]

The Negro renaissance in the United States was of capital importance in the development of Negritude. The writings of American Negroes were known outside the United States and commented upon by Negro intellectuals in France and the Caribbean.[48] And the renaissance exported not only its writings, but also some of its personalities. McKay, Cullen, and Hughes traveled in France, and a flow of Negro expatriates to that country started a Negro renaissance in Paris, with Josephine Baker and Sidney Bechet as the leading musical personalities. Richard Wright was later to become a prominent Negro expatriate in France. Negro intellectuals in France thus had the opportunity to meet their American counterparts.[49] It must be remembered, too, that Du Bois's Pan-African Congress, held in Paris in 1919, depended very much on the collaboration of Blaise Diagne, an influential Senegalese deputy.

But apart from these personal contacts, the Negro renaissance can be said to have led to Negritude as a movement, by setting precedents in all the areas of feeling in which the latter was to be given articulate expression. The literary movement that Negritude played a part in creating in Haiti provides a link between the two movements that is both historical and thematic. The American poets were thus not so much influences as precursors, whose work the French-speaking Black writers and intellectuals were to carry on to its logical limits.

The Haitian Literary Renaissance

The Haitian renaissance was a direct result of the occupation of the Republic by the United States in 1915. Whatever the tactical reasons for this gesture, the U.S. occupation created a colonial situation in Haiti and aroused a profound resentment among its intelligentsia. Apart from the complete takeover of the public institutions of Haiti, an element of color conflict was introduced by the racial attitudes of some members of the U.S. administration. The import of the occupation appeared clear— as the republic was the only state run by Black people in the Americas, the reversal of its sovereign position was generally interpreted in a racial light. Haiti thus came under White domination, and its intellectuals reacted along familiar lines.

Although Haiti had for about a century been an independent country, the very absence of direct White domination up to 1915 had made it a Negro republic, as far as the more sophisticated forms of cultural expression were concerned, only in a nominal sense. The Haitian elite, though proud of its people's political heritage and jealous of their independence, took its own cultural values exclusively from France and was far removed from the original culture of the ordinary folk. A deep cleavage thus existed between the intelligentsia and the masses. The U.S. occupation, however, brought a radical change in the mental outlook of the Haitian intellectuals. The process has been described by Naomi Garret:

> They had been made conscious, in a humiliating manner, of the racial characteristics which distinguished them from the powerful Americans in their country. To fight the feeling of inferiority that the Occupation had managed to engender within them, they turned within themselves and to their distant past to seek what there was, if anything, in their traditions and their heritage of which they could be proud. Here at last was something theirs, and inaccessible to the Americans.[50]

The reaction of the Haitians was to seek for themselves a sphere of thought and action outside American control, and thus to seek a "national soul." Their quest was to be facilitated by the writings of a most eminent scholar, the ethnologist Jean Price-Mars, who became their ideological leader. His book *Ainsi parla l'oncle*, though a scientific report of popular Haitian culture, was interspersed with comments in which he made clear the message he wished it to convey to his compatriots. Like Du Bois, Price-Mars saw in Haitian popular culture the common denominator, "the intimate essence," as he termed it, of the Haitian people. And, again like Du Bois, Price-Mars went on to recognize the African basis of this, and to advocate its acceptance as a functional part of the Haitian national heritage, in the hope that such a gesture would make the Haitians no longer colored Frenchmen, but "Haitians pure and simple, that is, men born under specific historical conditions." His main point was formulated thus: "We have no chance of being ourselves unless we do not repudiate any part of our ancestral heritage. Well, 80 per cent of this heritage is a gift from Africa!"[51]

Thus the sentiment of diminution by White rule led Price-Mars to place a specific situation within a larger context: cultural, historical, and racial. Naomi Garret has shown how strong the hold of Price-Mars's ideas was upon the younger generation of Haitian writers,[52] who reacted against their predecessors—considering them servile imitators of the French—and organized themselves around literary reviews with significant names like *La Relève* and *La Revue Indigène*.[53] Garret has also indicated how the American Negro poets of the renaissance were to exercise a determining influence upon the Haitians, through the articles in Parisian journals of writers like Frank Schoell on the American Negro phenomenon; through articles and translations by Haitians such as Dominique Hippolyte and Price-Mars (who had a fervent admiration for Du Bois); and through René Piquion's biographical study of Langston Hughes, with a selection in French of thirty-four of his poems:

> Like the American Negro writers of the 1920's, Haitians had become race conscious and were beginning to feel for their American brothers a kinship born of similarity of interests. It boosted their morale to discover that in their search for information about their African past, they were not alone; common cause had been found with American Negroes who, too, were ceasing to be ashamed of their heritage and

were able to look upon themselves and their brothers with objectivity.[54]

On the other hand, their French connection drew them into a
common stream with French-speaking writers from other parts
of the world, in particular from the Caribbean. Thus it was that
they became the first poets of Negritude as such, even before the
term had been coined, and occupied a prominent position in the
anthology compiled by Senghor which was to launch the movement.[55] The part of Haiti in the development of the movement
was well reflected by the election of Dr. Price-Mars as chairman
of the First Congress of Negro Writers and Artists, held in
Paris in 1956, and as president of the Society of African Culture
(SAC) created in 1959. Aimé Césaire's designation of Haiti as
the birthplace of Negritude is thus true in more than one sense.

INFLUENCES

An ironic aspect of Negro popular movements in Africa, as
well as in the United States, is the way in which Western elements acted as catalysts in the emotional reaction which produced nationalist feelings. Christian egalitarian teaching, for
example, helped to show up in the eyes of Black converts the
fundamental contradiction that separated White domination
from the avowed humanitarian principles of Western culture,
and to underline the rift between the objective practice and the
declared values of the White man. Toussaint Louverture's revolution in San Domingo was founded, by a similar process, on the
ideals of the French Revolution. A powerful emotional inspiration of nationalism was thus a disaffection for the White man,
judged according to his own principles.

Since the separatist churches in Africa and America were
syncretic, they were therefore never a pure return to original
forms of religious expression in Africa, much less in America,
where this was out of the question. Thus, once the Black man
had been dissociated in any way from his culture, a return to
any kind of complete authenticity became impossible. The acculturative process was irremediable.

On the above two points, popular movements were again to anticipate the intellectual movements, and what was true of the former became even more so for the assimilated Black intellectual. This truth is borne out by the tremendous influence which Western ideas and cultural forms have had on Negro intellectual movements, especially on Negritude. For, without any doubt, the progressive formulation of the movement made possible by the dominant currents of ideas in the West was in fact singularly favored by the intellectual and moral climate created in Europe in the aftermath of World War I.

The Intellectual Climate in Europe

One of the best chroniclers of this period in the intellectual history of Europe, the French critic R. M. Albérès, has declared: "European sensibility in the twentieth century is characterized by the belief that there exists a divorce between intelligence and reality, truth, or instinct."[56] Consequently, the dominating current in European intellectual life has been anti-intellectualism, and the man who helped to put it on a philosophical basis was Henri Bergson. His influence was important in creating a climate in which ideals that previous centuries had rendered "non-Western" could be accommodated within the European sensibility. Bergson's position as the "official philosopher" in France also had a direct consequence for French-educated Negro intellectuals.[57] His influence is apparent in the way Senghor employs concepts derived from Bergsonian categories like *intuition* and *élan vital* in his own writings on African culture.[58]

Anti-intellectualism also provoked a crisis of European consciousness, marked by a general calling into question of established institutions and of moral and religious values, and by a completely new vision of man. The surrealist movement developed out of this crisis and has left a permanent mark on the literature of Negritude, with Césaire as one of its foremost practitioners. But it was not so much the technical revolution as the social import of surrealism that came to have a meaning for Black intellectuals. By its aggressive iconoclasm, surrealism drew attention to the imperfections of Western society and helped to foster a radically critical outlook toward it, a lesson that was absorbed by the Blacks in their own movements of revolt.[59]

But a far more important Western influence was Marxism. For if surrealism could be considered, in the words of Gaëtan Picon, "a passionate enterprise of liberation,"[60] it was largely literary and individualist, and consequently offered no ideological direction, despite its revolutionary stand. Marxism, on the other hand, presented a comprehensive framework of social and political ideas. In Marxist concepts such as the *principle of contradiction, alienation,* and the *class struggle,* Black intellectuals found ready instruments of social analysis applicable to the colonial and "para-colonial" situation.[61]

Indeed, Western Marxists left nothing to chance in making Black intellectuals aware of the relevance of Marxist ideology to their situation. In 1916, Lenin had advanced the thesis that imperialism was "a direct continuation of the fundamental properties of capitalism in general," and Stalin followed this with an analysis of "The National and Colonial Question," in which the principles of national and cultural autonomy were reconciled with the ideal of proletarian solidarity. Anti-imperialism thus became an important part of the Marxist ideology. The Communist Party was at the height of its popularity in France in the 1930s and deployed tremendous efforts in the United States to win the adherence of the obviously discontented Negro population. Senghor has recounted how, as students in Europe, Black intellectuals were solicited by Marxist teaching:

> Indeed, right from the time of our arrival in Europe, we were subjected to Marxist propaganda. Some black students—especially the West Indians—had succumbed to its seduction. And they tried in turn to seduce us. They presented "scientific socialism" as the final solution to our problems, to all our problems. Under the guise of parliamentary democracy (they preached), a minority of bourgeois [elements] held in their hand the levers of power and wealth. They exploited, by oppressing them, not only their own people but also the immense flock of natives overseas. The solution to the problem was clear.

> It was up to us to join the army of the proletariat, and to struggle within its ranks. Once the "capitalist system" had been overthrown and the ownership of the means of production handed over to the workers, the colonized people would be at one stroke de-colonized, dis-alienated. They would recover, at the same time as their independence, the ownership of their material wealth and the freedom to promote the values of their civilisation.[62]

The influence of Marxism on Negro intellectuals on both sides of the Atlantic was profound and enduring. A good number of Negro writers have been, at one time or another, members of the Communist Party. The attraction of Marxism lay in its revolutionary character; and this emotional pull left a permanent imprint on the ideas of most of them. Even after the inevitable period of disillusionment with the Communist Party, due to its tactics and methods, the Marxist dialectic continued to inform the writings of Black intellectuals.[63]

Finally, the nature of literary activity in Europe has not been without consequence for the literature of Negritude. The years preceding World War II saw the development of a literature of causes, culminating in the outpouring provoked by the Spanish Civil War. This literature committed to political causes was to receive a tremendous impetus during the French Resistance; and, after the war, Jean-Paul Sartre developed the idea of *littérature engagée* in a series of essays on the nature of literature and on the relationship of the writer to society.[64] The two decades from 1930 to 1950 were dominated by the literary figures of Louis Aragon, Albert Camus, Paul Eluard, and Jacques Prevert.[65] It was inevitable that Black writers should have been strongly influenced by such poets and thinkers—especially Sartre, who was the first European apostle of Negritude—and others who were to have a direct hand in its formulation.

French writing thus had a marked social content in this period, and the literature of Negritude reflects the prevailing atmosphere in France. There was, however, an important distinction between the White writer and the Black, which Richard Wright pointed out at the time:

> The individual discovers that he is a sacrifice to
> society. This consciousness of sacrifice is develop-
> ing around two opposite poles: among the whites,
> the pole of psychological consciousness, among the
> blacks, that of the realistic-social.[66]

In other words, the poles of individual consciousness, for the
Whites, and of collective consciousness, for the Blacks, were
definitive.

THE CONTRIBUTION OF ANTHROPOLOGY

Although the intellectual climate in the West favored the
development of movements that questioned the fundamental
values of society, and Marxism, in particular, opened the way
for a revolt against imperialism, the determining factor which
provoked the Black counteroffensive and gave it validity was the
revision of the image of the Black man in modern anthropology. The development of a scientific method and an objective
approach, and the consequent evolution of the concept of cultural relativity, led Western ethnographers to a broader outlook
and a more sympathetic view of non-Western cultures.[67]

The work of Leo Frobenius was to play an important part
in the revaluation of Africa's culture and peoples. His *History of
African Civilisation* was the first serious attempt to credit the Black
race with a part in ancient Egyptian civilization, and a capacity for
developing more than rudimentary cultural institutions. Frobenius's attitude toward Africans was summed up in his enthusiastic exclamation, "Civilized to the marrow of their bones!"[68] The
writings of French ethnographers like Maurice Delafosse, Robert
Delavignette, Theodore Monod, Marcel Griaule, and later Placide
Tempels, in addition to the American Melville Herskovits, to
name but a few, were to give scientific authority to the growing
sentiment that the African cultures had been seriously underes-
timated, with prejudice against the Black man's human worth.[69]

The importance of the new ideas on Africa developed by
the anthropologists is threefold. In the first place, they gave an
important booster to the Black man's self-esteem and provided

scientific arguments for intellectuals to undermine the ideology of colonialism's *mission civilisatrice* [civilizing mission].[70] Quoting Frobenius in his pamphlet *Discours sur le colonialisme*, Césaire summed up the indictment of colonial rule with this epigram: "From colonization to civilization, the distance is infinite."[71]

In the second place, the anthropologists promoted in the West a new appreciation of African culture. Given the moral and intellectual climate of the interwar years, when Western man began to look outside his own culture for new directions in art and thought, the introduction of non-Western forms, and of African sculpture in particular, created an understandably profound impression. Leading artists and writers in Europe took up African forms of cultural expression, including literary styles; and jazz brought over by the Americans began to be considered a serious musical form.[72] In short, "The Negro was in vogue in Paris,"as Naomi Garret observes;[73] the African culture was becoming "respectable."

Finally, the anthropologists were to exercise a direct influence on the writings of some of the Black intellectuals. In this connection, Lucien Lévy-Bruhl's studies of non-Western forms of experience and knowledge furnished Senghor with a conceptual framework for his description of the Negro African mind. His controversial differentiation between Western man's "sight-reason" (*la raison-œil*) and the Negro African's "touch-reason" (*la raison-toucher*)[74] are based on Lévy-Bruhl's distinction between Western logic and "primitive" logic, as articulated in *La mentalité primitive* (1921).

Negritude thus owes an immense debt to the West, and this much Senghor has conceded: "Paradoxically, it was the French who first forced us to seek its essence, and who then showed us where it lay."[75]

TOWARD A FORMULATION

Negritude as a definite movement thus grew out of an emotional and intellectual ferment among African and Caribbean students and intellectuals living in Paris before World War II; it was gradually elaborated in a succession of journals,[76] and finally brought into focus in the postwar years. This ferment became significant because of the uneasy position that the Black intellectual occupied in French society. For there was a fundamental weakness at the heart of French colonial policy, which consisted of a selective and rigid assimilation of a Black elite, combined with discrimination against the rest of the colonized population.[77] This situation created in the elite a feeling that they were on sufferance, and generated within them a conflict of loyalties. Added to this was the fact that, even as elites, they could not always escape racial prejudice in White society, in which the Black man was an object of contempt. These contradictions are well expressed in this bitter line from Césaire's *Cahier*: "I salute the three centuries that uphold my civic rights with my blood minimized."[78]

The Black elite were thus assimilated intellectually and culturally, but never socially, and they could not become involved in and identify with the culture of their masters. As cultural hybrids, the only way out of their form of alienation was to fall back on ethnic loyalties. Their situation thus drew them together, and it is not difficult to understand their reaction. As Senghor put it in 1962:

> Early on, we had become aware within ourselves that assimilation was a failure; we could assimilate mathematics or the French language, but we could never strip off our black skins or root out our black souls. And so we set out on a fervent quest for the Holy Grail: our Collective Soul.[79]

The first sign of this reaction came in 1921, when a West Indian administrator, René Maran, published *Batouala*, based on his experience in the Congo. The novel won the coveted *Prix Goncourt* and caused a scandal, leading to the author's dismissal from the civil service. Although Maran, who was brought up and educated in France, rightly claimed to be French, he has since been acclaimed by other Black writers as a "precursor" of Negritude.[80] But such a title belongs more properly to another West

Indian, Etienne Léro, whose manifesto *Légitime Défense* (1932) indicated the way in which separate influences from America and Europe had converged upon the Blacks in France to inspire their reaction. In one passage, for instance, he wrote:

> The storm wind blowing down from Black America will soon wipe out from our Antilles the aborted fruits of a decaying civilisation. Langston Hughes and Claude McKay, the two revolutionary poets, have brought for us, tempered in red alcohol, the African love of life, the African joy of love, the African dream of death.

In another passage, Léro condemned the inauthenticity of West Indian writing:

> A foreigner would look in vain in this literature for an original or profound accent, for the sensual and colourful imagination of the black man, for an echo of the resentment as well as the aspirations of an oppressed people.[81]

And Léro went on to annex surrealism and Marxism to the cause he had set out to espouse.

Léro's poetry was neither original nor of a high quality.[82] But with this single manifesto he set in motion a process which was to outlive him, and to be prolonged by the efforts of three other poets: Aimé Césaire, Léon Damas, and Léopold Sédar Senghor. The three founded their own paper, *L'Etudiant Noir*, which appears to have brought together Africans and West Indians.[83] This was also the period in which Césaire produced his masterpiece, *Cahier d'un retour au pays natal*, published in a little known journal, *Volontés*, in 1939, in which the word Negritude first appeared in print. The original inventor of the term has been kept a close secret between the three poets, although Césaire is generally given credit for it.[84] The war soon scattered the group, but Césaire kept up their efforts with *Tropiques*, a journal he founded in Fort-de-France, where he had returned to serve as professor at the local *lycée*. He maintained a sharp commentary on the colonial situation in Martinique, his native island, complemented by a new determination, as can be seen in this excerpt from the article he wrote to launch *Tropiques*:

> The circle of darkness gathers, amid the cries of men and the howls of beasts. Yet we count ourselves among those who say "No" to darkness. We know that the salvation of the world depends also on us. That the earth has need of all her children. Even the humblest.[85]

It was in Martinique as a wartime refugee that André Breton, the leader of the surrealist movement, came to be acquainted with Césaire. As a result, a new bilingual edition of *Cahier* was published in New York, with a prefatory eulogy in which Breton acclaimed the poem as "the greatest lyrical monument of our time."[86]

After the war, the three men found themselves together again in Paris, as representatives of their territories of origin in the French National Assembly. The next step, however, was taken independently of the "triumvirate"—by Alioune Diop, a Senegalese who in 1947 founded the review *Présence Africaine* with the collaboration of the most eminent personalities in French literary and academic circles. This marked a decisive stage. *Présence Africaine* soon opened its own publishing section and helped to give a concrete formulation to the movement, by bringing out a series of works by Black writers and other scholars on African and Negro literature and problems. Special numbers such as *Le Monde Noir*, edited by the ethnologist Théodore Monod; *L'Art Nègre*; *Haiti*; *Poètes Noirs*; and *Trois Écrivains Nègres* (which included the first novel of Mongo Beti under the pseudonym Eza Boto) soon appeared to supplement the regular issues. Two important landmarks published by Présence Africaine were the French version of *Bantu Philosophy* (1949), and Cheikh Anta Diop's controversial work *Nations nègres et culture* (1954). The latter was a doctoral dissertation in which Diop, pursuing a trail already opened up by Frobenius, put forward the thesis that ancient Egyptian civilization was predominantly Negro.

Although the dissertation was rejected by the Sorbonne, the book made a profound impression upon Black people because of the boldness of its ideas and expression, and in European circles because of its erudition.[87]

Meanwhile, in 1948, Senghor had brought together, in his historic *Anthologie de la nouvelle poesie nègre et malgache de langue française*, the first lyrical expression of the movement, with an introduction in which he expatiated on the concept of Negritude. But it was the essay "Orphée noir" ("Black Orpheus"), which Jean-Paul Sartre contributed to the volume, that consecrated the term and gave the movement a start.[88] By the 1950s, a considerable body of literature and ideas had been produced. Césaire, Damas, and Senghor had been recognized as important figures in the French literary world, while others, including Jacques Roumain, Paul Niger, Joseph Zobel, Birago Diop, Jacques Rabemananjara; and, later, Edouard Glissant, Camara Laye, and René Depestre established themselves as Negritude writers.

The success of the Bandung Conference in 1955 inspired Présence Africaine to organize a cultural counterpart, and, in 1956, the First Congress of Negro Writers and Artists was held in Paris, with the express aim of defining a new, non-Western, cultural consciousness. As Alioune Diop put it in his opening address: "We of the non-European world have got, with the help of everybody, to stimulate new values, to explore together new worlds born out of the meeting of peoples." This Congress was mainly of a cultural character, with papers on different aspects of African and Afro-American cultures, although not without occasional attacks on the West and impeachments of colonial rule, "an enterprise of moral extermination" as Diop called it.[89] In short, this was a stocktaking and a tentative effort at Negro solidarity at the cultural level.

The Second Congress, which followed three years later in Rome, was of a far more political character. The theme, "The Responsibility of the Intelligentsia," was a direct reference to the colonial situation, and indicated a new attitude. The crises which marked French colonial policy and their consequences in France were probably connected with this development. Colonialism had at any rate become a burning question, made even more urgent by the rise of Ghana as the first African nation to become independent after the war. The spirit that dominated at this conference was thus expressed by Césaire: "We must hasten the process of de-colonization, that is to say, employ all means to hasten the ripening of a popular consciousness." And further on in his speech he declared: "As for us, in the particular situation in which we find ourselves, we are the propagators of souls, the multipliers of souls, and in the last resort, the inventors of souls."[90]

∽∽

Two facts stand out clearly from a consideration of the progressive development of Negritude, seen in its broad historical perspective. The first is that it was a movement of reaction against the Western cultural domination which was concomitant with political domination. As such, it appears as a remarkable example of counteracculturation. It seems perfectly clear, however, that without the pressure of colonial rule and the conflicts it created in Africa, and without the historical and social factors which dominated the situation of the Black population in America—that is, without the racial factor—the forms of reaction to culture contact among Black peoples summarized here would have had a completely different character. In this respect, the Haitian phenomenon illustrates how both political domination and racial difference, with the psychological problems this involves, have determined the nature of Black reaction to contact with the White man and Western culture generally. In short, Black cultural nationalism was inspired by a wish for freedom from both domination and contempt.

But this would be a very incomplete view of the situation. The complementary side of the Black man's response has been to turn to means which, at first sight and from a psychological point of view, afford him a compensation for the domination and humiliation to which he was subjected. The role of the Negro subcultures, leading progressively on both sides of the Atlantic to the myth of Africa among Negro masses and intellectuals, is thus tied to a defense mechanism. Yet it would be wrong to label this altogether an escape into fantasy. Although the intellectual movements developed out of very strong emotional conflicts, and they too produced their myths, they generally progressed further to a more constructive stage. Negritude, in particular, has evolved a framework of ideas, and its literature and ideology afford an insight into the intimate processes of the Black reaction to the West.

NOTES

1. Hodgkin (1956), p. 69.

2. Frazier (1957), p. 35.

3. For a discussion of this term, associated with Edward Wilmot Blyden, see my "Negritude and African Personality" in *The African Experience in Literature and Ideology* (1981), pp. 89-116.

4. See Balandier (1963), pp. 3-38.

5. See Frazier (1957), pp. 305-311.

6. See in particular Lanternari (1962).

7. Balandier (1963). The article he quotes by d'Arboussier was entitled "Les Problèmes de la culture," and was published in the special number of *Europe* (Paris), May-June 1949, devoted to Black Africa.

8. Balandier (1963), pp. 486, 441-442. Sentiments of racial solidarity were helped by the influence of American Negro "missions," but were inevitable in view of the racial discrimination to which the Africans were subjected. The racial factor assumed a preponderance in popular and intellectual movements of black people in the New World, and will consequently be discussed in that context. See also Balandier (1953).

9. This is Frantz Fanon's interpretation in *Les Damnés de la terre* (1961), which Sartre summarized in his preface by remarking that the colonized protect themselves from colonial alienation by reinforcing religious alienation.

10. Malinowski (1961), p. 158.

11. Kariuki (1963), p. 27.

12. Balandier (1957), p. 285.

13. See James (1938).

14. Césaire (1956), p. 44.

15. Quoted by Aimé Césaire in *Toussaint Louverture* (1956), p. 44. Delgrès and his followers in revolt were holding out against the French army, and preferred to blow themselves up with their fort rather than surrender.

16. Hughes (1958), "The Glory of Negro History—A Pageant," pp. 465 ff.

17. See Bastide (1958).

18. The problem of "Africanisms" in the New World has been given considerable attention; the best known studies are: Herskovits (1941) and Bastide (1960).

19. Jacques Roumain, "Guinée," translated by Langston Hughes in Bontemps and Hughes (1949), p. 365.

20. See Frazier (1949).

21. See Essien-Udom (1962), "The Nationalist Tradition," which offers a useful summary of American Negro forms of nationalism.

22. Burns (1949) gives a history of the development of this idea in his book *Colour Prejudice*.

23. Herskovits (1941), pp. 30-31.

24. Essien-Udom (1962), p. 17.

25. Frazier (1957), p. 311.

26. Abram Kardiner and Lionel Ovesey (1951), p. 363, concede as much when they write: "Marcus Garvey saw one important truth: that the Negro was doomed as long as he took his ideals from the white man. He saw that this sealed his internal feeling of inferiority and his self contempt."

27. Garvey (1923).

28. It is well known that Ghana's "Black Star" emblem is a legacy of Garvey's movements. But the activities of New World Negroes who *did* come to Africa, such as Dr E. W. Blyden, helped to diffuse ideas similar to his.

29. Césaire (1956), p. 31.

30. See Dollard (1949).

31. This image of Brazil propagated by Gilberto Freyre in his *Maîtres et esclaves* (1952) requires qualification today.

32. Bastide (1961), p. 36. Professor Bastide considers colored people in Brazil with particular reference to the ideology of *Négritude*, and shows that no real movement based on an African myth was able to extend beyond the national context, despite a Back to Africa slogan, "Volta na Africa."

33. See Coulthard (1962).

34. For example, Palés Mastos' poem, "Ñam-Ñam," in which this passage occurs:

> Asia dreams its nirvana
> America dances its jazz
> Europe plays and theorizes
> Africa grunts: ñam-ñam

Quoted by Coulthard, 1962, p. 33.

35. See Jahn (1958), p. 3.

36. Courthauld, p. 34.

37. Guillen (1959), pp. 5-9. The version here quoted offers slight variants on the original in *El Son Entero* (Buenos Aires, 1947).

38. The term "Negro" is used here in its accepted sense in the U.S.— that is, to denote any individual having in any way an African origin. The American Negro writer was often a mulatto, sometimes very light-colored, but in the circumstances was obliged to write under a racial "Negro" label.

39. See Park (1950) in his chapter "Cultural Conflict and the Marginal Man" and also Stonequist (1937).

40. Du Bois (1907), pp. 3-4.

41. Herskovits (1941), p. 2.

42. See Legum (1962), for more details of this aspect of Du Bois' activities.

43. Du Bois, quoted by Essien-Udom (1962), pp. 10-12.

44. Park (1950), p. 294. See also Wagner (1962) for a complete discussion of the period 1890 to 1940 (Dunbar to Hughes) in American Negro poetry.

45. Hawkins, "Credo," quoted by Park (1950), p. 296.

46. Cullen (1925), p. 36.

47. Bontemps and Hughes (1970), p. 88.

48. Césaire obtained his *Diplôme d'études supérieures* (MA degree), with a monograph on American Negro poetry. Léopold Sédar Senghor produced translations of Hughes and others.

49. Kesteloot (1968), p. 63, cites a letter of Senghor's, in which he mentions how contacts between American- and French-speaking Negro intellectuals were developed by the Nardal suisters, who published a journal, *La Revue du Monde Noir*, and kept a salon littéraire, at which Negro intellectuals from the United States, the Caribbean, and Africa were wont to meet.

50. Garrett (1963), p. 61.

51. Price-Mars (1928), pp. I-II, 20, and 210

52. Garrett (1963), p. 611, reports that in "separate interviews with many of them," the majority of the younger poets indicated "lectures by Dr Mars" as the great influence on them and their work.

53. The choice of the word "indigène" (the French colonial equivalent of "native"), is highly significant as a calculated gesture of defiance, the same attitude that was to produce "Négritude" out of the word "nègre," a term of contempt.

54. Garrett (1963), p. 84.

55. The poetry of the Haitian renaissance is discussed as part of the literature of Negritude, Chapter Two.

56. Albérès (1969), p. 11.

57. Henri Bergson was Professor of Philosophy at the Collège de France from 1900 until his death in 1941. His *Creative Evolution* probably exercised the greatest influence on Senghor and others.

58. A later influence on Senghor was the work of Pierre Teilhard de Chardin, to be discussed in Chapter Two.

59. The surrealists had adopted an anticolonial attitude in their reaction against Western society. In an open letter to Paul Claudel in 1925, they wrote, inter alia, "We heartily wish that revolutions, wars and *colonial insurrections* would come to wipe out this Western civilisation whose impurities you defend even as far as the eastern world," reproduced in Nadeau (1945), p. 296.

60. Picon (1960), p. 4.

61. Césaire (1958) describes the American Negro situation as "para-colonial" in his *Discours sur le colonialisme*. The fundamental identity between the colonial system and the caste system in the U.S. has been pointed out by the French sociologist Mickel Dufrenne (1953), p. 232, who remarks that they are both a perpetuation of the "master-slave" relationship, and concludes: "The hazards of history have only arranged that the United States have their colonies within!"

62. Senghor (1962), pp. 21-22.

63. Césaire resigned from the Communist Party after the exposure of Stalin by Nikita Kruschev at the 20th Congress in 1956. His *Lettre à Maurice Thorez* on this occasion has been analysed at length by Colin Legum (1962), pp. 104-10, in his *Pan-Africanism*. Senghor has affirmed on several occasions that Marxism is a Western ideology which has to be adapted in Africa.

64. These essays were first published in Sartre's review *Les Temps Modernes* and later under the title *Qu'est-ce que la littérature?* (1948).

65. Paul Eluard wrote the best-known poem of the French Resistance, "Liberté." (Eluard (1960, pp. 62 ff.) He was a personal friend of Césaire, and his death inspired one of the latter's greatest poems, "Tombeau de Paul Eluard" in *Ferrements*.

66. Wright (1947), pp. 1, 9.

67. A good example of the old approach to the question of culture is to be seen in T. S. Eliot's *Notes Towards the Definition of Culture* (1948).

68. Frobenius (1936), p. 14.

69. Delafosse (1922), Griaule (1948), Tempels (1949), Herskovits (1938).

70. As a Belgian administrator put it, "The colonizer conceived his relationship to the colonized as that of a civilized man to a savage. Colonialism is thus based on a hierarchy, assuredly elementary, but stable and sure" (quoted by Kesteloot, 1963).

71. Césaire (1958), p. 10.

72. The influence of African sculpture on Western art forms, especially on Picasso and Modigliani, is a well-known chapter of art

history. The influence of African literary forms is perhaps less appreciated, especially on Blaise Cendrars, whose *Anthologie nègre* appeared in 1947. Jazz has also influenced Western classical music through Stravinsky and Ravel.

73. Garrett (1963), p. 69.

74. Senghor (1959), pp. 249-79.

75. Senghor, (1962c).

76. Mme Kesteloot's account of Negritude in her 1963 publication is in fact based on its progressive development in these journals and reviews.

77. See Hodgkin (1956), pp. 33-40, for a fuller analysis of French colonial policy. There were also numerous cases of exactions, of which the most resented was the system of forced labor whose abuses were seen at their worst during the construction of the railway line from Brazzaville to Pointe-Noire (the "Congo-Ocean") in 1928-1933, at the cost of a great number of African lives.

78. Breton (1948), p. 65.

79. Senghor (1964), p. 54.

80. See Maran's preface to the second edition of *Batouala*, published in 1922.

81. Etienne Léro, "Misères d'une poésie," *Légitime Défense*, 1979, p. 12. This publication appeared as the first number of a projected review, but due to its "subversive" character, it was immediately suppressed by the French authorities.

82. For example, see Damas (1947) and Senghor (1948a). In "Black Orpheus" (1949), his preface to this volume, Sartre compares Lero's surrealism to that of Césaire, and concludes that the former showed no originality. However, there is no doubt that Césaire owes a lot to Léro, who can be regarded as his immediate ancestor.

83. Mme Kesteloot, whose documentation is otherwise complete, could not find a single copy of this paper, and had to rely on excerpts from another publication of Damas, and on testimonies.

84. Two other similar terms were also used by Césaire (1956b) in *Cahier d'un retour au pays natal*, "négraille" and "nigritie," the first being a pejorative term in common parlance, and the other an

invention. But in the crucial passages in the poem, the word *Négritude* is invariably employed.

85. Césaire (1941). The reference to "darkness" is, of course, to the war. For more about this review and the ideas developed in it by Césaire, with the collaboration of his wife Suzanne and other Caribbean intellectuals, see Kesteloot, 1963, p. 211. ff.

86. Breton (1948), p. 95.

87. Cheikh Anta Diop eventually obtained his doctorate with a dissertation entitled *L'Unité culturelle de l'Afrique noire* (1959) (*The Cultural Unity of Black Africa*), which was complemented by *Afrique noire précoloniale* (*Precolonial Africa*), 1960.

88. Sartre's essay "Orphee noir" is reproduced in *Situation III* (1949). An English translation by the American poet Samuel Allen was published by Présence Africaine under the title *Black Orpheus* (1964).

89. Diop (1956), pp. 11-12.

90. Césaire, "L'Homme de culture et ses responsabilités," *Deuxième Congrès des Ecrivains et Artistes Noirs*, pp. 117-118.

CHAPTER TWO
NEGRITUDE—LITERATURE
AND IDEOLOGY
❦

Pan-Africanism has been described as "essentially a movement of emotions and ideas,"[1] and this description is especially applicable to Negritude, which is its cultural parallel. Indeed, no better phrase could be found to sum up its double nature, first, as a psychological response to the social and cultural conditions of the "colonial situation"[2] and, second, as a fervent quest for a new and original orientation. In the former respect, the imaginative writings of the French-speaking Negro intellectuals offer a precious testimony to the human problems and inner conflicts of the colonial situation; in the latter respect, their ideological writings and other activities represent an effort to transcend the immediate conditions of this situation by a process of reflection.

THE LITERATURE

The literature of Negritude is dominated by the collective consciousness of the Black writer as member of a minority group which is subordinated to another and more powerful group within the total political and social order. The literary preoccupations of the movement revolve around this central problem, the Negro predicament of having been forced by historical circumstances into a state of dependence upon the West, considered the master society and the dominating culture. The literary themes of Negritude can be seen as a countermovement away from this state: they constitute a symbolic progression from subordination to independence, from alienation—through revolt—to self-affirmation.

ALIENATION

The theme of *exile* is the point of departure of the whole literary expression of Negritude, and in it is involved the most pathetic aspect of the French-speaking Negro intellectual's specific situation, which derives from the general political and cultural uprooting of Black people by colonial conquest. The overwhelming sentiment that dominates in this connection is the Black man's sense of separation from his own world and of being thrown into a world and a social system with whose cultural values he can strike no personal relation. The Black man recognizes himself as belonging to an *outgroup*, an alien in relation to the West, which controls the total universe in which he moves. For the French-speaking Negro writer, this situation is signified by his physical exile in Europe.

> Bless you, Mother,
> I hear your voice when I am given up to the
> insidious silence of this European night
> Prisoner under the white cold sheets tightly drawn,
> prisoner of all the inextricable anxieties that
> encumber me.[3]

This sentiment of belonging no longer to oneself but to another goes together with an awareness of inferiority, which becomes translated in social terms into a caste and class consciousness. The association between race and servitude is a constant theme in Negro literature, and occupies a prominent place in Negritude:

> I am a docker in Brooklyn
> Bunker-hand on all the oceans

Labourer in Cuba,
Soldier in Algeria.[4]

The economic exploitation of the race which defines it as a community and gives its members a group consciousness is a consequence of its original humiliation by conquest and slavery. The memory of slavery thus has a particular significance for Negro writers, especially for those of the Caribbean:

> And they sold us like beasts and counted our teeth...
> and they examined our genitals, felt the gloss and the
> roughness of our skin, pawed us, weighed us and put
> around our neck like tamed animals the strap of ser-
> vitude and of nickname.[5]

The Black man's principal role in Western history has thus been as an economic tool.[6] This is what Césaire, echoing Marx, has called "the reduction of the Negro to an object" (*la chosification du nègre*).[7] But although the Negro experience forms, in this light, part of the general Marxist conception of the "class struggle," the prevailing preoccupation of these writers was with the Black people as a race, not as a class.[8] They were concerned with the collective image of the Black man in the West and with his human status in the world. "The colonial system was based on a social division determined by the colour line,"[9] and it was maintained by a racial ideology which defined the Black man as inferior. The social relationship between colonizer and colonized was thus converted, as far as the Black man was concerned, into an opposition between *White* and *Black*, which acquired the moral values summarized by the South African Bloke Modisane in these words:

> White is right, and to be black is to be despised,
> dehumanized. . . classed among the beasts, hounded
> and persecuted, discriminated against, segregated
> and oppressed by government and by man's greed.
> *White is the positive standard, black the negative*
> (emphasis added).[10]

The cultural and political ascendancy of the White man, combined with the active denigration of the Black man, has thus had the effect of vitiating the latter's self-esteem, with profound psychological consequences, including shame and self-hatred.[11] The demoralizing effect of the caste system on the Black man has been given poignant expression in these lines by Léon Damas:

> My todays have each one for my yesterdays
> Wide eyes that roll with rancour and with shame.[12]

The Black man in the world thus suffered a negation of his human being. This was the external reality with which the literature of Negritude was concerned. But there is a more personal and intimate side to this theme of alienation, which has to do with the cultural situation of the assimilated Negro intellectual. The colonial enterprise was presented as a "civilizing mission," aimed at transforming the African by his progressive approximation to the ideals of Western civilization, specifically through education. This implied in most cases his dissociation from the basic personality pattern imprinted in him by his primary culture. Western education was thus an instrument of imposed acculturation, aimed at replacing the Black man's original modes of thought and feeling, which were attuned to his native norms, by another personality structure corresponding to Western norms.[13] The French policy of *assimilation* probably went furthest in this cultural hegemony, which was to some extent common to all the colonizing powers, of attempting to fashion the Black man—or at least a Black elite—into a foreign image. This problem is at the heart of the cultural and spiritual dilemma of the French-speaking Negro intellectual. In order to be acceptable socially in the Western world, it was necessary for him to deny a part of himself. Conformity to White ideals was only possible at the cost of a repression of his original self[14:]

> I must hide in the depths of my veins
> The Ancestor storm—dark skinned, shot with
> lightning and thunder
> And my guardian animal, I must hide him
> Lest I smash through the boom of scandal.

> He is my faithful blood and demands fidelity
> Protecting my naked pride against
> Myself and all the insolence of lucky races.[15]

The result was a division in his personality. The Haitian poet Léon Laleau has expressed this sentiment of the divided self in remarkable terms:

> This beleaguered heart
> Alien to my language and dress
> On which I bite like a brace
> The borrowed sentiments and customs of Europe.
> Mine is the agony
> The unutterable despair
> In breaking with the cold words of France
> The pulsing heart of Senegal.[16]

We touch here upon what Roger Bastide has called "the pathology of the uprooted man," and which Robert E. Park has observed in the cultural hybrid as part of the psychological results of culture contact and the acculturative process: "spiritual instability, intensified self consciousness, restlessness and malaise."[17] Damas has put this sentiment of malaise into verse:

> I feel ridiculous
> in their shoes
> in their evening suits,
> in their starched shirts,
> in their hard collars
> in their monocles
> in their bowler hats.[18]

This is a problem that was even more accentuated in the case of the Caribbean writers, whose non-Western cultural background was marginal, and whose racial stock, because of the total orientation of their society toward Western values, symbolized by Whiteness, was more a source of shame and frustration than it was for the Africans. The pressure upon Caribbean writers to deny their racial connections and to identify with Europe was even greater, though they were subject to the same discrimination as the Africans.[19] The West Indians' sentiment of exile is thus intensified by a feeling of rootlessness, which Césaire expresses with the symbol of the island itself:

> Island of the blood of Sargassoes
> island, nibbled remains of remora,
> island, backfiring laughter of whales,
> island, specious word of mounted proclamations,
> island, large heart spread out
> island ill-jointed, island disjointed,
> all islands beckon
> all islands are widows.[20]

The Black man, and especially the intellectual, found himself a man no longer in his own right, but with reference to another, thus estranged from himself; in exile, not only in a political and social sense, but also spiritually. The whole colonial existence appears as one long paling of the Black self, an "ambiguous adventure," as Cheikh Hamidou Kane has put it. A man divided between two worlds, his overriding aspiration thus became, in the words of Kane's tragic hero, Samba Diallobé, "nothing but harmony."[21]

REVOLT

A situation of oppression offers the victim a range of reactions limited by two opposite poles—total submission or total refusal—but the exact nature and degree of this reaction will depend upon the experience and the disposition of the individual. The colonial situation as a whole was a collective political and cultural oppression of Black people, yet it cannot be said that it was felt uniformly as such. The Black intellectuals were in fact privileged in comparison with the masses, as far as the more external conditions of life were concerned, and it is quite conceivable that in some cases their consciousness of the fundamental injustice of the system in which they lived was limited, if it existed at all.

But the mental conflict into which the French-speaking Negro intellectuals were plunged as individuals probably made them aware that their dilemma was inherent in the whole colonial situation. Thus they were forced, despite assimilation, to identify with the colonized rather than the colonizer:

> But if I must choose at the hour of testing,
> I have chosen the verset of streams and of forests,
> The assonance of plains and rivers, chosen the
> rhythm of blood in my naked body,
> Chosen the trembling of balafongs, the harmony
> of strings and brass that seem to clash,
>
> I have chosen my toiling black people, my
> peasant people, the peasant race through
> all the world. [22]

The literature of Negritude became, as a result, a testimony to the injustices of colonial rule and an expression of the Black man's resentment:

> An immense fire which my continuous suffering and
> your sneers
> and your inhumanity,
> and your scorn
> and your disdain
> have lighted in the depths of my heart
> will swallow you all.[23]

The tone changes often from this kind of menace to one of accusation. The poetry of David Diop best illustrates this indictment of colonial rule:

> In those days
> When civilization kicked us in the face
> When holy water slapped our tamed foreheads,
> The vultures built in the shadow of their talons
> The blood-stained monument of tutelage
> In those days
> There was painful laughter on the
> metallic hell of the roads
> And the monotonous rhythm of the

> *pater noster*
> Drowned the howling on the plantations.[24]

Accusation in turn becomes a criticism of Western society as a whole, and, in this respect, the contradiction of "war and civilization" became a powerful weapon. Senghor's *Hosties noires*, for example, is a collection of war poems in the tradition of Wilfred Owen, but Senghor reveals a particular view of European war when he speaks with sarcasm of having been "delivered up to the savagery of civilized men."[25] The shortcomings of Western society, both within and without, furnished that element of disenchantment which made it possible for Negritude to develop an attitude of refusal toward the colonial system:

> I shout no to class
> no to the taint of soot
> no to the humid floor
> no to the glass furnace
> no to damped lights
> no to love paid for in bank notes.[26]

Protest, accusation, and refusal lead inevitably to a call to arms:

> But when, O my people,
> winters in flames dispersing a host of birds and ash,
> shall I see the revolt of your hands?[27]

Protest and threats of revolt are in themselves an indirect form of defense, a verbal means of projecting violent reaction which cannot be physically realized. Although the militancy of Negritude was an explicit response to a real situation (and the agitated character of a good deal of this writing indicates that the situation was often felt as real personal experience), it has no more than a symbolic value. Its real significance, however, lies elsewhere, for it does in fact reveal the hidden mechanism of response to oppression. The resentment of the Black man against domination tends toward retaliation, and, as Fanon has shown, his consciousness as a colonized man is suffused with violence.[28]

In the work of Césaire, this element is translated through poetic terms into an apocalyptic vision:

> And the sea lice-ridden with islands
> breaking under rose fingers
> flame shafts and my body
> thrown up whole from the thunderbolt.[29]

The surrealist technique is here employed in a manner appropriate to the alienated condition of the Black man. It offers the Black poet a means of projecting his dream of violence, and becomes in fact a symbolism of aggression. A corresponding side to this aggressiveness is the way in which the Black poet responds by wilfully identifying himself with Western symbols of evil:

> I seek the thousand folds of the oceans
> witnesses of savageness
> and rivers where beasts go to drink
> to make for myself a face
> that would scatter vultures.[30]

Negritude here borders on nihilism. Yet nihilism is not characteristic of the movement as a whole; more often than not, it represents a defiant truculence, as in this passage, where Damas operates a literary reversal of situations in a way reminiscent of Nietzsche:

> The White will never be negro
> for beauty is negro
> and negro is wisdom
> for endurance is negro
> and negro is courage
> for patience is negro
> and negro is irony
> for charm is negro
> and negro is magic
>
> for joy is negro
> for peace is negro
> for life is negro.[31]

In this respect, one of the most striking technical innovations of Negritude has to do with the reversal of color associations in the Western language which was the only tongue accessible to most of them—French—as in this example from Césaire's *Cahier*:

> a solitary man imprisoned in white
> a solitary man who defies the white cries of
> white death
> TOUSSAINT TOUSSAINT LOUVERTURE
> He is a man who bewitches the white hawk of
> white death
> He is a man alone in the sterile sea of white sand.[32]

A reversal of Western symbols implies as well a reversal of the concepts associated with them. The revolt of Negritude appears also as a refusal of Western values, regarded as oppressive constraints. The Christian religion, in particular, comes under continual attack, and this theme has had an original and refreshing treatment in the comic novels of Mongo Beti, in particular, *Le pauvre Christ de Bomba*.[33] Western morality is also set in contrast to the African's sensuality, presented as natural and uninhibited.

It can be remarked that, in general, the theme of revolt in the literature of Negritude represents a reinforcement of the antagonism created by the colonial situation, between the White master and the Black subordinate. It is a way of underlining an opposition that was implicit in the colonial human context. It is not, however, an end in itself, as Sartre has observed, but rather part of a movement toward a more constructive vision.

Rediscovery

The rejection of Western political and cultural domination in the literature of Negritude represents also a severing of the bonds that tie the Black man to Western civilization. A corollary to this claim for freedom from the West is the quest for new values. Revolt becomes not only a self-*affirmation* but also a means of self-*differentiation*:

For myself I have nothing to fear I am before
Adam I claim descent neither from the same lion
nor from the same tree I am of another
warmth and of another cold.[34]

The quest for new values thus leads the Black writer to self-definition in terms that are non-Western, and the association between the Black race and Africa acquires a new meaning: instead of being a source of shame, it becomes a source of pride. This is the ultimate end of Negritude, and much of the literature is dedicated to a rehabilitation of Africa as a way of refurbishing the image of the Black man. The psychological function of this, as well as being a counter to the Negro's inferiority complex, is to permit an open and unashamed identification with the continent, a poetic sublimation of those associations in the Negro's mind which constitute for him a source of mental conflict in his relationship with Western culture: a process of self-avowal and self-recognition. This view of the movement is best supported by the writings of the West Indians, whose collective repression of Africa, as has been pointed out, has been the more painful:

Africa, I have preserved your memory, Africa
you are in me
like the splinter in a wound
like a totem in the heart of a village.[35]

A myth of Africa developed in consequence out of the literature of Negritude, which involved a glorification of the African past and a nostalgia for the imaginary beauty and harmony of traditional African society, as in Camara Laye's evocation of his African childhood.[36]

This strain in Negritude is probably charged with the greatest emotional force. Senghor, for instance, infuses into his well-known poem *Black Woman* a feeling that is more filial than erotic, due to his identification of the continent with the idea of woman in a way that lends to the image of Africa the force of a mother figure:

Naked woman, Black woman,

> Clothed with the colour which is life, with
>   your form which is beauty,
> In your shadow I have grown up; the gentleness of
> your hands was laid over my eyes
> And now, high up on the sun-baked pass, at the heart
> of summer, at the heart of noon, I come upon you,
>   my Promised Land,
> And your beauty strikes me to the heart like the
>   flash of an eagle...
>
> Naked woman, Black woman,
> I sing your beauty that passes, the form that I
>   fix in the Eternal,
> Before jealous Fate turns you to ashes to feed the
>   roots of life.[37]

In a poem by another writer, Bernard Dadié, despite the use of conventional Western imagery, Africa is celebrated in cosmic terms:

> I shall weave you a crown
> of the softest gleam
> bright as the Venus of the Tropics
> And in the feverish scintillation
> of the milky sphere I shall write
> in letters of fire your name
> O, Africa.[38]

The romanticism of the African theme in Negritude illustrates certain functions and characteristics of "nativistic movements" as analysed by Ralph Linton,[39] but in literary rather than ritualistic form, that is, at a sophisticated level. Yet a purely sociological and "realistic" view would miss the profound significance of this aspect of Negritude. In any case, realism is a purely relative term applied to literature, and has little relevance to poetry;[40] but apart from this, the African theme went far beyond a purely compensatory mechanism in that it was also a genuine redis-covery of Africa, a rebirth of the African idea of the Black self. This opening up of the African mind to certain dimensions of its own world which Western influence had obscured appears to be in fact the most essential and the most significant element in the literature of Negritude. The way in which the best of these poets came to root their vision in African modes of thought has given a new meaning to the traditional African worldview.[41] It is of interest to note that Césaire's celebrated poetic formulation of Negritude is in fact taken from a Bambara symbol of man in a telluric union with the universe:

> My Negritude is not a stone, its deafness hurled
> against the clamour of the day,
> my Negritude is not a speck of dead water on the
> dead eye of the earth,
> my Negritude is neither a tower nor a cathedral
>
> it thrusts into the red flesh of the earth
> it thrusts into the livid flesh of the sky.[42]

The West Indian is of course at one remove from the living center of traditional African humanism, which is essential to the poetry of the African writers of Negritude, as in Senghor's works;[43] and has perhaps been expressed in its purest and most authentic form by Birago Diop in his famous poem "Souffles":

> Listen more often
> To things than to beings;
> The fire's voice is heard,
> Hear the voice of water.
> Hear in the wind
> The bush sob
> It is the ancestors' breath.
>
> Those who died have never left,
> They are in the woman's breast,
> They are in the wailing child
> And in the kindling firebrand
> The dead are not under earth.
>
> They are in the forest, they are in the home
> The dead are not dead.[44]

The literature of Negritude tends toward a point where it can coincide with the traditional mythical system of thought in Africa. This does not imply that the coincidence is perfect or that it is always genuine; what is significant about it is the "backward movement" toward an end from which Western culture had originally pulled the African. Negritude, as literature, retraces a collective drama as well as a spiritual adventure, involving a quest for the self.

From a social angle, its importance is mainly symbolic and functional. In the historical context in which it developed, the Black writer incarnating his despised and oppressed race is the mediator of a new self-awareness. The racial exaltation of the movement is mainly a defense;[45] the use of an African myth represents Black ethnocentrism, an attempt to recreate an emotional as well as an original bond beneath the contingencies of a particularly difficult historical experience.

The alliance of the imaginative and the political in Negritude relates the movement to African nationalism. Nationalism hardly ever corresponds to an objective reality; but it is, nonetheless, a powerful emotional attitude, and literature has always been an outstanding vehicle for dominated people to give voice to their group feelings.[46] But imaginative writing, even with an explicit political content, implies a group mind rather than group action; it is essentially inactive. At the literary level, Negritude remains largely subjective, and it was the ideology that attempted to establish objective standards of thought and action for the Black man, in general, and for the African, in particular.

THE IDEOLOGY

The non-imaginative writings of French-speaking Negro intellectuals to a great extent run parallel to the literature. They are determined by the same sentiments, and are, consequently, in the main, a formulation in direct language of the attitudes expressed in symbolic terms in the imaginative writings. The distinction lies in the fact that, whereas the literary works simply express these attitudes, the nonliterary writings formulate and define them.

The majority of the books, essays, articles, and speeches that constitute what may be called the ideological writings of Negritude are straightforward polemics: protest writing, testimonies, and direct attacks on colonialism. A typical example is Albert Tévoédjré's essay *L'Afrique révoltée*, which is a violent denunciation of colonial rule, with particular reference to Dahomey, the author's place of origin. Even here, the main source of grievance appears to be cultural rather than economic or social:

> I shall always regret the fact of having been obliged to learn French first; to think in French while being ignorant in my own mother tongue. I shall always deplore the fact that anyone should have wanted to make me a foreigner in my own country.[47]

An even more forceful attack on colonialism is contained in Césaire's famous pamphlet *Discours sur le colonialisme*, which takes up the question in original terms by demonstrating the evil effects on both colonizer and colonized of a system which limits to the West the idea of man as promoter of values:

> Never was the West, even at the time when it shouted the word loudest, further removed from being able to assume the responsibilities of real humanism— humanism of a world-wide scope.[48]

It was not enough, however, to denounce colonialism; it was also considered necessary to contest its foundations, and especially the racial and cultural ideas by which it was rationalized.

SOCIETY, HISTORY, AND CULTURE

The subordinate role of the Negro in Western society had been justified mainly by the allegation that Africa had made no contribution to world history, had no achievements to offer. The logical conclusion drawn from this idea was put by Alioune Diop in this way:

> Nothing in their past is of any value. Neither customs nor culture. Like living matter, these natives are asked to take on the customs, the logic, the language of the colonizer, from whom they even have to borrow their ancestors.

The Western thesis that the African had no history implied for the Black man that he had no future of his own toward which to look. A good deal of the propaganda effort of French-speaking intellectuals was, as a consequence, devoted to a refutation of this unacceptable proposition. Cheikh Anta Diop's writings stand out in this respect. His book *Nations nègres et culture*, for example, is an impassioned, heavily documented attempt to show that ancient Egyptian civilization was in fact a Negro-African achievement, and thus to prove that the West owed its enlightenment to Africa. The conclusion to the principal section of his thesis is worth quoting in full, as it illustrates the tenor of the whole book:

> The Egyptian origin of civilisation, and the Greeks' heavy borrowing from it are historical evidence. One wonders therefore why, in the face of these facts, the emphasis is laid on the role played by Greece, while that of Egypt is more and more passed over in silence. The foundation for this attitude can only be understood by recalling the heart of the question.
>
> Egypt being a Negro country, and the civilisation which developed there being the product of black people, any thesis to the contrary would have been of no avail; the protagonists of these ideas are certainly by no means unaware of this fact. Consequently, it is wiser and surer purely and simply to strip Egypt of all her achievements for the benefit of a people of genuine white origin.
>
> This false attribution of the values of an Egypt conveniently labelled white to a Greece equally white reveals a profound contradiction, which is not negligible as a proof of the Negro origin of Egyptian civilisation.

> As can be seen, the black man, far from being
> incapable of developing a technical civilisation, is in
> fact the one who developed it first, in the person of
> the Negro, at a time when all the white races, wal-
> lowing in barbarism, were only just fit for civilisation.
> In saying that it was the ancestors of Negroes,
> who today inhabit principally Black Africa, who
> first invented mathematics, astronomy, the calendar,
> science in general, the arts, religion, social organisa-
> tion, medicine, writing, engineering, architecture...
> in saying all this, one is simply stating the modest and
> strict truth, which nobody at the present moment
> can refute with arguments worthy of the name.[49]

The whole thesis is based on an implied correlation between
history and culture which determines the nature of society, and
of the individual; and its intention was to prove that the African
was essentially a technical man—*homo faber*. However, by sum-
marily ascribing all civilization to the Black man in this way,
Diop proceeds in the field of scholarship in the same fashion as
Léon Damas in the poem cited above—by reversing the hierarchy established by the colonizer, without contesting the basis
on which it was founded. It is, in a way, a total acceptance of the
Western measure of evaluation, namely technical achievement.

Negritude may be distinguished from other efforts to rehabilitate Africa by what can be termed its ethnological aspect,
which attempted to redefine its terms, and to reevaluate Africa
within a non-Western framework. Here the concept of cultural
relativity was to help in sustaining a campaign whose purpose
was to establish the validity of African cultural forms *in their own
right*. This explains the preoccupation of the French-speaking
Negro intellectuals with anthropology, a preoccupation which
reveals itself in the series of special issues published by Présence
Africaine, especially the two remarkable volumes *Le Monde Noir*
(1951) and *L'Art Nègre* (1952). The former, edited by Théodore
Monod, brought together a number of articles by eminent scholars, both European and African, on various aspects of African
cultural expression as well as their ramifications in the New

World, in such a way as to suggest not only their originality but their worldwide ramifications.

The accent was almost invariably placed on the nonmaterial aspects, on those intangible elements which could distinguish the African's approach to the world from the Western, and which might seem to underlie his conscious existence as well as his material productions. Thus, African traditional beliefs and, in particular, the native forms of religion received strong emphasis. African "animism" tended in general to be placed on an equal footing with Christianity, though curiously enough by an effort of reconciliation in most cases. The most noteworthy example of this kind of procedure is perhaps a paper by Paul Hazoumé, in which the Dahomean conception of God is likened to that of John the Evangelist.[50]

The anthropological interests of Negritude came to the fore at the First Congress of Negro Writers and Artists, whose express purpose was to make a total inventory of the Negro's cultural heritage, in an effort to define a Pan-Negro cultural universe. This was at best a very delicate, if not impossible, undertaking, as the discomfort and reserve of the American participants at the conference was to make clear. Two main lines of thought emerged from the deliberations of this conference. Foremost in the minds of the organizers was the will to demonstrate the specific character of traditional African institutions and beliefs as well as of African survivals in America, in a way that refuted the Western thesis of inferiority. The purpose of this was made clear by the Haitian Emmanuel Paul:

> It was from this [African] past that colonial authors undertook to make the black man inferior. But what we look for from these studies is precisely the awakening of a historical consciousness embracing the millennial past of the race. These black people scattered all over the world who, even under the pressure of the West, still hesitate to deny themselves, have need of this source of pride, this reason for clinging to life.[51]

Secondly, and as a consequence, the concern with the past implied a process of self-appraisal, as a solid basis for self-definition. The Malagasy writer Jacques Rabemananjara declared:

> The deliberations [of this Congress] have no other purpose than to assemble and to select material for dialogue. First among ourselves, with the aim of knowing ourselves more, of grasping, through our diverse mentalities, customs, and countries of origin, the essential human note, the ineffable human warmth that unites us. [52]

These efforts cannot be said to have produced a common cultural denominator, but their significance lay rather in the attitude that inspired them. In direct response to the intolerance that characterized the cultural policy of the colonizer, Negritude developed into a vindication and an exaltation of cultural institutions which were different from those of the West; it was thus a conscious attitude of pluralism. The corollary was a rejection of *assimilation* and a claim to cultural autonomy and initiative.

Alioune Diop expressed this aspect of the movement in the following terms:

> Unable to assimilate to the English, the Belgian, the French, the Portuguese, to allow the elimination of certain original dimensions of our genius for the benefit of a bloated mission of the West—we shall endeavour to forge for this genius those means of expression best suited to its vocation in the twentieth century.[53]

Politics and Race

These efforts to rehabilitate African history and to reevaluate African culture were a conscious reaction to the ideology that sustained colonial rule. But the central pole of the colonial situation was political domination rather than cultural supremacy. The next step after a demand for cultural autonomy was logically a corresponding demand for political independence.

The arguments for an explicit political stand came mainly from the Marxist elements in the movement, especially at the Second Congress in Rome. Frantz Fanon's address to this meeting contained an unequivocal summary of their point of view:

> In the colonial situation, culture, denied the twin support of nation and state, withers away in a slow death. The condition for the existence of culture is therefore national liberation, the rebirth of the nation. [54]

However, if a certain political awareness was an implicit part of the cultural offensive of the French-speaking Black intellectual, which placed Negritude in close relationship with African nationalism and Pan-Africanism, it is nonetheless quite clear that Negritude remained essentially a cultural and intellectual movement, albeit with political implications. The French-speaking Negro elite tended more toward an elaboration of ideas concerning the Black man's place in the world than toward the actual mobilization of the masses for an immediate and definite political goal.[55] Negritude was thus at the most an ideological movement with remote political purposes. Its link with nationalism is all the same certain in that a special *rationale* was developed along with it; it thus furnished the most important *mystique* of African nationalism.

In so far, then, as it is an answer to a certain combination of circumstances, the product of a historical situation, Negritude is another cultural and political myth: the expression of a justified self-assertion swelling into an exaggerated self-consciousness, extending into an assiduous cultivation of the Black race.[56] That Negro nationalism on both sides of the Atlantic should have been based on a vehement racial consciousness can be imputed to the racialism that grew out of and which often came to underlie White domination: Black nationalism can in the final analysis be reduced to a challenge to White supremacy. Negritude, by confronting White domination with Negritude's own racial protest and zealous partisanship of the Negro race, did more than draw together the sentiments and attitudes that went with

Black reaction and embody them in a heightened form: it moved in fact very distinctly toward a racial ideology.

Even here, most of the ideas expressed by French Negro intellectuals are limited to a refutation of the racial ideology of colonialism. For if, in the literary works, the exaltation of the Black race rises to dizzy heights, it has not been reproduced in the nonliterary writings with anything like the same abandon. In the single case of Senghor, this aspect of Negritude acquires a certain intellectual dimension. So preeminently do his ideas emerge on this question that his conception of Negritude demands separate consideration.[57]

SENGHOR AND THE THEORY OF NEGRITUDE

Senghor's Negritude starts out as, and essentially remains, a defense of African cultural expression.[58] It presents itself first as an elaborate apology before it becomes an exposition and a personal view of Africa: it is a *passion* that is later *rationalized*. Nonetheless, his ideas over the last quarter century present a coherent and consistent pattern.

On several occasions, Senghor has defined Negritude as "the sum total of African cultural values," something perhaps more than the simple relation of the African's personality to his social and cultural background. For, although Senghor never speaks of an *essence*, he speaks of a *Negro soul*—a special spiritual endowment of the African which is, in some respects, shared by the Negro in the New World, and is therefore a racial mark.[59]

Senghor describes and defines the African's distinctive qualities mainly by opposition to the Western, often by setting a positive value on what the West derided in the African, sometimes proceeding by grounding his own thinking in modern currents of Western thought, which he then turns against the West for the benefit of his arguments. He has written, for example:

> Discursive reason merely stops at the surface of things, it does not penetrate their hidden resorts, which escape the lucid consciousness. Intuitive

> reason is alone capable of an understanding that
> goes beyond appearances, of taking in total reality.[60]

It is this line of thought that forms the basis for Senghor's justification of the African's nonrational approach to the world. He has boldly annexed Lévy-Bruhl's studies on "primitive mentality" to argue the validity of the African's ways of thinking. He seizes in particular upon the French anthropologist's "law of participation"[61] and proceeds to use this in his own formulation of the African's mode of experience, which he presents as essentially one of feeling—of a mystical sympathy with the universe: "The African cannot imagine an object as different from him in its essence. He endows it with a sensibility, a will, a human soul."[62] For Senghor, this African mode of apprehending reality through the senses rather than through the intellect is at the root of his direct experience of the world, of his spontaneity. The African's psychology helps to determine a different form of mental operation from the Western, a different kind of logic:

> The life-surge of the African, his self-abandonment
> to the other, is thus actuated by reason. But here,
> reason is not the eye-reason of the European, it is
> the *reason-by-embrace* which shares more the nature
> of the *logos* than *ratio*.

He goes on to state, "Classical European reason is analytical and makes use of the object. African reason is intuitive and participates in the object."[63] Senghor has made this distinction a constant theme in his writings.

The "law of participation" that, according to Senghor, governs the African's sensibility, is basically emotive. He has pushed this conception of the African mind to a point where emotion has become its cardinal principle. "Emotion is African, as Reason is Hellenic," he exclaimed, and though this statement has been given careful nuances by him (for the benefit of his critics) he still leaves no doubt about this aspect of his theory of Negritude: "It is this gift of emotion which explains Negritude... For it is their emotive attitude toward the world which explains the cultural values of Africans."[64]

Senghor points to creative works to demonstrate the presence of a unique African sensibility which animates them, and insists above all on the privileged position of rhythm in African artistic expression. Rhythm is for him the expression of the essential vitality of the African:

> The architecture of being, the internal dynamism which shapes it, the system of waves which it sends out towards others, the pure expression of vital force... For the Negro-African, it is in the same measure that rhythm is embodied in the senses that it illuminates the Spirit.[65]

In his exposition of the African mind, Senghor lays emphasis on its intensely religious disposition, on the African's "sense of the divine," on "his faculty of perceiving the supernatural in the natural."[66] The African's mystical conception of the world is for Senghor his principal gift, and derives from his close links with the natural world. Because the African "identifies *being* with life, or rather with the *life-force*," the world represents for him the manifestation in diverse forms of the same vital principle: "For the universe is a closed system of forces, individual and distinct, it is true, yet also interdependent."[67] Lévy-Bruhl's law of participation is here allied to Fr. Temple's "Bantu Philosophy" to produce a conception of the African worldview as a system of participating forces, a kind of great chain of vital responses in which Man, the personification of the "life-force," is granted a central position: "From God through man, down to the grain of sand, it is a seamless whole. Man, in his role as person, is the centre of this universe."[68] For Senghor, this is not an abstract system but an existential philosophy and indeed a practical view of life; Negritude is for him not only a way of being, but also a way of living. He therefore extends his theory of the African personality to explain African social organization.

Senghor believes that the African society is an extension of the clan, which represents a kind of mystical family, "the sum of all persons, living and dead, who acknowledge a common ancestor."[69] Thus African society has a religious character—it is not so much a community of persons as a communion of souls. Where, therefore, Western culture insists on the individual, African culture lays emphasis on the group, though without the loss of a sense of the person.[70]

Senghor's theory of Negritude is not really a factual and scientific demonstration of African personality and social organization, but rather a personal interpretation. An element of speculation enters into his ideas, which lays them wide open to criticism. His more subtle formulations often have a specious character; besides, the most sympathetic reader of his theories cannot fail to be disturbed by his frequent conflation of race and culture, especially in his early writings. On the other hand, these weaknesses are due to the circumstances in which his ideas developed. In assessing the objective differences that cut off the African from Western man, his concern is to make a positive reevaluation of realities which the West considered negative.

Furthermore, Senghor's political career has given his theory of Negritude a practical significance—from polemics, it has evolved into a form of social thought, for his social and political thought are set within the general framework of his cultural philosophy. It is in the name of the innate spiritual sense of the African that he rejects the atheistic materialism of Marxism as unfitted for and irrelevant to the African situation.[71]

In a certain sense, therefore, Senghor may be justified in designating his theory of Negritude as a cultural and not as a racial philosophy. At any rate, it is not an exclusive racism. Senghor's views on the African, and even on the whole Negro race, open out toward the larger perspectives of a broader humanism. Here he has been influenced by Pierre Teilhard de Chardin's philosophy of the convergence of all forms of life and experience toward the evolution of a superior human consciousness, which has given Senghor a pole around which he has developed his idea of "a civilisation of the Universal."[72] His defense of cultural and racial mingling (*métissage*) is founded on this key concept, which is summed up in the following passage:

> The only "pan-ism" which can meet the demands of
> the 20th century is—let us proclaim it boldly—pan-

humanism, I mean a humanism which embraces all men at the double level of their contributions and their comprehension.[73]

The African Presence and the Black Millennium

An ideology, when it becomes explicit, is a kind of thinking aloud on the part of a society or of a group within it. It is a direct response to the actual conditions of life, and it has a social function, either as a defensive system of beliefs and ideas which support and justify an established social structure, or as a rational project for the creation of a new order. The latter type of ideology, even when it includes a certain degree of idealism, also implies a reasoned program of collective action; it becomes the intellectual channel of social life.

The literature and ideology of Negritude were by their nature revolutionary, or at the very least radical. Because they spring from a need to reverse an intolerable situation, they are moved in the first instance by a negative principle. They are a challenge to the common lot which Western expansion had imposed on non-Western man, especially the Negro, whose experience—dispersal, subjugation, humiliation—illustrates the worst aspects of contact with the White man. For Black people had in common an experience which, in the words of James Baldwin, placed in the same context their widely dissimilar experience. He explains:

> What they held in common was their precarious, their unutterably painful reaction to the white world. What they held in common was the necessity to remake the world in their own image, to impose this image on the world, and no longer be controlled by the vision of the world, and of themselves, held by other people. What in sum black men held in common was their ache to come into the world as men.[74]

In the circumstances, it is not surprising that this "ache" should have developed sometimes into an intense collective neurosis. The dilemma in which history placed the Black man, and from which the intellectual movements could not escape, was that Negro nationalism of any kind was bound to be even more irrational than any other, for it was to a considerable degree a gesture of *despair*.

This negative aspect of Black reaction to White rule has left a mark on Negritude, even in its development of positive perspectives. A contradiction, purely emotional in origin, bedevils the movement, which, in its crusade for the total emancipation of Black people, has sought to comprise within a single cultural vision the different historical experiences of Negro societies and nations.

It would be a mistake, however, to dismiss the movement as a futile and sectarian obsession with self—as a kind of Black narcissism. In the larger context of Negro experience, it represents the ultimate and most stable point of self-awareness. For, although its expression has sometimes been exaggerated, it has always had an intellectual content. In the African political context, its role as the ideological spearpoint of African nationalism has been sufficiently emphasized. Its profound significance in the cultural and social evolution of Africa has been perhaps less appreciated.

Negritude represents an African crisis of consciousness, its most significant modern expression; it is the watershed that marks the emergence of a modern African consciousness. African "messianism" and Negritude represent the ritualistic and the intellectual facets of the reaction to the same historical, social, and cultural stimulus. Their forms have varied. In African messianism, tradition remains the basis of social behaviour, despite borrowings from Western religion, which are absorbed only so far as they will fit in. The reverse is true of Negritude: despite its championship of a nonrational tradition, it remains rigorously rational. Senghor's Negritude, for example, is an anti-intellectualism mediated by the intellect, and the whole movement is expressed through a Western mode focussed on African realities. In short, Senghor's Negritude is a break with tradition: although African in content, it is Western in its formal expression.

The movement thus marks a transition in the nature of collective expression in Africa—from the millennial forms and the religious undercurrent on which traditional Africa had relied for human accomplishment, to the secular intellectually centered approach to the world by which modern thought is characterized. It marks a "desacralization" of African collective life, an attitude out of which have begun to flow new currents of ideas for tackling present-day African problems. This is what Balandier observed as "the progression from myth to ideology" in Africa.[75] Although this progression has been continuous, and although, as L. V. Thomas has remarked, "the originality of modern solutions is inspired by the specific character of former times,"[76] the transition is nonetheless real. African messianism was an archaic reaction to a new situation; Negritude was a far more appropriate response, adapted to the modern age.

It thus forms an essential and significant part of an African revolution which is marked not only by the emotions it has liberated and the ideas it has generated, but also by the forms it has assimilated. The profound character of the transition can best be appreciated by comparing the respective visions of the Absolute in African messianism and in Negritude. The former was supernatural and apocalyptic—essentially an eschatology. The idealism of Negritude from the beginning tended toward an earthly utopia:

> We Africans need to know the meaning of an ideal, to be able to choose it and believe in it freely, but out of a sense of personal necessity, to relate it to the life of the world. We should occupy ourselves with present questions of world importance, and, in common with others, ponder upon them, in order that we might one day find ourselves among the creators of a new order.[77]

In their search for identity, the adherents of Negritude have had to accept and explore to the fullest their particular situation. But, although preoccupied with a sectional and limited interest, they were inspired by a universal human need for fulfilment. In this, they have never strayed from the central, enduring problem of the human condition.

Notes

1. Legum (1962), p. 14.

2. The term "colonial situation" is used here to denote the global situation of Black people as it affected the writings of French-speaking Negro intellectuals. It has already been spelt out in Chapter One how the position of the Negro in the United States was readily assimilated to the domination of other black populations by Western colonial powers.

3. Senghor (1964b), p. 29.

4. Camille (1956), p. 53.

5. Césaire (1956), p. 93.

6. See Williams (1966).

7. Césaire (1956), p. 22.

8. Gunnar Myrdal (1944), pp. 667 ff. has observed that racial solidarity is more marked among U.S. Negroes than class consciousness. He speaks therefore of a "caste struggle," thus making the economic status of the American Negro secondary to the ethnic classification, in his analysis of the Negroes' place in U.S. society.

9. See Raymond Kennedy, as quoted in Linton (1945), p. 308: "The colour line, indeed, is the foundation of the entire colonial system, for on it is built the whole social, economic, and political structure."

10. Modisane, "Why I ran away," in Hughes (1960), p. 26.

11. The psychological implications of racial discrimination for the Black man in White society have produced numerous studies. This question seems to have been best summarized by John Dollard (1949), p. 184: "The upshot of the matter seems to be that recognizing one's own Negro traits is bound to be a process wounding to the basic sense of integrity of the individual who comes into life with no such negative views of his own characteristics." The genesis of Negro "self-hatred" is discussed at length by Roger Bastide (1950), pp. 235 ff. in his chapter on «Le Heurt des races, des civilisations et la psychanalyse."

12. Damas (1963), p. 45.

13. For the theoretical basis of these remarks, see Kardiner (1946) and Dufrenne (1953).

14. See Mannoni (1950), pp. 10-30.

15. "Totem" in Senghor (1964b), p. 10.

16. Laleau, Leon. "Trahison." Samuel Allen (trans.) in Drachler and Herskovits (1963), p. 195; French original in Senghor (1948a).

17. Roger Bastide's "Problèmes de l'entrecroisement des civilisations et de leurs oeuvres" in Gurvitch (1963), p. 319; and Park (1950), p. 356.

18. "Solde" in Damas (1962), p. 39.

19. See Henriques (1951); and Harris and Wagley (1958). Mittelholzer (1950) and Lamming (1955) offer sensitive inside views of this Caribbean problem.

20. Césaire (1961), p. 90.

21. Cheikh Hamidou Kane, (1961). See Reed (1963) for an analysis of the theme of cultural conflict in the African novel.

22. "For Koras and Balafongs" in Senghor (1964b), pp. 13-14.

23. Regnor C. Bernard, "Nègre," as quoted and translated in Courthauld (1962), p. 81.

24. David Diop, "Les Vautours" in Coups de Pilon (1960), p. 8.

25. Senghor (1948b), p. 115.

26. René Depestre, "Quand je crie non," quoted in Garrett (1963), p. 19.

27. Roumain (1945). The titles of the collections of poems by French Negro writers speak manifestly of this mood: Les Armes miraculeuses (Césaire), Coups de pilon (David Diop), Feu de brousse (Tchikaya U. Tam'si), Balles noires (Guy Tirolien), and so on.

28. Fanon (1961), Chapter One. Georges Balandier and Roger Bastide have also both drawn attention to this phenomenon, highlighted by the influence of the Apocalypse on "messianic" movements. See Balandier (1963) and Bastide (1950), p. 262.

29. Césaire (1946), p. 25.

30. Belance, "Moi nègre," quoted by Garrett (1963), p. 178.

31. Damas (1956), p. 52. The same reversal of situations occurs in Camara Laye's The Radiance of the King (1959), where Clarence the white man goes through a succession of adventures in supplication of the attention of a Black king.

32. Césaire (1956b), p. 46. Sartre (1964), p. 27 observed, in connection with the problem posed to the black poet by his use of a European language: "Let him open his mouth and he condemns himself, except in so far as he sets himself to destroy the hierarchy" (that is, of the "coupled terms black-white").

33. This theme is also a favorite one with English-speaking African writers. Okigbo (1962), p. 35, calls the Angelus "the bells of exile". J. P. Clark (1962), p. 46, writes in, "Ivbie," almost a poem of Negritude:

    Is it ruse or truce
    That peace which passeth all understanding?

34. "Visitation" in Césaire (1946), p. 53.

35. Roumain (1945), p. 53.

36. Laye (1955).

37. Senghor (1964b), p. 6.

38. Dadié (1956).

39. Linton (1945). See also his chapter on "The Distinctive Aspects of Acculturation" in Linton (1940), pp. 501-20.

40. It is not suggested by these remarks that the romanticism of Negritude was without its abuses. But this is a question for literary criticism, which must content itself with judging the aesthetic value of the finished product rather than legislating for the writer about his raw material. Besides, like any other literary school, it has produced its uninspired writers. .

41. See Jahn (1961), especially Chapters 5 and 7, and Taylor (1963), for an extensive discussion of this question.

42. Césaire (1956b), p. 71.

43. See Beier (1959). Beier concludes his study with the following observation: "Senghor is not merely a Frenchified African who tries to give exotic interest to his French poems; he is an African who uses the French language to express his African soul."

44. Translated by Anne Atik in Drachler and Herskovits (1963), p. 95.

45. See Memmi (1957), p. 174.

46. See Kohn (1944). The analogy between Negritude and other nationalist literatures has been drawn, principally by two writers: Bernard Fonlon (1978), who compares Negritude to similar

movements in Irish nationalism; and Thomas Melone (1962), in which Negritude is compared to the literature of the German revival in the eighteenth and nineteenth centuries.

47. Tévoèdjré (1958), pp. 114-15.

48. Césaire (1958), p. 65.

49. Cheik Anta Diop (1954), p. 253.

50. Hazoumé (1956), pp. 233-251. See also the collected volume, *Des Prêtres noirs s'interrogent* (Paris, 1957), for a similar approach to African religious beliefs.

51. Paul, (1956) p. 152.

52. Rabemananjara (1956), p. 28.

53. Diop (1959a), p. 41.

54. Fanon (1959, p. 87.

55. Balandier (1962), p. 93, observes that, in the development of African political myth, "the accent was placed more on... cultural liberation... than on political liberation."

56. The following observation by Louis Wirth about minorities' reaction to their situation should be kept in mind when considering Negritude: "One cannot long discriminate against a people without generating in them a sense of isolation and of persecution, and without giving them a conception of themselves as more different from others than in fact they are." Quoted in Linton (1945), p. 348.

57. No other member of the movement has elaborated Negritude so fully as Senghor. As a matter of fact, Césaire himself prefers to regard Negritude as a historical stand, as an attitude, rather than as a comprehensive system.

58. The title of one of Senghor's early articles is significant: "Défense de l'Afrique noire" (1945).

59. See Senghor (1964), pp. 22-39.

60. Preface to Birago Diop, *Les Nouveaux contes d' Amadou Khoumba*, in Senghor (1964), p. 246.

61. See Lévy-Bruhl (1936), pp. 23-27.

62. Senghor (1964a), p. 24.

63. Senghor (1962a), pp. 3-16. See also translation by John Reed and Clive Wake in Senghor (1965), p. 33.

64. Senghor (1962a), pp. 3-16.

65. Senghor (1964a), pp. 212-13.

66. Senghor (1964a), p. 27.

67. Translations by John Reed and Clive Wake in Senghor (1976), p. 37.

68. Senghor (1976), p. 43.

69. Senghor (1976), p. 43.

70. See Senghor (1961), pp. 71, 123-24.

71. Senghor (1962b), pp. 17-31.

72. Senghor (1962b), p. 33 ff.

73. Senghor (1961), p. 108.

74. Baldwin (1992), p. 2.

75. Balandier (1962), p. 93.

76. Thomas (1965), p. 19. See also Ogot (1963) for a study of the same progression in African political organisation and attitudes.

77. Diop (1947), p.14.

CHAPTER THREE
NEGRITUDE REVISITED
❧

The concept of Negritude has had a singular career. First launched by Aimé Césaire in his long poem *Cahier d'un retour au pays natal*,[1] the term itself was taken up and developed by Jean-Paul Sartre in his essay "Orphée noir," written as a preface to Senghor's anthology of French-speaking Black poets.[2] Sartre's purpose in this essay was not so much to define its content, or even to clarify its meaning, as to explore its various and extensive implications within a unified philosophical perspective. Sartre discerned in the poetry of the writers with which he was concerned the expression of a common sentiment deriving from their multiple reactions to the colonial situation and to the overall historical experience of the Black man. He identified this sentiment as "the Negro's affective attitude to the world" and went on to define Negritude in terms of his existentialist philosophy as "the being in the world of the Negro."[3] He saw the movement as the emergence of a distinct consciousness of the Black man resulting from the relationship between his historical and sociological determination, and his responses to the specific factors and active elements in his experience of the world; in other words, as the dynamic interplay between his "situation" on one hand, and his "freedom" on the other.

For Sartre, therefore, Negritude was from the beginning only a relative phenomenon, embracing the experience of a particular category of men in a definite context. It was therefore subject to the historical process. This accounts for his Hegelian view of the movement as an antithetical stage in a dialectical progression: "the theoretical and practical affirmation of white supremacy is the thesis: the position of Negritude as an antithetical value is the moment of Negativity."[4] The significance of the movement lay for him in its character as a kind of positive negation whose ultimate direction was the resolution of the original Black and White conflict at a higher level of collective awareness and action, in a new synthesis that would be the "realisation of the human society without racism."[5] It is therefore clear that Sartre considered Negritude not as an essentially negative movement, as Fanon was to later complain,[6] but rather as a purely contingent phenomenon.

The subsequent development of the concept of Negritude has, however, taken it beyond this limited and relative definition. The term itself has tended to acquire a multiplicity of meanings, engendering a certain ambiguity as to its actual content. Its most immediate application is to the literary school constituted by French-speaking Black writers, to designate what apparently is their common literary purpose and vision, and in a further extension of the term to denote certain forms of textual practice defining a distinctive style of the school.[7] But the intimate relationship between the literary concerns of these writers and the wider social and political issues involved in the Black experience has also given the term a political connotation. Negritude appears in this light as the French equivalent of the Pan-Negro movement, corresponding in some important respects to the Pan-African movement among the English-speaking Black intellectuals and nationalist leaders.[8] The points of coincidence which bind Negritude to these other movements have their roots in the global reaction of Black people to their experience in relation to the Western world. But through the specific orientation of the French-speaking writers, and in particular the individual stamp which Léopold Sédar Senghor has imprinted upon their attitudes and ideas in his own elaboration upon them, Negritude has evolved into a distinctive system of contemporary African thought. Senghor has developed the concept to such an extent that, while taking in these other meanings and implications of a historical character, it now appears as a whole system of thought: as the formulation of an African conception of the universe, and of a mode of existence founded upon this fundamental conception.

The specific meaning that Senghor has tended to attach to the term is that of a cultural and spiritual endowment of the Black man, an original quality deriving from the common African source. According to him, this quality provides the denominator of the Black race, defines a common ground, as it were, of feeling and of experience from which the varied patterns of cultural expression in the Black world receive a kind of primordial determination. Negritude functions as a synonym of the "collective soul" of all the Black peoples, the underlying substratum, deriving ultimately from the African heritage, to which the personality of both the African and the Black man in the New World can be reduced. When Senghor defines Negritude, then, as "the sum total of African cultural values," he adopts a different perspective from Sartre. He sees it as a *permanence*, as the informing principle of a stable African being expressing itself through his culture, which then becomes, so to speak, its "objective correlative."

There is an obvious disparity, and even conflict, between the definitions of Sartre and Senghor, which, though not easy to reconcile, is not difficult to understand. Sartre was using the term to designate the movement of a collective feeling in the definite context of a historical situation. The aspiration of the French-speaking Black intellectuals toward a new experience of their African antecedents was for him no more than an element, albeit a powerful one, in this movement. It indicated a tendency toward an objective which had no real meaning for him since it did not constitute a reality to which he could relate in any profound sense. Moreover, the essentially dialectical turn of his intellect predisposed him to an almost exclusive concern with the "dynamics" of the movement. Senghor's definition, on the other hand, is a reversal of the dialectical scheme put forward by Sartre. Rather than a tendency, the African term becomes the point of departure and remains the substantial element in the historical and spiritual progression implied by the collective vision of the Black man as represented by the concept of Negritude.

It could be argued that this reversal operated by Senghor arises out of a need to give Negritude a more concrete foundation than that of a transient sentiment or attitude, to give the concept a more definite substance than that of a limited historical stand—hence, the direction of his efforts toward a rigorous, as well as comprehensive, formulation of the concept over the years. Yet it must also be admitted that Senghor's viewpoint is not unnatural, and, by making Africa, and the Black man generally, the central preoccupation of his intellectual application, he gives to his theories a greater measure of relevance and interest, perhaps, than does Sartre.

At all events, it is clear that the two viewpoints are not, in the long run, mutually exclusive, and that the total significance of Negritude lies indeed in its compatibility with the two definitions of the concept proposed by the two men. In other words, the varied interpretations and implications of the term itself attest to the comprehensive character of the movement and to its immediate involvement in the historical experience of the Black man. At the same time, while characterized as a historical phenomenon with its origins in definite sociological factors, it is also the reflection, seen as a body of ideas embraced within a single concept, of the effort of a social group to pose its experience on a level higher than that of the immediate, to project itself beyond the historical moment so as to achieve a fuller and deeper understanding of its experience, and ultimately of itself. The literary and ideological writings of the French-speaking Black writers amount therefore to an introspective movement, while the theories of Senghor constitute an extensive effort to give their movement a foundation by creating a fundamental framework of ideas.

THE COLONIAL EXPERIENCE

The sociology of knowledge has accustomed us to seeing ideas in their functional setting, in their specific correlation with their sociological determinations and directions. In the case of the Negritude movement, the connection between the experience which gave birth to it, the sentiments and attitudes which this experience produced, and the ideas which as a result germinated in the minds of French-speaking Black intellectuals, is a direct one. Between, first, the factor which gave some kind of uniformity and consistency to the collective existence of Black people within the Western world; second, that which in a more limited way particularized the experience of the French-speaking intellectual within the larger context of the "Black world"; and, third, the global world view which the most articulate among them came to develop, there exists what one might call a *sociological continuum*: a straight line of development from a collective feeling to a collective idea. Negritude corresponds perfectly to Karl Mannheim's description of ideology as a "thought in the service of a wish." It arose out of a complex of mental images which fulfilled a felt need, and was developed into a systematic and self-sustaining ideology which is, in the last resort, an intellectual projection of this need. This double perspective of the movement also confers on it a singular significance in the development of contemporary ideas in Africa: first, as a response to the colonial situation in which Black people were involved; and, second, as a movement of the collective mind beyond this situation toward the definition of new terms of reference for the Black experience and, in particular, for the African consciousness in the modern world.

The reaction of the Black man embodied by Negritude thus takes on its full historical meaning when considered against the background of the colonial situation which determined the specific character of the experience and existence of Black peoples. It would be tedious to elaborate upon this notion of "the colonial situation"; what is essential to bear in mind is the racial component which characterized it, the relationship between the White dominator and the Black subject, in other words, the *master-slave relationship*. The main foundation of this relationship was political. Colonial rule implied the deliberate suppression of the political identity of the colonized, with all the social and economic implications which this entailed. From a sociological perspective, the colonial situation implied, as Balandier has pointed out, a state of tension and conflict,[9] underlined by the racial differentiation of the parties involved in this conflict. It can thus be said that the relationship of the Black man to his White dominator was based upon a racial antinomy in which the colonizer and the colonized represented the opposite terms. This explains the fact that White domination came eventually to rest upon a racial ideology, a hierarchy of values and a system of symbols by which colonial rule was rationalized, and which aimed at a mental and spiritual alienation of the Black man. For Negritude cannot be understood without considering the deep injury to the self awareness of the Black man by which colonial rule in Africa, and the political and social domination of Negro communities in America, came to be sustained. The consistent denigration of African cultures and societies, and the deliberate demoralization of the Black man wherever he was, constituted not simply a rationalization of White domination but, indeed, an overwhelming assault upon the consciousness of the Black man, a direct and crushing attack upon his subjectivity. It is this global alienation of the Black man in the Western world, in both objective and subjective terms, which gave a fundamental unity to his experience, and which serves as the wider framework of the racial consciousness expressed in Negritude. This implied simply the discovery of the negative position of the Black man in the modern world, and a reaction, at first emotional and later rationalized, against this situation.

What was to give the reaction of the French-speaking Black writers its specific character and indeed its motive power, however, was their peculiar cultural and social situation in the context of assimilation. So much has been said already about the problems of assimilation that it would be unnecessary to develop them here. Two points need to be considered, however, in order to understand the orientation of Negritude.

The first point concerns the psychological impact of the French policy of assimilation on the Black intellectual. Because the responses of the adherents of Negritude to their integration into French culture have so often been expressed in symbolic rather than concrete terms, it is often taken by its critics that these problems existed merely in an abstract form. The intensely felt nature of the cultural dilemma of the assimilated individual, the reality of the psychic disruption involved in his situation, is not often fully appreciated. We cannot now very well represent to ourselves the mental and spiritual tension with which the men of the generation of Senghor and Césaire had to live, nor understand perfectly how immediate to them was the dilemma of social and cultural duality with which they were confronted. For assimilation in the colonial context meant for them not only a cleavage in their social awareness, which increased the normal pressure of social constraint, but also a blurring of their normal feeling of attachment to, and inner involvement with, social norms. It was not only the demoralizing impact of colonial ideology, but also the disruptive effect of the double system of social values, that accounted for the double consciousness of the assimilated Black intellectuals, engendering in them an acute sense of disharmony. When it is also considered that the values of their native backgrounds conflicted often with those proposed by their assimilated culture, it will be realized that they were in fact faced with a real problem, not only of meaningful social participation, but a more profound one of identity.

The effect of assimilation upon these individuals was thus to place them in a mental state in which they experienced not simply an estrangement from themselves, but indeed an instability in their very mode of existence. Rendered sensitive to the devaluation of the Black race by colonial domination and its corresponding ideology, and made uncomfortably self-conscious by the essential ambivalence involved in their integration into the culture of their colonial master, it is hardly surprising that the element of personal feeling that often lends a poignant and pathetic note to Negritude, as in Cheikh Hamidou Kane's novel *L'Aventure ambigue*[10] should have run so deeply in the literature. For many of the French-speaking Black writers and intellectuals, to give vent to their *malaise* as assimilated individuals was to respond to an inner compulsion. The metaphysical element of alienation in the literature of Negritude derived, then, from a real and concrete sociopsychological foundation.

The second aspect of assimilation to which attention needs to be drawn is intimately bound up with the first, and has to do with the political and social significance of French colonial policy with regard to the Black elite. This policy tended to equate political rights with cultural conformity and thus overtly to identify the submission of the Black man to colonial rule with submission to Western values. The French-speaking Black writers who developed the ideology of Negritude belonged to the elite created by the advent of Western culture, inasmuch as this culture had become, by reason of the political and social supremacy of the White man, the basic reference point for values in colonial society in Africa. In a sense, therefore, the colonial situation implied the ascendancy of European culture over African and Africa-derived cultures. This association of culture and politics is emphasized in the French policy of assimilation by the very fact that political participation was made open in principle to the Black man—provided he could justify his claim to full social existence in terms of the values of the colonizer. This explains the fact that the cultural preoccupation of the French-speaking Black elite was more pronounced than in the case of their English-speaking counterparts. The social and economic motivation of nationalism is perhaps no less intense in the development of Negritude than in that of other reactions against the colonial situation. But the political component of the nationalist consciousness of the French-speaking Black intellectuals was less marked because, as a class, their experience of the "state of dependence" with regard to the colonizer was felt in cultural rather than political terms. Nonetheless, the political basis of colonial rule was apparent enough to them, and it is easy to understand why the already uneasy sentiments of the assimilated individual came to be crystallized around social factors, and why the quest for identity among the French-speaking Black intellectuals also came to have political significance. "For it is an apparent fact," writes Balandier, "that among colonial peoples, the quest for norms coincides with the quest for autonomy."[11] For the moral, cultural, and spiritual control of the White man came to underlie his social and political control in the mind of the Black elite, and it is this sentiment that accounts for the passionate search for a new spiritual orientation for the Black man with which Negritude was preoccupied.

SELF-REFLECTION AND SOCIAL COMMITMENT

The specific preoccupations and even obsessions that figure as the leading themes in the imaginative and ideological writings of the French-speaking Black intellectuals are too well known to need restatement here.[12] It will therefore be enough, I believe, to highlight and to discuss what I consider to be the main direction of their attitudes and thinking—namely, the creation of a new order of experience for the Black man—and to relate them to the dominant trends in modern African thought.

The direct link—that of cause and effect—between the literary expression of Negritude and the colonial situation explains what appears at first sight as the most striking aspect of its content, its documentary character. Literature is here employed as the representation in artistic terms of a social experience and becomes essentially an imaginative exploration of an objective collective situation, and the transposition of reality into symbols expressing a collective sentiment. This objective relation between the literature of Negritude and the colonial situation confers on it a special value as a testimony to the inner realities of the colonial experience, and explains the direction of the ideas evolved by the movement. For its immediate significance lies in the fact that it reflects not only the impression within the collective mind of a social reality, but also a new activity of this mind toward some kind of intimate understanding and toward an organization of its experience. It is perhaps in the literature of Negritude that we see most clearly the movement of the African mind toward itself, the necessary narcissism that results in the working out of a new self at the intellectual level. The literature represents a process of conscious self-reflection at the level of artistic symbols.

The deliberate character of this process is often overlooked, or not emphasized enough. The whole attitude expressed in the symbolism of Negritude, the state of mind involved with the descent into the depths of the self made by these writers, is centered upon the fact of Blackness which epitomizes the external reality of the Black man's existence. Because Blackness stood as a symbol of his existential plight, it was, as Sartre has observed, inevitable and, indeed, under the circumstances, imperative, that the Negritude poet should undertake to recreate himself by fastening upon this racial fact in order to endow it with a new meaning. The action is indeed a unilateral one, and its essential import is that the poet has decided to *will* himself into a new existence and into a new being, by imposing upon his Blackness a new, positive connotation. Thus Aimé Césaire, the archpoet of Negritude, exclaims:

> My Negritude is not a stone, its deafness thrown against the clamour of the day
> My Negritude is not a film of dead water on the dead eye of the day...
> It thrusts into the red flesh of the soil
> It thrusts into the warm flesh of the sky
> It digs under the opaque dejection of its rightful patience.[13]

What these lines convey is first and foremost the sense of the Black subject coming alive as a responsible being. What they register is the inner progression of his consciousness as it is stimulated into a new awareness and issues forth into a new and determined gesture of defiance and self-fashioning. And the mood of exultation here proceeds from the heightened feeling of life, expressed in organic terms, communicating itself to the poet's senses as he strides into the new stance which he proposes to his race. This same conscious progression from passivity to a new activity can be seen in the intense transformation that is depicted in these lines from another poem by the same poet:

> And the mines of radium buried deep in the abyss
> of my innocence will burst into grains in the manger
> of birds.[14]

Césaire's lines are highly representative in their transmission of the lively and consuming restlessness of spirit that characterizes, in greater or lesser measure, the work of the most accomplished of the Negritude writers. This is a quality that derives from their immediate engagement, within the innermost recesses of their feelings, with the state of mental and spiritual disruption implied by the colonial situation, and against which, through their literary activity, they began to struggle.

The imaginative writings of the French-speaking Black intellectuals can be said to offer a simplified view of the relationship between art and social reality by presenting the former as a direct reflection of the latter. In this view, artistic creation is seen clearly as the translation of social perception into imaginative symbols, reducing the complex web of human and social relations into images which constitute the essential quality of the experience that they determine—in other words, into their most immediate manifestations within the collective consciousness. And it is by the same token that we can take the literature of the Black consciousness as the elaboration of a distinctive new Black subjectivism. This is the aspect of Negritude to which Sartre drew attention when he defined it as an attitude to the world. But I believe the literature of Negritude has more than a purely subjective significance, for its meaning extends further than the establishment of a new state of mind. The very involvement of this literature in a social situation gives it the kind of active significance which Sartre himself attributed to literary creation when he wrote:

> in a collectivity that is continually taking hold of itself,
> judging itself and undergoing a metamorphosis, the
> written work can be an essential condition of action,
> that is, the moment of the reflective consciousness.[15]

By consciously ascribing a social and political purpose to their work, French-speaking Black writers sought to make as explicit as possible the social function of literature which Sartre recognizes as implicit in the art form. However, the political importance of the imaginative expression of Negritude does not reside so much in this purely verbal stance, as in the active correlation of artistic creation, which remains a formal substitute for action, with political activity and thinking. Many of the writers sought to make their literary work an integral part of their political action to such an extent that art became for them the mediator of political commitment.

Insofar, then, as the literature of Negritude was the reflection of social consciousness, serving as the wellspring of political intentions, it was functional and active. In the imaginative writings of the French-speaking Black writers, the distance between literature, considered as the passive expression of experience, and political myth, defined by Georges Gurvitch as "image-signals calling to action,"[16] became significantly narrowed. The literature was already then beginning to fulfill the function of ideology; its manifest purpose was not simply to register the Black man's experience in the modern world, but also to define for him what L. V. Thomas has called "a new manner of being in history."[17]

NÉGRITUDE AND AFRICAN MYTH

To the tendency observed above toward an active social purpose established in the imaginative writings of Negritude, the ideological writings give definite form and substance. The intimate reciprocity between artistic and ideological expression in Negritude is most clearly established by the development of the African myth, which seems to provide the unifying element in the sentiments and thinking of the French-speaking Black writers. It brings out most clearly the symmetry at a symbolic level between the active factors in these writers' experience of the colonial situation and their responses to them.

Mythmaking is an essential activity of the human mind and an important element of collective life. The role of the imagination in formulating the responses of men to the conditions of existence, to the various determinations which they have to endure, has always been a preeminent one. Even more relevant is the social function of myths, which serve as agents in the fusion of minds on which, in the long run, collective participation depends. It is generally through the symbols that any given collectivity provides for its members that they are able to develop meaningful involvement with each other, that a group mind is able to emerge out of the interpenetration of their various and separate modes of consciousness.[18]

When this observation is borne in mind, it becomes easy to understand the special significance of the African myth in the literature of Negritude and in the development of its ideas. The symbolic value of Africa as the antithesis of Europe, already proposed by colonial ideology in negative terms, acquires a new meaning and a new force in the reversal of the colonial order and in the creation of an alternative system of social symbols with which the Black subject can identify. Africa consequently serves as the positive pole upon which the historical and racial consciousness expressed in Negritude comes to be centered. This is obvious enough and should explain the romanticism which characterizes the African theme in the work of the French-speaking Black writers. Their intention to create a new image of Africa could not possibly accord with the kind of objective appraisal of the African heritage that the critics of Negritude have demanded of these writers. It is thus futile to demand of them a disinterestedness that was precluded by their peculiar situation.

The whole process of the revaluation of Africa in Negritude takes on ideological significance, however, not only in relation to the historical context in which the enterprise was undertaken, but also because we are faced here with more than a simple negation of colonial ideology; it is a movement toward the differentiation of the Black man as such, and of the African, in particular. A new conception of the African on the basis of his cultural heritage, and of his special place and possible role in the world emerges. The import of this is again quite clear: it represents a conscious effort to reactivate the Black man by bringing to the level of his consciousness and will his inherent sense of his own value and potential. If, therefore, the Negritude movement has been erected upon a novel image of Africa—a Black *mystique*—it is a *mystique* with a definite social aim: to create out of a community of experience and feeling a new community of values and destiny.

The movement from the imaginative to the intellectual expression of the African myth consists in the hardening of an attitude and its firm realization in an idea. Thus the theoretical elaboration of Negritude is a development upon the subjective element which underlies the literature, sharpening it and giving it ideological focus.

The writings of Léopold Sédar Senghor constitute the most systematic effort at giving this ideological aspect of Negritude both a unity and an autonomous dimension. What Senghor strove to achieve through the doctrine was an enlargement of the African consciousness. With him, Negritude acquires a broader perspective than that afforded by the colonial question. It becomes a vision of the race, which embraces history only to transcend it, by relating Black people, and specifically the African, to the universal order. In Senghor's hands, Negritude is turned into an introspective process in terms not only of existence, but also of being.

It will not be possible to deal here at any length with the theory of Negritude as expounded by Senghor,[19] but we might restate some of the main points along which the theory runs. It seems clear that Senghor in fact develops Negritude theory along the same line of progression as its literary expression—that is, from a reversal of the hierarchy of symbols which sanctioned the colonial enterprise to an affirmation of the positive quality of being African and, by extension, Black. From the distinction he makes between the psychology and mode of apprehension of the African and that of the European, Senghor has derived a whole philosophy of African values. What he has distinguished as the "participating reason" of the African is placed at the heart of an apprehension of reality which determines a differentiated worldview. In Senghor's explanation, this worldview consists of a belief in a hierarchy of forces animating the visible world and all proceeding from a single vital principle as a supranatural order (what he terms "le surréel"). The African in his psychological disposition is a sensory being, open through his pores, as it were, to the universe. His relation to the world is of a sensual order, one of an organic sympathy with the whole of creation. His mode of knowledge is therefore intuitive rather than rational; hence, his spirituality derives from his affectivity. The distinctive quality of the African, and the psychophysiological basis of Negritude, is for Senghor this emotive endowment, "this essential human warmth, which is a presence within the life of the world."[20]

The moral values deriving from this sense of sympathy with the universe, this immediate participation in the cosmic life, constitute for Senghor the spiritual framework of African social organization. His treatise on African socialism can be summarized as a demonstration of the processes by which the African's mystical values are manifested in social terms, given objective expression in the world of interpersonal relations. In Senghor's theory of Negritude, the African's social universe is the projection into the human world of the mystical world of vital forces.[21]

It is principally in his development of the concept of African socialism that Senghor's effort to give a substance to Negritude appears most clearly. We see a stream of ideas developing from a system of rationalizations; the desire to reverse a given situation gives rise to a new conception of the self, ultimately taking shape as a worldview. For, in this development, we are presented with not simply a series of assertions about the African mind or observations about African society, but rather with a social philosophy whose fountainhead is an ontological vision. There is also a marked transfer of certain categories associated with the political and the mystical into the sociotheoretical so as to give it something of a sacred sanction, a transcendental dimension, as it were. The point here, then, is that Senghor's formulation of Negritude tends toward an absolute vision of the race founded upon an African mystique: cosmology is thus borne out of a contingent situation.

The main significance of this development seems to me to be what it reveals of the underlying motivations which direct Senghor's thought processes in his philosophical elaboration of Negritude. It is not only a matter of considering their source in those sentiments and attitudes expressed in the imaginative writings, and in particular, in the poetry, with its emphasis on vital values, on a certain pagan dynamism and the consequent recourse to traditional African mythologies as the touchstone for a fresh and primary vision of the world. Its significance also derives, and primarily, I believe, from the deliberate and conscious emphasis laid by Senghor on values that, though not unknown in Western civilization, have always been considered contradictory to its dominant trend and spirit. Also of importance is his manner of ascribing these values to African civilization in order to differentiate the African from Western man. Yet his fundamental preoccupation is not simply to establish an absolute opposition between the two, but rather to stress their complementary nature and, ultimately, their unity in a new humanism. It is instructive in this regard to consider the connection between Senghor's theory of Negritude and those currents in European thought from which the theory derives some of its leading concepts.

In many ways, Négritude is a latter-day romanticism, an African variant of the anti-intellectual tradition within European thought. But it represents an originality, in that the line of division between the clarity and rigor of the classical mind, and the self-abandonment of the romantic mind is now drawn between two different civilizations, and their associated two distinct races. This distinction itself can be attributed to some extent to the influence of writers such as Gobineau, for whom the notions of race and culture were synonymous, and who believed in the distinctive character of the race as the moving spirit of each civilization. In particular the idea of an organic belonging to the nation developed by Maurice Barrès in France, notably in his novel *Les Déracinés*, seems to have marked the thinking of Senghor rather deeply.[22] Now, this mystical idea of race and nation inherited from nineteenth-century European nationalist ideology forms the basis of the conception of African identity in Negritude and is overlaid by other ideas stemming from the Western romantic tradition. These ideas tended to confer a value upon what one might call the "nonrational categories" and to establish the validity of nondiscursive modes of knowledge. The result is the progressive exaltation of the imagination as an autonomous faculty, different from the intellect, and if not superior at least equal to it, in its own special sphere of operation.

We recognize here the current of thought which, starting with Rousseau, was to find in the person of Coleridge one of its principal theorists, and whose philosophy has been described as "the intellectual centre of the romantic movement."[23] Subsequent developments in the intellectual milieu of Western Europe were to reinforce this current. With the disillusionment with realism and order, the romantic imagination became dominant in the literature of Western Europe, finding a culmination in the irrationalism of the surrealist movement. Meanwhile, dissatisfaction with the positivist doctrine led to Bergson's sustained reexamination of the logical intelligence and his affirmation of the importance of intuition as a mode of knowledge. Nor must one forget the tremendous impact of Freud and his theories on the active role of the subconscious in our total experience. It cannot be said that these developments have led to a total abandonment in the West of the traditional adherence to the canons of logical intelligence, or by any means established the primacy of what one may subsume under the general term of the "romantic intelligence." Nonetheless the latter trend has established for itself a certain prestige, and even acceptance, to such an extent that an opening within the Western intellectual tradition had been secured for the serious consideration of doctrines which took as their frame of reference the nonrational.

Closely allied to this relationship of Senghor's theory with the romantic tradition in the West is the direct influence of the anthropologists, who not only furnished him with some of the terms with which he elaborates the theory, but also supplied some of the spirit that animates it. The broad division between the logical mentality of the West and the mystical and "participating" reason of non-Western man can be identified as a direct derivation from the writings of Lévy-Bruhl. Moreover, Father Tempels's application of Bergsonian philosophy to the Bantu accounts for the central position of the notion of "vital force" in Senghor's formulation of Negritude. The increasingly permissive attitude on the part of European scholarship to non-Western cultures that anthropology helped to foster was, however, only possible through the gradual acceptance of the idea that there was more within man and within the world than was contained in Western rationalism. The spirit of relativity was already abroad before its confirmation by anthropology, which demonstrated the different patterns of culture and of experience that could be found within the human community. The import of all this, in philosophical terms, is the denial of the universal value of the traditional norms and categories obtaining in the Western thought.

What gives coherence to all these separate threads in Senghor's philosophy is his conscious erection into a whole system of thought of these elements which, though significant, had remained subsidiary in Western culture, and his claim to their African specificity. The intuitive and imaginative paths to knowledge which the Western poets had claimed, since the early nineteenth century, as their exclusive realm, are thus given a wider application. Wordsworth's "organic sensibility" and Whitman's "cosmic passion" find a new abode, so to speak, in the African mind.

But if Senghor's immediate purpose is to effect a sharp differentiation between the African and the European by reference to a dominant spirit of their respective cultures and the attitudes that they determine, his ultimate aim is to demonstrate their reciprocal values within a larger unity. His insistence on the validity of the mystical faculty as a normal rather than exceptional mode of experience in non-Western cultures is intended to offer a wider scope for a new humanism that would embrace all the cultures in the universe. In this vision of a "civilisation of the universal," in which Teilhard de Chardin's philosophy plays a major role, the African mentality and consciousness would complement those of the West, bringing forth a new humanism in which the values of the head have been finely counterbalanced with those of the heart. It is in my view in the light of this complementary synthesis of the modes of feeling and of thought that one should now understand Senghor's well-known phrase: "Emotion is African, as Reason is Hellenic."[24]

NEGRITUDE AND THE MODERN WORLD

When one considers the line of development in Negritude from collective sentiment to theory, one is struck by the considerable distance between its original impulse and the attitudes of which it is a reflection, and its elevation, in Senghor's development of its theory, to the status of an independent system of thought with its own autonomous value outside of and beyond the historical and sociological factors by which it was generated. In effect, although in the first instance it can be considered a strategy to meet the exigencies of history, it is developed in the writings of Senghor into a full statement on the nature of the African mind and of its means to knowledge, in other words, an epistemology.

The objections to Negritude, and in particular to Senghor's formulation of it, have always been leveled from this angle. These objections concern generally the stretching of the theory beyond its sociological context in order to give it a philosophical orientation.[25] And, indeed, it is perhaps the misfortune of Senghor that in his successive elaborations upon the concept of Negritude, his poetic temperament should have impelled his ideas toward a form of idealism. This objection is particularly relevant where his social philosophy is concerned, for there is a discrepancy, and perhaps even a fundamental contradiction, between the philosophy considered as a plan of action, and its theoretical basis in what is, essentially, an imaginative vision. Hence, considered from a sociological perspective, Negritude appears to be a static philosophy, inasmuch as it postulates the constancy of an African mentality, an irreducible African "soul." The emphasis that Senghor lays on the distinctive nature of the Black man is seen by some critics to imply not only a too ready acceptance of racial theories developed in Europe,[26] but also a denial of the necessary progression of African culture from the mystical to the scientific and rational stage of development. Senghor's Negritude does not appear to these critics therefore to be situated within what has been termed a "diachronic perspective."[27] And precisely because it exalts the traditional values of Africa, whose essence it endeavors to clarify, and whose categories it attempts to establish, it is held to be a retrograde and conservative philosophy, one that is reactionary in its social implications. In this respect, in particular, it has been described as an ideology of a new middle class attempting to inhibit an authentic social revolution, as an *ideology* in the Marxist sense of the word: an elaborate system of mystifications.[28] In all these objections, the main concern is to judge the philosophy of Senghor in relation to immediate social problems. Negritude does not seem to these critics to have, from this point of view, an empirical significance. This is what appears most readily in the attacks of the Marxists, whose materialist bent necessarily pits them against any doctrine that implies any kind of idealist orientation. They therefore tend to dismiss Negritude as metaphysical, irrational, and nonscientific, in much the same way that the early Marxists dismissed the Slav socialists as either immature or reactionary dreamers.[29]

There is a good deal of misunderstanding involved in these objections, as well as a certain partisan dogmatism. But it can be admitted that the circumstances in which the concept of Negritude developed have made it fluctuate between a progressive utopia and a conservative ideology. Moreover, in the postcolonial era, it has not only lost much of its topical relevance, but has also been exposed to the trial of practical issues through the fact that its most articulate exponent has also been a Head of State. Very few ideas can come out of such a trial unscathed. The main weakness of the theory lies, however, in its absolutism. The paradox of Senghor's thought is that, while on the theoretical plane it opens a broader perspective of human development for the Black subject, it does not in reality present a progressive aspect in sociological terms, and appears indeed to lie outside the realm of empirical and historical factors. It is, even as social philosophy, somewhat abstract. When Senghor remarks for instance: "the very being of being is to persevere in one's being,"[30] it appears that he is unable to recognize the relative character of his own thinking. Certainly he has anchored his Negritude to the ideas of Teilhard de Chardin and foresees its mutation in its progressive integration into the "Civilisation of the Universal." But his conception of Negritude makes it appear as something immanent in the historical process, as a Black essence realizing itself more fully in the cosmic consciousness prophesied by Teilhard, being merely prolonged and not transcended, and therefore retaining its fundamental identity.[31] Apart from the intangible nature of such a proposition, this conception is also at variance with the bent of modern historical intelligence, with its pronounced dialectical inclination.

Yet there is another angle from which to view Negritude and to appreciate its achievement and enduring interest. As an intellectual movement, it forms part of a long and steady reaction to the impact of Europe, and represents the final fruition of a process that dates back practically to the first contact between Africa and Europe. The new African who has progressively emerged from this contact and who was placed at the heart of the confrontation between two different world orders has had to seek through intellectual and emotional means a resolution of the conflict inherent in this situation. The African could not begin to take stock of himself until he had been confronted with an outside image of himself. He could not begin to think about himself until his mind was intruded upon and divided between two conflicting frames of reference. It was this pressure on the African's psyche, which conditioned his attitudes as he was forced through the web of historical events, that is so well demonstrated in the Negritude adventure.

We know that African nationalism has its roots in this intro-spective movement. The idea of an African world was finally crystallized in the imagination of the African as much through the transformation of the African's self-awareness as through political mobilization. All through the nineteenth and the early years of the twentieth centuries, the rising African bourgeoisie had begun to justify its claims to political rights and to self-determination for the continent by refashioning the African image. And, although the cultural ideas developed in this phase of African awakening were a function of the social and political aspirations of the new African elite, they represented more than nationalist thinking. They implied, as well, a full statement of the conditions and prospects of the African's existence in the modern world, with reference to his past heritage. As Robert July has put it, this African reaction represented "a thoroughgoing examination of man and society in West Africa."[32]

This is the general direction of modern African thought which finds a culmination in Negritude. As set out by Senghor, it is certainly the most fundamental expression of the effort of the modern African at self-understanding and self-projection, and his theories on the African personality constitute an advance of a qualitative kind on previous attempts to define a collective *ethos* in modern Africa. This advance can best be illustrated by comparing Senghor with Edward Wilmot Blyden, his most considerable predecessor, and whose ideas most closely parallel Senghor's own among the early ideological leaders of Africa. Blyden had touched upon practically every aspect of the African personality that Senghor pronounced upon in his day. But Senghor's ideas cannot by any means be considered a mere restatement of those of Blyden, who believed in the unique quality of race and therefore in the special genius of the African.[33] Although his belief in a spiritual endowment of the African anticipated the ideas of Senghor, it was left to the latter to refine his predecessor's conceptions of the African mind, to analyze its manner of responding to the world, and to enunciate an African mode of experience. Similarly, Blyden, as well as other African ideological leaders after him, had presented almost a century before Senghor a conception of a distinct and original African system of social values and organization. Senghor, benefitting from modern social theories, developed this conception into a comprehensive social philosophy with relevance for the contemporary situation in Africa today.

For Negritude, with the theory of African socialism derived from it, is meant as an instrument in the service of an African renewal. It takes its place in the general effort now prevailing in Africa at creating a meaningful collective existence in the modern context. As Senghor himself put it some years ago:

> The problem with which we, Africans in 1959, are confronted is how to integrate African values into the world of 1959. It is not a case of reviving the past so as to live on in an African museum. It is a case of animating this world, here and now, with the values that come from our past.[34]

What distinguishes Senghor's intellectual endeavors from all others, however, is his manifest intent to go to the roots of those values which we are more or less aware of, and thereby to delineate the African's originality. In contrast to other African political and ideological leaders, whose entire thinking and action were focused upon immediate issues, Senghor wanted to illuminate with the vivid light of the intellect the foundations in the African mind on which African reconstruction could be effected. The common source of his and Nyerere's African socialism cannot be disputed, whatever the difference in their final positions. This source is a personal interpretation of the traditional system of values and social life in Africa. Both are attempts to rethink in modern terms, and to adapt the spirit of traditional Africa to modern conditions.[35] But, in Senghor's case, we discern an effort to see more than the manifestations of this spirit, to comprehend it as a phenomenon in its ultimate essence, before attempting to integrate it within the scheme of collective life. Thus, where others assert the originality of African cultural expression, Senghor affirms the specificity of the African mind which underlies it. It is in this sense that his theory of Negritude can be considered the decisive stage in the intellectual elaboration of a modern African identity and consciousness.

Notes

1. Césaire (1968).

2. Senghor (1948a).

3. Sartre (1964), p. 41.

4. Sartre (1964), p. 60.

5. Sartre (1964), p. 60.

6. Fanon (1967), pp. 134ff.

7. See Jahn (1961) and Jahn (1968), pp. 251-262.

8. See Decraene (1959).

9. Balandier (1966), p. 44.

10. Kane (1961).

11. Balandier (1966), p. 44.

12. For a schematic exposition of these themes, see Chapter Two above.

13. Césaire (1983) p. 101.

14. Césaire (1946), p. 8.

15. Sartre, 1947.

16. Gurvitch (1963), p. 124.

17. Thomas (1963), p. 383.

18. See "Représentations individuelles et représentations collectives" and other articles in Durkheim (1967).

19. For a fuller exposition, see "What is Negritude?," in Irele (1981), pp. 67-88.

20. Senghor (1964a), p. 317.

21. Senghor (1964b).

22. See Kohn (1944) and Ploncard d'Assac (1965).

23. Hough (1970), p. 84.

24. Senghor (1976), p. 33.

25. For a fuller review of these objections, see "The Negritude Debate," Chapter Four of this volume.

26. See Mezu (1968), pp. 173-76.

27. Mudimbe (1967).

28. See for example, Armah (1967) and Fanon (1968), pp. 167-69.

29. See in particular Marton (1966), pp. 3-10.

30. Senghor (1976), p. 97.

31. Senghor (1962b).

32. July (1968), p. 18.

33. See Lynch (1967).

34. Senghor (1976), p. 78.

35. See Nyerere (1968).

Chapter Four
The Negritude Debate
❦

There is a sense in which the development of Negritude, both as a movement and as a concept, has been marked by a fundamental irony. This irony stems from the fact that the first extended discussion and systematic formulation of Negritude was provided by Jean-Paul Sartre. In many ways, it was Sartre's brilliant analysis in the essay "Orphée noir" that consecrated the term and gave Negritude the status of one of the most important ideological concepts of our time. At the same time, it can be argued that his very formulation has been in large measure responsible for the ambiguity that has surrounded the term and generated the controversy that Negritude has attracted to itself ever since.

The starting point of Sartre's analysis is the complex of emotions and attitudes expressed in the poetry of the first generation of French-speaking Black poets brought together in the 1948 anthology by Senghor.[1] These emotions and attitudes, related as they were to a historical experience common to all Black people, were subsumed under the term Negritude, coined by Aimé Césaire and first used by him in the long poem *Cahier d'un retour au pays natal*. In exploring the universe of feelings of which the poetry was a representation, Sartre was led also to examine the various meanings suggested by the term and to offer a comprehensive interpretation of its significance.

His trenchant summing up of Negritude as "the Negro's affective attitude to the world" underlines his understanding of the movement as a response to the specific pressures of a historical situation, as a means for the Black man to take his place in history as an active agent rather than as a suffering object. Sartre develops this aspect of the movement as follows:

> *La situation du noir, sa "déchirure" originelle, l'aliénation qu'une pensée étrangère lui impose sous le nom d'assimilation le mettent dans l'obligation de reconquérir son unité existentielle de nègre ou, si l'on préfère, la pureté originelle de son projet par une ascèse progressive, au-delà de l'univers du discours. La Négritude, comme la liberté, est point de départ et terme ultime: il s'agit de la faire passer de l'immédiat au médiat, de la thématiser.* (p. xxiii)

> [The situation of the black, his original "laceration," the *alienation* that a foreign way of thinking imposes on him, in the name of assimilation, all oblige him to reconquer his existential unity as a negro,—or, if you prefer, the original purity of his project, through a gradual *askesis*, beyond the universe of discourse. Negritude, like liberty, is a point of departure and an ultimate goal: it is a matter of making negritude pass from the immediate to the mediate, a matter of *thematizing* it. (Bernasconi, 2001, p. 125)]

Sartre further discerns in this progression of the Black consciousness toward a full awareness of its determining history a positive manner of transcending experience, of living the world in its fullest implications. This leads him to the well-known formulation of Negritude, in terms of his existentialist philosophy, as "the-being-in-the-world of the Negro" (*l'être-dans-le-monde-du-noir*).

It was perhaps to be expected that Sartre's interpretation would be closely related to his own philosophical and ideological preoccupations at the time when he wrote the essay, and generally his discussion refers to an ethical and philosophical tradition of radicalism of which he has been one of the most distinguished contemporary heirs. This radical approach was moreover perfectly suited to any understanding of the actualities of the global experience of the Blacks as represented in the poetry Sartre was examining.

However, Sartre deviates from this course for a while, in order to consider other aspects of Negritude. Taking his cue from Senghor, he devotes the entire middle section of his essay to an examination of the term as the fundamental reference for the Black poet in his "existential project." Thus he writes:

> *Cette méthode...est la loi dialectique des transformations successives qui conduiront le nègre à la coïncidence avec soi-meme dans la Négritude. Il ne s'agit pas pour lui de connaître, ni de s'arracher à lui-même dans l'extase mais de découvrir à la fois et de devenir ce qu'il est.* (p. xxiii)

> [But this method...is the dialectical law of successive transformations which lead the negro to coincidence with himself in negritude. It is not a matter of *knowing*, nor of his ecstatically tearing himself away from himself, but rather of both discovering and becoming what he is. (Bernasconi, 2001, p. 125)]

Sartre goes on to distinguish between what he calls "objective Negritude," which expresses itself in the customs, the arts, the songs and dances of the African populations, and the "subjective Negritude" of the Black poet, which corresponds to the movement of his sensibility toward the scheme of spiritual values defined by those elements of the African civilization that stand as the objective references of his original identity. And it is precisely Sartre's understanding of this movement that gives point to the title of his essay. As he puts it

> *Ainsi sont indissolublement mêlés chez le vates de la Négritude le thème du retour au pays natal et celui de la redescente aux Enfers éclatants de l'âme noire. Il s'agit d'une quête, d'un dépouillement systématique et d'une ascèse...Et je nommerai "orphique" cette poésie parce que cette inlassable descente du nègre en soi-même me*

97

fait songer à Orphée allant réclamer Eurydice à Pluton.
(p. xvii)

[Thus the theme of return to the native country and of redescent into the glaring hell of the black soul are indissolubly mixed up in the *vates* of negritude. A quest is involved here, a systematic stripping and an *askesis*... And I shall call this poetry "Orphic" because the negro's tireless descent into himself makes me think of Orpheus going to claim Eurydice from Pluto. (121)]

In this light, Negritude begins to appear as something more than an active confrontation with history, more than a strategy, so to speak, to meet the pressures and vicissitudes of the collective existence, rather as a term or facet of an original being which gives sanction to the historical gesture of the Black poet. Sartre himself elaborates on this aspect. Analyzing the symbolism employed by the poets, as expressive of an original mode of apprehension, he comes to the following conclusion:

Si l'on voulait systématiser, on dirait que le Noir se fond à la Nature entière en tant qu'il est sympathie sexuelle pour la Vie et qu'il se revendique comme l'Homme en tant qu'il est Passion de douleur révoltée. (p. xxxv)

[If one wished to systematize, one would say that the Black blends with whole of Nature, in as much as he represents sexual congeniality with Life, and in as much as he claims he is Man in his passion of rebellious suffering. (133)]

Although Sartre finds a parallel between this vitalism and the Dionysian cult of ancient Greece as celebrated by Nietzsche, he seems to regard it as a specific endowment of the Black and as the essential quality of Negritude. And relating this to the poetic expression of the French-speaking Black, he asks:

Est-ce une explication *systématique de l'âme noire
ou un Archetype platonicien qu'on peut indéfiniment
approcher sans jamais y atteindre?* (p. xl)

[Is it a systematic *explanation* of the Black soul or a
Platonic Archetype which one can approach indefi-
nitely without ever attaining it? (137)]

But, although Sartre here appears to envisage Negritude from
an essentialist point of view, it turns out that in fact his emphasis
is elsewhere, and it is here that some of the ambiguity in his
analysis resides. For Negritude is, for Sartre, not so much the
expression in time of a definite collective personality and mode
of understanding peculiar to the Black, but a contingent phenomenon, the provisional outcome of the tension between the
Black man's *situation,* on the one hand, and his *freedom,* on the
other. The sympathy which Sartre appears to exhibit for an idealist notion of a *Black soul* proves illusory; his emphasis on the
historical and ideological significance of the concept emerges
more clearly toward the end of his essay:

*Du coup la notion subjective, existentielle, ethnique de
Négritude "passe," comme dit Hegel, dans celle—objective, positive, exacte—de prolétariat.* (p. xl)

[After that, the subjective, existential, ethnic notion
of *negritude* "passes," as Hegel says, into the objective,
positive, and precise notion of the *proletariat.* (137)]

And, further on, he sums up the matter in the following terms:

*En fait, la Négritude apparaît comme le temps faible d'une
progression dialectique: l'affirmation théorique et pratique
de la suprématie du blanc est la thèse; la position de la
Négritude comme valeur antithétique est le moment de la
négativité. Mais ce moment négatif n'a pas de suffisance
par lui-même et les noirs qui en usent le savent fort bien;
ils savent qu'il vise à préparer la synthèse ou réalisation de
l'humain dans une société sans races.* (p. xli)

[In fact, Negritude appears as the minor moment of a dialectical progression: the theoretical and practical affirmation of white supremacy is the thesis; the position of Negritude as an antithetical value is the moment of negativity. But this negative moment is not sufficient in itself, and these blacks who use it know this perfectly well; they know that it aims at preparing the synthesis or realization of the human in a raceless society. (137)]

In concrete terms, then, Sartre suggests in his essay that the felt intensity of Black poetry, related as it is to a specific historical experience, serves to endow that experience with a tragic beauty and symbolic resonance, but that its true direction and meaning reside in its defining for the race a truly historic mission. For Sartre, Negritude is simply the effort to create a new and positive mode of historical existence and consciousness for the Black race, in a perpetual tension between the actualities of its collective experience, and the humanizing tendencies of its collective will and intention.

Sartre's essay was to exercise a remarkable influence not only in making Black poetry known to the French, but also in establishing Negritude as a significant contemporary ideology. It provided not only the main themes of its later development as a concept, notably in the writings of Senghor, but also, arising out of its bristling ambiguities, the lines along which much of the controversy on Negritude has run. There is a further paradox involved here, for Senghor's formulation, while representing a further expansion of some of the themes which Sartre's essay threw up in such magnificent profusion, shows in fact a clear divergence from Sartre in its emphasis. In an important respect, Senghor elaborates in his essays on these themes in order to gather them, as it were, into a focus upon what seemed to him, as an African, the essential point: the affirmation of Negritude as a concept designating the collective personality of the Black race, as a quality essential to the race, and only incidentally involved in a particular history which it transcends.

Thus, while Senghor does not lose sight of the historical context of Negritude as a movement involving the expression of

a new spirit of Black assertion relative to the political and sociological conditions of the Black experience, he tends rather to a
definition of the concept itself in terms that are fundamentally
essentialist. For him, Negritude represents a mode of being and
denotes the cultural and spiritual endowment of the Black man,
a basic groundwork of the collective personality deriving from
the common African origin. Where Sartre's emphasis falls on
the "subjective Negritude," which is historical and contingent,
Senghor sees this simply as an inner compulsion, arising from
the circumstances of history, toward self-affirmation, and therefore as a purely secondary aspect of Negritude. For Senghor,
the act of self-affirmation itself is related, more importantly, to
a common consciousness of shared cultural and moral values
and of psychological traits original to the race—hence his most
common definition of Negritude as *"l'ensemble des valeurs du
monde noir"* ("the totality of the values of the Black world").

There is a clear shift, therefore, from Sartre's understanding
of Negritude as a phenomenon subject to the laws of a historical
dialectic, to a view of Negritude as a unique endowment of the
Black soul, with an objective expression in those specific features
of the African civilization which make it a distinctive, organic
whole, and which are the determinants of a special disposition of
the Black race. Where, for Sartre, Negritude is pure contingence
and becoming, for Senghor, it appears more as an irreducible
essence of the collective identity.

It is instructive to contrast the views of Sartre with those
of Senghor because their divergence on the essential definition
reveals not merely a difference of personal intellectual disposition but, more fundamentally, of interests and involvement in
the subject. The essential motivation of Senghor's efforts was to
rehabilitate African civilization and, through it, the Black race.
Though Sartre shows some sympathy for this consideration and
makes some concession to it, his final emphasis, as we have seen,
does not rest on a new appraisal of African culture, to which
he was an outsider, but rather on the possible historical role of
Black men in a political and social revolution whose ideological
seeds were sown in Europe. Senghor's interests lay elsewhere,
and if he conceded a historical significance to Negritude, it was a

significance that derived from a unique situation of the race, not to be confounded with any other. This much is made clear in the following lines:

> La voix de l'Afrique planant au-dessus de la
> rage des canons longs
> ....
> Est-ce sa faute si Dieu lui a demandé les prémices
> de ses moissons
> Les plus beaux épis, et les plus beaux corps élus
> patiemment parmi mille peuples?[2]

> [The voice of Africa hovers over the rage of long
> cannons...
> Is it her fault if God has demanded the first fruits of
> her harvests
> The prettiest shoots, the handsomest bodies carefully
> Chosen from thousands of peoples
>
> Senghor, trans. Dixon, 1991, p. 65)]

This view of the race as singled out for a unique historical and moral mission derives from an absolute vision of the race which Senghor expresses in another poem:

> Pour tous ceux-là qui sont entrés par les quatre
> portes sculptées—la marche
> Solennelle de mes peuples patients! leurs pas se
> perdent dans les sables de l'histoire.[3]

> [For all those who have entered by the four carved
> doors
> The solemn march of my long-suffering people
> Their steps are lost in the sands of Time.
>
> Senghor, trans. Dixon 1991, p. 78)]

In other words, the special experience of the race, the particular character of Black history, is merely a facet of a collective being that, in its foundation, remains outside history. Senghor's theory of Negritude, as elaborated in some key essays collected in *Liberté I* (1964) and diffused throughout his prose works, rests therefore on this essential vision of the race.

The main lines of this theory are now well established and can be briefly summarized, in order to place them within the context of the controversy that they have aroused. As is well known, Senghor's thinking is based on an emotive theory of the African personality, from which he derives his explication of the modes of apprehension that are original to Africa and characteristic of its culture and societies. Senghor has consistently argued that, by virtue of the traditional African's situation within the organic milieu which determines a specific psycho-physiological constitution, he is endowed with a special force of response to the outside world, with a mode of feeling which generates a form of sensuous "participation" in nature and which affords him an immediate grasp of the inner quality of reality. This form of experience, proceeding from a faculty which, after Bergson, Senghor has termed *émotion*, establishes a direct and intense relation between the experiencing mind and the object of its experience; it leads therefore to a fuller apprehension of reality than is afforded by the limiting forms of mental operations associated with the discursive method, and to which, since the ancient Greeks, Western civilization has given an ascendant position in its approach to the world. The following extract is a characteristic statement of this point of view:

> *Ici, les faits naturels, surtout "les faits sociaux ne sont pas des choses." Il y a, cachée derrière eux, les forces cosmiques et vitales qui les régissent, animant ces apparences, leur donnant couleur et rythme, vie et sens. C'est cette signification qui s'impose à la conscience et provoque l'émotion. Plus justement encore, l'émotion est la saisie de l'être intégral—conscience et corps—par le monde de l'indéterminé, l'irruption du monde mystique—ou magique—dans le monde de la détermination. Ce qui émeut le Négro-africain, ce n'est pas tant l'aspect extérieur de l'objet que sa réalité profonde, sa sous-réalité, non pas tant son signe que son sens.*

[Here, natural facts, especially social facts, are not
"things."[4] Behind them lie cosmic and vital forces by
which they are governed, animating them, imparting to them color and rhythm, life and meaning. It
is this significance that is forced upon consciousness
and which triggers emotion. More correctly, emotion
is the flooding of the whole being—consciousness
and body—by the indeterminate world, the irrup-
tion of the mystical—or magical world—into the
determinate world. What moves the African is not
so much the external aspect of the object as its profound reality, *its sub-reality*,[5] not so much the *sign* as
the *sense*.][6]

The whole framework of African sensibility and expression
rests on this postulate in Senghor's theory and determines the
African worldview in his formulation. The strong sense of sympathy with the universe which the African's participating relation with nature affords leads to a conception of the world as
a system of vital forces, linked as it were in a hierarchical order
within a "great chain of being." The African's mode of apprehension is thus mystical, and is sustained by a sense of the sacred,
in which reverence for the dead and a belief in the continuing
life of the ancestors also play a significant part. All this, in turn,
informs the moral values of African societies and determines
their characteristic form of social organization, which rests on a
close and intensely spiritual sense of community. The social universe appears therefore as translation into practical terms of the
values that derive from a profound level of spiritual experience.

Senghor's theory of Negritude rests on what might be
termed an *African epistemology* and embraces a distinction long
acknowledged, even in Western thought, between two different
modes of knowledge: on the one hand, the intuitive and symbolic,
which Senghor attributes to African civilization as its distinctive
mode, and, on the other, the rational and scientific, which, again,
he ascribes to the West: "L'émotion est nègre, comme la raison
est hellène" ["Emotion is African as Reason is Hellenic"].

But for all the sharpness of this dichotomy, it does not appear
that Senghor wishes to postulate an irreconcilable opposition

between the two modes. Although in his writings the question is not given the proper clarification that it requires, there is nonetheless the constant suggestion that he sees the two modes as complementary and their interaction as necessary to the full development of the life of man. Senghor's distinction acquires its sharpness from his insistence on the need to recognize certain aspects of African forms of life and expression which had been taken as indications of the African's inherent inferiority to the European, and Senghor points to these as essential in any consideration of human experience that would understand it in its wholeness. He does not hesitate to reinforce his case by reference to those currents in European thought that, in reaction against the dominant rationalism, had attempted to arrive at a more subtle and more complete view of life by resorting to nonrational categories. In this sense, Senghor's exaltation of the mystical and intuitive allies with the anti-intellectual protest within Western thought against rationalism and scientism, in a specific effort to rehabilitate the traditional civilizations of his native continent.

This point leads us to a consideration of a special character of Senghor's theory that has to do with his position as a poet. It is evident that, for all his borrowing of terms and concepts from contemporary psychology and philosophy, Senghor's formulations derive less from a rigorous investigation of the nature of the African personality and its social expressions than from a personal feeling for the native civilization that stands behind him. In his conception of Negritude, these values are directed toward a spiritual vision of man and the universe. The need to rehabilitate African civilization meets here with the poet's requirements for a scheme of spiritual reference for his individual poetic expression. The metaphors with which Senghor habitually decks out his theory are indeed only slightly less opaque than those that animate his poetry; in one as in the other, they serve to convey a personal feeling for a world of primary experience, for a mythical intuition of a reality that transcends the material world and the historical process.

Thus, Senghor's theory fulfills a double function—as an ideological revaluation of African civilization, and as the intellectual foundation and reference, derived from a living culture, of his poetic thought and mythology. For Senghor, traditional African civilization provides the active model of a significant form of human experience and thus serves as a source of inspiration for his individual spiritual vision. The ideas that go into his theory of Negritude spring as much from a desire to understand the nature of that inspiration as from a need to present a new and positive image of Africa to the world.

The concept of Negritude has come today to be associated with the name of Senghor. Yet the first major attack on the concept was directed not at Senghor but at Sartre. This is perhaps not surprising, since Sartre himself was the first to give some encouragement to the systematic elucidation of the notion of a *Black soul*. At all events, it is in a 1953 review of "Orphée noir" by an African student, Albert Franklin, in a special issue of *Présence africaine*, "Les Etudiants noirs parlent," that we find the first extended questioning of this notion and of the associated ideas which Sartre developed around it.[7] Franklin offered a series of objections to Negritude, both as a concept and as a historical force, and attempted a systematic refutation of it as an inherent racial attribute. His objections are framed within an avowedly Marxist viewpoint, and his arguments are based on a rigorous economic and materialist explanation of the differences between African and European civilizations, and on varying patterns of social psychology—of the personalities and attitudes which they may be thought to determine. Thus, examining the notion that the African (and, by extension, the Black man) is endowed with a sense of community as a *racial inheritance*, whereas the European is predisposed to a morality of individualism, he writes:

> Mais il est faux d'y voir les effets d'on ne sait quelle vertu originelle de l'Essence Noire. D'autre part, si le Blanc (Européen ou Américain) est devenu individualiste, ce n'est pas davantage grâce à une vertu originelle de l'Essence Blanche. Dans le premier comme dans le deuxième cas, ce sont les niveaux organiques des deux économies respectives qui sont les causes et le soutien matériel.[8]

[But it is wrong to see here the effect of some pur-
ported original quality of the Black Essence. Moreover, if the White man (European or American) has
become individualist, it is not due either to an original quality of the White Essence. In the first case,
as in the second, it is the respective level of development of the two economies that are the causes and
the material base.]

In a similar vein, Franklin attacks what he sees as a complacent
idealism in Sartre's essay: it appears to concede the racial character of some of the traits which mark out African civilizations
and, as a consequence, the personality of the African—a sense
of rhythm, an organic sense of life with a strong sexual character,
a mystic approach to the natural universe and the cult of the
ancestors, all of which are assimilated in the concept of Negritude. For Franklin, these traits are merely conditioned by the
level of technical competence achieved by the traditional civilizations, destined to be transcended as African societies evolve, and
a new modern consciousness emerges within these societies. In
particular, Franklin attacks the distinction which Sartre appears
to make between the *intuitive* approach of the Black man to
reality and the *intellection* of the White: he rejects the image of
the African civilizations as being essentially nonscientific and
nontechnical.

But Franklin's overriding concern is political. He is plainly
preoccupied with the ideological and political implications of
these notions, which appear to him to buttress the colonialist
myth of the Black man and to sanction his continued subjugation by the White. His conclusion is unequivocal in its rejection
of Negritude as a serviceable concept for Blacks in the colonial
struggle:

> Dans cette lutte, la Négritude n'est pas faite pour nous
> aider, puisqu'elle est repos, captation magique du monde,
> c'est-à-dire abandon, angoisse, désespoir.[9]

[In this struggle, Negritude is no help to us, for it
is repose, magical reception of the world, in other
words, self-abandon, anguish, despair.]

Franklin's article holds special interest for any consideration of
the Negritude controversy. For although, on balance, it reveals
a misunderstanding of Sartre's real position, it shows up the
ambiguities in which Sartre enveloped the term, and lights up
with singular clarity the very paradox of his position. Beyond
that, it anticipates with remarkable prescience the very objections which were to be brought against the concept of Negritude
as it was developed further by Senghor in the two decades or
so that followed the appearance of Sartre's essay. From the scattered intimations of the possible lines of the development of the
concept in Sartre's essay, Franklin's review marked out for attack
those very points which Senghor himself was to elaborate later
into a comprehensive theory. It thus foreshadowed the pattern
of the controversy that Negritude was later to generate. While
Franklin accepts the necessity of creating a new image of the
Black man as a psychological reference in the struggle against
colonialism and racism, he also indicates that the delineations
of such an image, its very character, cannot be a matter of indif-
ference to the reflecting consciousness of the Black intellectual
caught in the colonial experience. It is this very question that can
be considered to be at the heart of the Negritude controversy.

In the debate that has attended the development of Negritude as a concept, perhaps the most extreme form of the cleavage between adherents and antagonists has been that created by
the initial hostility of a significant section of English-speaking
intellectuals to the movement as a whole. It seems indeed as if
the very degree of elaboration with which Senghor in particular
presented his theory has created a climate in which his ideas
have been met with incomprehension and, indeed, a certain
skepticism.[10] This initial reaction of the English-speaking intellectuals was summed up by Ezekiel Mphahlele in the following observation: "For us, Negritude is merely intellectual talk, a
cult." Mphahlele expands on this somewhat laconic view of the
movement by stressing the differences between the cultural situ-

ations of the French- and English-speaking Africans within the colonial system:

> It is significant that it is not the African in British-settled territories—a product of indirect rule and one that has been left in his cultural habitat—who readily reaches out for his traditional past. It is rather the assimilated African, who has absorbed French culture, who is now passionately wanting to recapture his past. In his poetry, he extols his ancestors, ancestral masks, African wood carvings and bronze art, and he tries to recover the moorings of his oral literature; he clearly feels he has come to a dead end in European culture, and is still not really accepted as an organic part of French society, for all the assimilation he has been through.[11]

That the negritude ideology was on the whole irrelevant had always been Mphahlele's view. Reviewing Janheinz Jahn's report of the Paris Conference he had written: "Whether or not Richard Wright has exorcized his African gods or Senghor finds the inspiration he wants in his African past and present, does not matter to anyone else except the two writers. The African must resolve the 'conflict' in himself as an individual. This struggle will make the literary content of his work." [12] And two years later, reviewing South African anthropologist Simon Biesheuvel's *Race, Culture and Personality*, he pointed obliquely to the inadequacy of the negritude concept and indeed of any all-black generalizations to the South African cross-breeding:

> Born into oppression as we Africans are in South Africa, we are keen to seize the tools that keep the white man in power; we are at grips with a brutal present. The past has been used against us by the white man and we have no time to sit and brood about it, even though we reject certain European values and cling to certain of our own that we still cherish. But we don't think for twenty-four hours of the day on which we are going to adopt or throw aside on any occasion. Three hundred years is a long

> time in terms of cultural cross-breeding, and we have
> been unconsciously taking and throwing away and
> sifting. Senghor's people haven't had that experience.
> It is well that Dr. Biesheuvel talks of 'African person-
> alities,' which phrase has no pretention to a mystical
> unified whole.[13]

It would not be difficult to show that Mphahlele's distinction between francophone Africans and Africans colonized
by the British is not only inadequate as an explanation, but it
also ignores the facts of the historical development of a theory
of Africanism as an integral aspect of African nationalism in
British-controlled Africa. For although the concept of *African
personality* as it emerged in the writings of the English-speaking
African intellectuals in the nineteenth century, and particularly
in the work of Edward Wilmot Blyden, did not receive the same
degree of elaboration as that of Negritude, it contained the same
elements of racial and cultural awareness as Negritude was
later to express in a more comprehensive form, and was thus a
significant precedent.[14] It is nonetheless true that the cultural
problem did not lead to the same kind of self-dramatization
among English-speaking Africans as among the adherents of
Negritude, a situation which inspired the well-known *boutade*
by the Nigerian dramatist Wole Soyinka: "The tiger has no need
to proclaim its tigritude."

Soyinka was later to develop his attack on Negritude in less
elliptical terms. In his book *Myth, Literature, and the African
World*, he reproaches its adherents with failing to pose the question of African civilization in terms proper to it:

> The fundamental error was one of procedure: Negri-
> tude stayed within a pre-set system of Eurocentric
> intellectual analysis both of man and society and
> tried to re-define the African and his society in those
> externalized terms.[15]

Soyinka argues that this procedure was induced by the defensive
attitude of the theoreticians of Negritude toward the ideological
affirmation of European superiority in the realm of intellectual

and technological endeavor, such that they were forced into a romanticism that was essentially a system of countervalues opposed to those impregnably held, as it appeared, by Western civilization. The movement of self-affirmation, which the Nigerian playwright approves in principle, thus coincided in Negritude with an oversimplified view of human difference which, in his opinion, does not effect a decisive break with the structure of European thinking on human and social problems. The result is a curious confirmation, even within its very revolt against Europe, of European judgments and attitudes. Soyinka puts the matter thus:

> Négritude trapped itself in what was primarily a defensive role, even though its accents were strident, its syntax hyperbolic and its strategy aggressive. It accepted one of the most commonplace blasphemies of racism, that the black man has nothing between his ears, and proceeded to subvert the power of poetry to glorify this fabricated justification of European cultural domination. Suddenly, we were exhorted to give a cheer for those who never explored the oceans. The truth however is that there isn't any such creature.[16]

It is plain that Soyinka reads into Senghor's texts a meaning that their author could never remotely have intended, and even if the rhetoric which Senghor often employs to express his ideas lays open his thinking to this kind of distortion, it must be said that Soyinka is less than fair to Senghor here. But Soyinka's critique is significant, coming from a writer who shares with Senghor a common interest in restoring to modern consciousness that primal order of the imagination which they both recognize as a privileged mode of experience within African civilizations.

Soyinka's critique of Negritude goes beyond a mere expression of antagonism arising out of a difference of intellectual background, as is the case very largely with Mphahlele, to a questioning of the very theoretical foundations of the concept. In this respect, he is adding his voice and the authority of his position to a chorus of objections that have arisen from all sides and especially among the younger generation of French-speaking African intellectuals since Franklin's essay appeared. These objections in the main take up the points already made by Franklin with a new amplification, and are directed specifically at Senghor, whose personality has become intimately associated with the concept.

Perhaps the most important charge against Negritude is the one that underlies Soyinka's criticism, namely, its apparent acquiescence in the stereotype of the Black man as a nonrational creature. This charge had been developed at considerable length in the late sixties by another Nigerian, Sebastian Okechukwu Mezu, in his study of Senghor's poetry.[17] In Senghor's ideas concerning the emotive disposition of the Black man, Mezu discerns a throwback to the thinking of Gobineau and, more generally, an uncritical acceptance of the theoretical and ideological discriminations between races by which the notion of White superiority is sustained. The close similarity in both conception and presentation between certain aspects of Senghor's theory of the African personality, with its insistence on the "principle of participation" in its mode of apprehension, and that of "primitive mentality" put forward by Lucien Lévi- Bruhl, is seen by Mezu as a form of ideological complicity with the colonial system.[18] Mezu's criticism of the derivative nature of Senghor's theory has been further extended by another commentator, Yenoukoume Enagnon, in what amounts to a philosophical critique of Senghor's Negritude that denies its value as an original system of thought: "*la Négritude reste un appendice négrifié de la philosophie idéaliste de Bergson, aménagé par Teilhard de Chardin*"[19] ["Negritude remains a negrified appendix of the idealist philosophy of Bergson, readjusted in the light of Teilhard de Chardin."]

These various objections concern what one might call the *fabric* from which Senghor's theory of Negritude is woven. More important have been the attacks directed against the very content and practical implications of the theory. The most representative attack on Negritude, from this point of view, is that developed by Marcien Towa in his short book *Léopold Sédar Senghor: Négritude ou Servitude*, whose title is sufficiently eloquent of its author's intention. Towa's discussion of Negritude is based essentially on an interpretation of Senghor's poetry which relates both to his theoretical writings and to the different phases of his political activity. In this way, Towa attempts to establish a congruence between the dominant attitudes that appear to him to underlie Senghor's poetic expression—attitudes of conciliation and accommodation—and the ideological significance of Senghor's theory within the colonial context. For him, this significance amounts to an acceptance of a subservient role for the Black man in the scheme of human affairs and a collaborative attitude to the White man's domination. Towa proceeds from an examination of Senghor's poetical themes to this conclusion regarding those options that have marked the evolution of Senghor the politician. Thus, after considering the volume *Ethiopiques*, Towa concludes:

> *L'insistance sur la sensualité du nègre, son émotivité, son incapacité technique etc....coïncide avec l'opposition active du poète contre toute idée d'indépendance, opposition qui marquera toutes ses démarches politiques durant la période qui va de 1947 à 1958.*[20]

> [The insistence on the Black's sensual nature, on his emotive disposition, on his technical shortcomings...matches the active opposition of the poet to every idea of independence, an opposition that marks all his political activity during the period from 1947 to 1958.]

This manner of establishing a correspondence between the themes and ideas of a writer and the events and choices of his real life is of course legitimate, but in the particular instance fails to carry real conviction because Towa's procedure is based on a less than sensitive reading of Senghor's poetry and on a somewhat summary consideration of the details of Senghor's political life and activity during the period he alludes to. Towa is, however, on firmer ground when, in the last chapter of his book, he turns to a direct analysis of Senghor's ideas as embodied in the theoretical and ideological conception of culture from which the Negritude theory draws much of its impulse. Towa's critique is intended primarily to draw out the practical implication of such a conception for contemporary Africa, as it appears to him to arise from Senghor's theory:

> Acculé à s'adapter à l'univers technico-scientifique que l'Europe fait surgir autour de lui, le nègre ne trouverait dans son patrimoine biologique aucune ressource lui permettant de relever le défi, ni immédiatement ni à terme. Senghor ne voit d'issue que dans l'acceptation de la tutelle blanche, en attendant que la spécificité biologique du nègre se dilue et disparaisse par métissage dans une humanité sans races.[21]

> [Compelled to adapt to the technical and scientific universe that Europe has conjured up all around him, the African can find no resources in his biological inheritance that enables him to meet its challenge, either in the immediate or in the long term. Senghor sees no solution except an acceptance of the White man's tutelage, in the expectation that the biological specificity of the Black will be diluted and disappear through race mingling in a humanity without races.]

The point of Towa's critique is made with even greater emphasis by Stanislas Adotévi in his frankly polemical book *Négritude et Négrologues*, which contains the most comprehensive and the most vigorous attack on Negritude. Adotevi's objections to the theory are presented with a marked disregard for organization, but with a vehemence that translates a mood of accumulated impatience into open animosity. Like other writers before him, he rejects the notion of an irreducible Black soul:

> [La Négritude] suppose une essence rigide du nègre que le temps n'atteint pas. A cette permanence s'ajoute une spécificité que ni les déterminations sociologiques ni les variations historiques, ni les réalités géographiques ne confirment. Elle fait des nègres des êtres semblables partout et dans le temps.[22]

[(The theory of Negritude) presupposes a rigid essence of the Black race unaffected by time. To this permanent state is added a specific nature that neither sociological determinations nor historical variations nor geographical realities bear out. Negritude makes of Black people the same everywhere and through all time.]

Beyond the abstract notion of a collective being of the race outside history, Adotévi's attack is directed here against the sociological references of the concept of Negritude. The notion of a unified African universe, constituting a moral and spiritual whole distinctive of the race and set apart from other racial wholes is struck at, as it were, at the base—the empirical facts revealing the rich diversity of African values and forms of expression are thus adduced as evidence of the fundamental infirmity of the notion. Adotévi proceeds from this to a critical review of Negritude's various claims to express the truth of the African personality and situation. He attacks in particular the recourse to traditionalism as an unrealistic, regressive appeal to an inheritance that no longer has a value for the contemporary African, observing: "*C'est dans l'inadéquation de ces notions aux problèmes africains que se trouve la clé des difficultés que soulève la négritude.*" ("It is in the inadequacy of these notions to meet African problems that is to be found the key to the difficulties raised by Negritude.") For Adotévi, the criterion of judgment is not only the objective value and coherence of Senghor's theory, but also its relevance to the immediate preoccupations of the African populations. He goes further by attributing to Negritude, and its derivative, African Socialism, a particular significance in the postcolonial context, for he sees both as part of an elaborate system of mystification, as an ideological construction in the Marxist sense, intended to mask and preserve vested interests: "*La Négritude doit être le soporifique du nègre. C'est l'opium. C'est la drogue qui permettra à l'heure des grands partages d'avoir de "bons nègres."*[23] ["Negritude has to be the soporific of the Black. It's the opium, it's the drug that enables one, at the point of sharing out, to retain one's good Negroes"] (45).]

115

The various judgments of Negritude discussed here represent a fair summary of the reactions that have been provoked
by Senghor's efforts to formulate a comprehensive theory of the
Black personality and to endow such a theory with a meaning
for contemporary African life. What seems clear from these
reactions is that, while the original stance of Negritude as a
form of Black self-affirmation is accepted, the particular terms
of Senghor's formulations in his development of the concept, as
well as the practical orientation of the theoretician himself, in
his position as a political leader, are viewed with distrust. This
explains the attempt by many critics of Negritude to draw a distinction between Senghor's form of Negritude and what they
take to be Césaire's continued adherence to the original project.
Thus, René Depestre writes:

> La Négritude, avec Aimé Césaire, père du concept qu'il
> a défendu et illustré tout au long d'une oeuvre exem-
> plaire, était avant tout une prise de conscience concrète
> de l'oppression, comme chez Guillén, Fanon, Roumain,
> Damas, etc., c'est-à-dire une recherche passionnée
> d'identification de l'homme noir profané par des siècles
> d'esclavage et de mépris.[24]

> [With Aimé Césaire, father of the concept, which he
> has defended and illustrated throughout an exem-
> plary career, Negritude was above all a concrete act of
> taking consciousness of oppression, as with Guillén,
> Fanon, Roumain, Damas etc...that is, a passionate
> quest by the Black people, violated by centuries of
> slavery and contempt.]

Seeking to drive a wedge in this way between Césaire and
Senghor is made all the simpler by the fact that Césaire himself
has made no attempt to develop a theory, though his poetry
draws much of its force from many of the ideas that inform Senghor's theory. This limitation of the Martinican poet's Negritude
to symbolic expression rather than conceptual formulation has
preserved him from the attacks discussed here, all of which reveal
a preoccupation with giving to the notion of African personality

and culture an active and efficient value, indeed, a revolutionary significance. This position was well represented at an early stage in Fanon's statement to the effect that

> *La culture négro-africaine, c'est autour de la lutte des peuples qu'elle se densifie, et non autour des chants, des poèmes ou du folklore.*[25]
>
> [African culture—it is around the struggle of the people that it will take shape, not around songs, poems or folklore.]

Fanon's position is perhaps the most extreme taken on the question, and is characteristic of his uncompromising insistence on the primacy of political action, in the colonial situation, over the cultural. It represents a reversal of the priorities which Senghor has attempted to establish in his efforts to promote a new consciousness on the part of the Black man through a revaluation of African civilization as a condition for his political and social emancipation. In a more general perspective, Fanon's statement also sums up the underlying postulates of nearly all the critics of Negritude: they proceed from what one might call a *positivist* standpoint, involving a materialist view of society. In their concern with achieving an immediate sense of reality, they have little or no sympathy for any theory of African development that does not appear to bear a direct relation to an objective and practical scheme of historical action in the contemporary world. The appeal to a racial consciousness based on a new appraisal of the potential of African civilization to create a new order of life and expression for Black peoples appears to them to be too remote from the exigencies of the moment to be of any practical and immediate significance.

Despite the continuing attacks leveled against it, it is undeniable that the concept of Negritude has acquired a historical and ideological value of the first importance and, with the literature associated with it, remains the most comprehensive and coherent effort of reflection upon the African and the Black situation. Its impact upon modern African thought has been far-reaching. Indeed, what the debate around the concept has demonstrated is the special power it has exercised in Black intellectual circles on both sides of the Atlantic. In a more limited perspective, its significance in the movement toward independence has received a recognition acknowledged in these terms by one of the younger African intellectuals:

> Ce retour aux sources négro-africaines a consacré effectivement les valeurs nègres de civilisation. Et la Négritude, par conséquent, a permis de souder les consciences des peuples noirs et les a mobilisés pour les luttes anticoloniales et libératrices.[26]

> [This return to African sources has put a seal on the values of African civilization. Consequently, Negritude has helped to bind the consciousness of Black peoples and mobilized them for anticolonial, liberation struggles.]

Within a broader perspective, the Negritude movement can also be said to have defined the terms of a projection of the African consciousness into a future in which African development is intimately bound up with the conditions of human evolution in the modern world. Senghor's ideas have constantly been oriented toward such a future, in which African civilization will play an original and significant role in what he calls "la civilisation de l'Universel." And the awareness of the necessary integration of modern values into the framework of an original African scheme of life and expression forms an essential part of the intellectual adventure of Negritude. That this awareness has become an accepted element of African thinking is borne out by this statement by another member of the younger generation:

> La renaissance africaine, pour exprimer son africanité, son authenticité et la conscience d'elle-même, devra s'assimiler la modernité selon ses propres termes. Cet effort implique sinon une révolution du contenu des cultures africaines, du moins leur transformation profonde, leur actualisation.[27]

> [In order to give expression to its Africanity, its authenticity and its self-awareness, the African

Renaissance will have to assimilate modernity on
its own terms. This effort implies, if not a revolution
of the content of African cultures, at least their profound transformation, their refashioning.]

In conclusion, it may be said that the literature of Negritude has
given expression to the lived actualities of the Black experience.
Furthermore, by promoting the concept of an original racial
specificity, it has provided the collective consciousness with the
fundamental basis for the confrontation by Black people of a difficult history and their determination to create for themselves a
new mode of historical being.

NOTES

1. L. S. Senghor, *Anthologie de la nouvelle poésie nègre et malgache*,
   1948). Page references are to the second edition (1969).

2. Senghor, "Chant du Printemps," in *Hosties Noires* (1948).

3. Senghor, "Le Kaya-Magan," in *Ethiopiques* (1956).

4. An allusion to Durheim's celebrated injunction in *Les Règles de la
   méthode sociologique*, to treat soical facts as "things."

5. Senghor's use of the term *"sous-réalité"* is a way of distinguishing
   the epistemology he attributes to the African from *"surrréalisme"*
   associated with Western experience.

6. L. S. Senghor, "De la Négritude. Psychologie du Négro-africain,"
   Diogène, No. 37 (1962), pp. 3-16.

7. Albert Franklin, "La Négritude: réalité ou mystification? Reflex-
   ions sur 'Orphée noir," in *Présence Africaine*, No. 14 (1953), p.
   287-303. Prior to that, however, a mulatto intellectual born in
   Mali, Gabriel d'Arboussier, secretary of Houphouet-Boigny's
   Rassemblement Démocratique Africain before the latter cut
   its ties with the Communist movement, had published an essay
   entitled "Une Dangereuse Mystification: La Théorie de la négritude," in *Nouvelle Critique*, (June 1949), pp. 34-47. In 1952,
   d'Arboussier was expelled from the R. D. A., but after independence, he became Minister of Justice in Senegal.

8. Ibid., p. 289.

9. Ibid., p. 303.

10. Consider for example Richard Wright's incredulous dismay as he listened to Senghor's expostulations about negro intuition and surreality at the Paris Conference of 1956. His own contribution dealt with "Tradition and Industrialization: The Plight of the Tragic Elite in Africa," in *Présence Africaine*. 8/9/10 (1956), pp. 347-360. As he had hoped to be faced with what he called "emancipated," intellectually liberated Negroes, his bitter disappointment is conspicuous in the report of the discussions printed in the same special issue of *Présence Africaine*. See also his *Black Power* (1954).

11. Ezekiel Mphahlele, *The African Image* (1961), p. 25-26.

12. *Ibadan*, No. 2, 1958, 36-37.

13. *Black Orpheus*, No. 7 (June 1960), p. 57.

14. For a fuller discussion of this point, see the chapter "Négritude and African Personality" in my book, *The African Experience in Literature and Ideology* (1981), p. 89-116.

15. Wole Soyinka, *Myth, Literature and the African World* (Cambridge: Cambridge University Press, 1976), p. 136.

16. Ibid., p. 129.

17. S. Okechukwu Mezu, *Léopold Sédar Senghor et la défense et illustration de la civilisation noire* (1968).

18. Op. cit., pp. 173-176. On this point, see Mezu, "Senghor, Gobineau et l'inégalité des races humaines," *Abbia*, 26 (1972), pp. 121-41.

19. Yenoukoumée Enagnon, "De la 'philosophie senghorienne ou du charlatanisme philosophique à l'usage des peuples africains," *Peuples Noirs—Peuples Africains*, I, 3 (1978), pp. 11-49.

20. Marcien Towa, *Léopold Sédar Senghor: Négritude ou Servitude* (1971), p. 79-80.

21. Ibid, p. 109.

22. Stanislas Adotévi, *Négritude et Négrologues* (1972), p. 45.

23. Ibid., p. 118n. On the anti-Negritude movement in Francophone Africa, see also Barbara Ischinger, "Négritude: Some Dissident Voices," *Issue*. 4, 4 (1974), pp. 23-25

24. René Depestre, "Haïti ou la Négritude devoyée," *Afric-Asia*. No. 5/6 (January 1970).

25. Frantz Fanon, *Les Damnés de la terre* (1961), p. 176.

26. Alpha Sow, "Prolégomenes," in *Introduction à la culture africaine*, (Paris: Editions 10/18, 1977), pp. 16-17

27. Pathé Diagne, "Renaissance et problèmes culturels en Afrique," in Sow, op. cit., p. 291.

CHAPTER FIVE
CONTEMPORARY THOUGHT
IN FRENCH-SPEAKING
AFRICA
❧

In the introductory pages of his short book *Feuerbach and the End of German Philosophy*, Friedrich Engels provides an interesting testimony as to the impact which *The Essence of Christianity* had upon his and Karl Marx's generation of German intellectuals. Engels's testimony not only throws light on a significant moment in the development of the ideological system to which he made such an important contribution, but also, in broader terms, illustrates the correlation between the political and social conditions of a historical period and the movement of ideas of which it is a reflection. In the particular instance of mid-nineteenth century Germany, and with specific reference to the development of Marxism as a system of thought, Engels's testimony points to the realization among young German intellectuals about the lack of a real correspondence between the idealism of established German philosophy, in particular its Hegelian brand, and the social and economic transformations that were then taking place. Feuerbach was thus an important stage in the reaction against Hegel, of which Marx's dialectical materialism was to be, in one particular direction, a culmination. The full import of this reaction came, then, to be a profound transformation of the mental universe which would ultimately lead to a significant revolution of thought.[1]

A comparable development in the realm of thought is taking place in Africa today, a development which will, I believe, have implications for the way in which we as Africans perceive ourselves and our position in the modern world; for the way in which we not only conceive our collective historical being, but also our possibilities within the historical process as it unfolds in our own time.

Put quite simply, this development involves a complete rethinking of the tenets and assumptions that have gone into the formation of African attitudes and found an articulation in the prevailing intellectual reaction to the colonial experience. The terms in which the investigation of the African experience has so far been carried out are being questioned and revised, and the set of problems perceived by an earlier generation of African and Black intellectuals is now being supplanted by a new set of problems, raised by the younger generation. In other words, there is beginning to be a redefinition of what one might call the "African problematic," and this redefinition appears to be related to the changed realities of the contemporary African situation in the postcolonial era. A new perception of African problems is thus emerging, affecting as a consequence the mental processes which were implied in the emergence of the nationalist consciousness.

This development is most evident in the way the movement of ideas has been proceeding among French-speaking African intellectuals. The clearest indication is provided here by the steady buildup of the reaction against the Negritude movement and the ideas it propagated, especially through the writings of Léopold Sédar Senghor. I propose, therefore, to examine this phenomenon, by placing it in a perspective that sees it as an evolution not so much in historical terms, but rather as a process— a dialectic, if one prefers—having a certain coherence which derives from an immediate relation to the course of a general African experience.

When one considers the broad movement and the main points of emphasis in modern African thought,[2] it seems clear that it has so far been dominated by a single problem—that of *identity.* By this, I mean that, for generations of African intellectuals urged by the very pressures of the colonial experience to direct their intelligence toward the fact of this experience and to consider its implications for themselves and their fellow Africans, the central theme of their reflection has been that of self-definition. The intellectual response to European conquest and domination took the form of a long and sustained effort on the part of the Westernized elite to situate themselves anew in relation to their cultural and spiritual antecedents as defined by their African environment, and to apprehend in themselves an essential African nature—obscured by the cultural and spiritual impositions of the dominant European civilization—in order to reestablish a profound correspondence with their original sources of being.

Though often posed in these abstract terms, the problem of identity as perceived by these intellectuals was of course bound up with the concrete effects upon every African involved in the colonial encounter. But it was not divorced from the social interests of the rising African bourgeoisie. As the example of the Gold Coast intellectuals clearly indicates, cultural nationalism subserved immediate political and economic ambitions, providing a rationale for them.[3] But it is also important to consider that the prominence which African intellectuals have regularly given to the problem of identity has been a function of their cultural and psychological situation as a class. For the African intellectual is an individual at the meeting point of two cultures. It is probably safe to say that the successive generations of intellectuals who came to maturity within the colonial system experienced the contradictions of the system most directly as an intense psychological and moral tension, a tension they interpreted as a form of spiritual alienation. They tended therefore to subsume all the other concrete issues that contributed to the objective reality of their situation—the political, social, and economic issues of colonial dependence—under the single problem of recovering a unified consciousness of the self.

We find the most vivid dramatization of this tendency in Cheikh Hamidou Kane's novel *L'Aventure ambiguë*, whose hero, Samba Diallo, is the prototype in modern African literature of

125

the Westernized African torn between two worlds and the conflict of values which each represents. In Kane's novel, the trauma of European conquest in the various areas of life and expression within an African social formation is perceived ultimately in sole relation to a disruption in the hero's being and consciousness; thus, his existential plight represents the thematic focus, the significant structural level of the novel.[4] The example illustrates the affective coloration of the intellectual reaction to colonialism and conditions an idealist orientation in African thinking, which comes to provide the terms of a whole discourse around the issue of identity.

There was of course an objective dimension to the African intellectual's preoccupation with the problem of identity. Colonial domination was not only a political fact, but represented as well the imposition of global constraint upon the colonized society; it also effected a general reordering of life, producing social and cultural tensions that were reflected in the consciousness of the individual and, through the interpenetration of minds, in a collective cultural malaise. The so-called messianic movements in Africa, as elsewhere, attest to the comprehensive nature of cultural resistance by the colonized. They also define the conditions for the emergence of the more restricted form of reaction among the intellectuals, which appears, in sociological terms, to be an articulated form of counteracculturation.

If the quest for an original integrity of being came to dominate African thinking, it was not only because it fulfilled a psychological need, but also because it served to answer the system of rationalizations by which Western ideologues sought to justify European domination of other races.[5] The cultural argument was a major plank of imperialist ideology. The myth of Black/African inferiority could not but provoke an anxiety in the African intellectual, who encountered it at every turn as part of the process of his intellectual formation within the colonial educational system and, indeed, as a regular feature of his colonial experience. More than this, the myth could not but induce in him a process of self-exploration, touching upon the quality not only of his individual mental dispositions, but also of the entire cultural and spiritual inheritance in his African background. The implication here is that the terms of reference for African self-reflection were determined by the fact of its opposition to the ideology of imperialism. What has been called modern African philosophy starts as a polemical form of thought, a counterthesis, placed in historical and logical relation to the scheme of ideas and representations by which the colonial system was sustained. The sociological significance of modern African thought, in its preoccupation with the problem of identity as the intellectual focus of a whole movement of counteracculturation, is thus complemented by its ideological significance as the elaboration of a whole system of countervalues.

It is necessary to recall these elements, which define the framework of development of modern African thought, in order to place the Negritude movement in its proper historical perspective. The special significance of Negritude resides in the particular quality of its formulation of the "African problematic," that is, of a long-standing question about the place and role of the African in a world dominated by the West. This implies in fact a certain progression, in that the theory of Negritude gathers up the various strands of the process of African self-exploration into a focused articulation, into a unifying concept of African and Black identity. To place this progression in a clear light, it is enough, I believe, to indicate the way in which Edward Wilmot Blyden's notion of the "African personality" is given complex elaboration in Senghor's Negritude and transformed into a full-fledged theory of African being.[6]

In considering Negritude itself, we need to distinguish between two acceptations of the term. In its first and general sense, the term refers to the phenomenon of Black awakening, as a global response to the collective situation. Associated with this sense is Jean-Paul Sartre's definition of Negritude as "an affective attitude to the world,"[7] that is, a subjective disposition expressive of the Black man's total apprehension of his peculiar situation. Sartre not only related the Black man's apprehension to the historical conditions of his existence as a member of an oppressed race, but, basing his analysis on the character of the Black poetry in French which was the immediate occasion of his definition, Sartre went on to give an active significance to the

Black *prise de conscience*, seeing in this the passage from an unre-
flected experience to a reflexive consciousness. It indicates, therefore, a collective revolutionary project destined to transform the
conditions of the Black man's existence and thus, ironically, to
eliminate the need for a self-directed consciousness on the part
of the Black subject himself. We might say that Sartre's definition situates Negritude in a relative perspective while intending
to accord it a universalizing purpose and significance.

The other sense of the term emerges from Senghor's formulation of Negritude as a concept and can be considered a special
case—a restricted sense within the general one. In effect, for
Senghor, the term in its proper reference designates an attribute
of the Black man, specific to the race in its timeless constitution
as a distinct branch of humanity. Senghor insists on the distinction between "subjective Negritude," which corresponds to
Sartre's definition, and "objective Negritude," which denotes an
African mode of life and values and the fundamental adherence
of the Black man's basic personality to this reality. Negritude in
this sense seeks to grasp the singular wholeness of the varied
"patterns of culture"[8] that characterize African societies as well
as their derivations in the New World—that is, an underlying
principle which may be said to define a common spirit of African
civilization.[9] Along this range of references, the term points ultimately to the conception of a unique racial endowment of the
Black man.

Senghor's Negritude rests upon a theory of culture and is
grounded in a firm correlation between race and culture. This is
not to say that Negritude is a racial theory in the sense that it is
an exclusive vision of a race and the way of life associated with
it. There is, however, an explicit postulation of an intimate relationship between the biological constitution of the Black race
and the cultural works it has produced in history. For Senghor,
culture has a racial character to the extent that culture is the
effect of a total response by man to his environment, a response
that involves his total being, including his organic constitution,
which represents a structure of equilibrium between the physical determinations of the environment and the human pressures,
immediate and spiritual, upon that environment. The process

of adjustment to the milieu left its impress on the African in such a way as to determine a racial character in all Black men.[10] Senghor has often had recourse to certain notions of character study to distinguish the Black race from the other races to explain the observable differences between human groupings in terms not merely of their external aspects but of the common internal dispositions which they are thought to express and which affect modes of living. Whatever this approach is worth, the point remains that Senghor's theory of Negritude is predicated on the idea of a lively reciprocity between racial character as conditioned by an original formative milieu and the different cultural forms to be found in the world.

What Senghor calls the "physiopsychology of the African," the result of his timeless insertion within a certain milieu and his organic adaptation to that milieu, thus conditions a distinctive mode of apprehension. That mode itself finds objective expression not only in characteristic cultural forms, but also in the superstructural sphere of collective life in the realm of thought and values. The emotive disposition of the African, for example, appears as the principal factor in the pronounced mystical outlook of man in the African world, an intense religiosity that expresses a total grasp of life in the universe. At the imaginative and spiritual level of collective expression, this outlook receives an elaboration in those mythical representations and symbolic schemes which define a particular structure of being and consciousness. In proposing this view of African life, which also has implications for his interpretation of traditional forms of social organization in Africa, Senghor gives to his theory of Negritude the dimension of a cosmology.

For reasons which will become apparent later, it is important to draw attention to the contribution made by Father Placide Tempels's exposition of the so-called Bantu philosophy to the architecture of Senghor's theory. As we have seen, Tempels extracted a coherent worldview from the mores of the Baluba (in present-day Democratic Republic of Congo.) The crux of this philosophy is an ontology in which being is conceived not as a static notion but as *force*, with the universe seen as an interrelation of forces within the whole realm of existence. According to this primordial scheme, everything that can be thought to exist is endowed with vital force and contingent upon certain factors that may intervene in the course of existence.[11]

It is not surprising that Tempels's theory features prominently in Senghor's Negritude, into which "Bantu philosophy" is integrated in such a way as to demonstrate a distinctive African form of spirituality. The attraction of Tempels's work resides not only in its apparent vindication of the African claim to an elevated system of thought, but also in its provision of a conceptual framework for this African mode of thought. The vitalist emphasis of Bantu philosophy ties in very well with the epistemology implicit in Senghor's Negritude, and its postulation of a hierarchy of forces attributes to the African a comprehensive world view which presupposes characteristic structures of mental projection. In his assimilation of Bantu philosophy into a general scheme of ideas concerning the nature of the African, Senghor's purpose is to present, through Negritude,an independent African system of thought, a distinctive African humanism.

In the preindependence period, Negritude was the dominant ideology in Francophone Africa, and, thanks to the personality of Senghor, it maintained an ideological presence whose ongoing importance is attested by the attacks that continue to be directed against it. The peculiar force of Negritude stems from the fact that it formed so comprehensive a system of ideas that, in one way or another, it responded to African interests in the colonial situation and thus came to serve as a significant ideological reference—in both a positive and a negative sense—for the intellectual activity of French-speaking Black intellectuals, the point of departure of the new African discourse. We may even go further to observe that Negritude was the most complete expression of the African state of mind in relation to the colonial experience.

Senghor's method, as we have seen, consisted in seeking a validation of this concept by reference to an "objective Negritude" of the African's collective cultural expression, as documented in the ethnographic literature devoted to African societies. Senghor's example inspired a line of development in French African intellectual activity that came to have important consequences for its subsequent direction. This line of development involved what amounts to an entire school of scholars, who, in the wake of Tempels, devoted their attention to the investigation and elucidation of traditional thought systems in an effort to derive from them a distinctive African philosophy.

The most notable effort in this connection was perhaps that of Alexis Kagame, who sought to follow up Tempels's work by verifying within his native Rwanda culture the Belgian missionary's theory of Bantu ontology. In his book *La Philosophie bantu-rwandaise de l'être*, published in 1956, Kagame adopted an original approach, which consisted of analyzing the Rwanda language in an effort to demonstrate the existence among its users of a different and more precise grasp of the notion of being than the one that had been suggested by Tempels. Kagame pointed out that this notion was rendered in the abstract by the radical *-ntu* and in its manifestations or modalities by four terms derived from it: *Umuntu*, which designated man—a being endowed with intelligence; *Ikintu*, anything without intelligence; *Ahantu*, space-time; and *Ukuntu*, modality—such as quantity, quality, and relation.[12] Kagame maintains that, for the user of the Rwanda language, these terms prescribe a universal order and correspond to the world of experience. Moreover, they represent not only an order of essences but also an order of concepts and thus provide an image of the mental structure which the language itself determines in its users. The ontology of the Rwandans is thus present in the grammatical structure and the semantic field proposed to them by their language; it has an effect on thought processes comparable to that of classical Greek on the pioneers of Western philosophy and, in particular, on Aristotle. Kagame goes on to claim that the Rwanda conception of the world based on this ontology is explicit, having found expression in the oral tradition of the people and constituting an effective factor of their indigenous forms of social organization and total cultural life. In a subsequent work, *La Philosophie bantu comparée*, Kagame recognizes the cultural unity of the area covered by the Bantu family of languages, not only in terms of their common use of classifiers, but also in what he describes as "the mental organization of the symbol of ideas, the categorization of beings and whatever else exists, the conception of the world of the existence of what lies beyond."[13]

Kagame's exploration of the Bantu worldview takes him well beyond Tempels, whose theory of "vital force" he refutes; but he does appear to remain within the same perspective, for he too seeks to establish the reality of a distinctive African mode of thought and existence. Quite apart from the theoretical merits of the case he makes, the ideological import of his point of view cannot be denied. It becomes even more manifest in the work of other Francophone African scholars concerned with Bantu philosophy as a specific problem or as part of a general construction of an authentic African system equivalent to that of Western philosophy.[14] All this effort came in the wake of Negritude, and reflects its spirit, its attempt to give a conceptual form to an immediately felt sense of African identity.

The same spirit animates the work of Cheikh Anta Diop, the foremost representative of another group of scholars whose activity runs parallel to that of the philosophers. This group may be described as the historical school of the Negritude movement. It may come as a surprise to see Cheikh Anta Diop associated in this way with Senghor, but the rapprochement is justified by the fact that his work takes its place and meaning from the same context of cultural nationalism as that in which Negritude was generated. What is more, Diop occasionally employs some of the latter's conceptual terms. In a more fundamental way, Diop's work addresses itself to the same problem of African identity which preoccupied writers in the Negritude tradition.

Diop has called his method *historical sociology*, but no neat label can be attached to his approach, which draws on his vast erudition with foundations in the natural sciences and the humanities. The range of Diop's scholarship is evident in his first work, *Nations nègres et culture*, which can be said to have attained the status of a classic in Black intellectual circles.[15] It is easy to explain the success of this book, for it contains the most overt and vigorous challenge to the cultural argument of the imperialist ideology; its firm nationalist stand is still able to elicit a deep African response even today. As is well known, the primary objective of the book is to demonstrate the Negro origins of ancient Egyptian civilization and thus to refute the argument that the Black race had produced no great world civilization; however, the discussion extends beyond an argument for this thesis to a demonstration of the continuity between ancient Egyptian civilization and the contemporary cultures of Black Africa.

A full exposition of Diop's thesis cannot be undertaken here, but it is not without interest to chart the lines of his thinking for an understanding of its mechanisms and its course. It is essential in this respect to stress the fact that Diop's presentation of his thesis was in fact the intervention of an African in a debate that had long been going on in Western scholarly circles about the racial character of the ancient Egyptians. His contribution was motivated by a dissatisfaction with the point of view espoused by European scholars who seemed (to him) to have gone deliberately against the evidence in classifying the Egyptians among the White races. Diop attributes this point of view to the effect of racial prejudice against the Black race and credits it with producing a falsification of history. An element of racial indignation thus permeates Diop's discussion, lending to his work a strong polemical tone which may be thought incompatible with objective scholarship, but which, under the circumstances, was necessitated by the force of the established ideas with which he was contending. Diop raises important issues of historical method in his assault upon the prevailing ideas, showing up the system of rationalizations by which they were constructed. The least that can be said is that *Nations nègres et culture* succeeds in reopening the whole question about the racial origin of ancient Egyptian civilization.

In two subsequent works, *Antériorité des civilisations nègres* and *Parenté génétique de l'Egyptien pharaonique et des langues négro-africaines*,[16] both of which must be seen as complementary to the first work, Diop further develops his arguments for considering ancient Egyptian civilization as essentially a creation of the Black race. This he does by marshalling an array of evidence drawn from a formidably diverse range of special fields: archaeology, paleontology, physical anthropology, classical European studies, historical and comparative linguistics, as well as the central field of Egyptology itself. It is impossible to judge the value of the evidence—internal and external—without some specialized knowledge in this vast area of scholarship. It is possible to note, however, that Diop's examination of ancient Egyptian institutions and thought provides him with a cultural argument for postulating an essential affinity between the forms of social organization and the cosmology of the ancient Egyptians and those that appear to characterize the traditional African world. It is in this respect that he comes closest to Senghor, both in his vision of the African world as a unified whole and in his acquiescence with the theory of Tempels as regards the vitalist conception of the world. The cultural argument leads Diop to the following categorical affirmation:

> The identity of Egyptian culture and Black culture could not be more evident. It is by reason of this essential identity of genius, culture and race that all Black men can today legitimately link their culture to ancient Egypt and build a modern culture on that basis. It is a dynamic, modern contact with Egyptian antiquity that will enable Negroes to discover more and more each day the intimate relationship between all Blacks on the continent and the mother valley of the Nile. It is by means of this dynamic contact that the Negro will arrive at the profound conviction that these temples, these forests of columns, these bas-reliefs, this mathematics, this medicine, all this science, are indeed the works of his ancestors and that it is incumbent upon him to recognize himself completely in them.[17]

For all the ideological flavor of this statement, it would be a limited view of Diop's purpose to see in this passage merely a simple reversal of established Western prejudices against the African and the Black race. It is certainly true that Diop appears here at pains to demonstrate that Africans have had a past of great technical and intellectual achievement. Elsewhere, he makes the point that Western civilization owes an original debt to Africa through the direct influence of ancient Egypt on its early formation in classical Greece. But the real thrust of Diop's affirmation lies in another direction. The cultural argument is accessory to a much wider project: it serves to establish ancient Egyptian civilization as a retrospective reference and primordial model of African existence and endeavor. Diop's purpose is not merely to refute the theory of Black inferiority by presenting the African in the image of technical man, but, more significantly, to provide a broader perspective upon African collective experience and identity, with this identity being defined not as an intangible entity of his racial being but as an effective presence in the world. In this perspective, the colonial experience itself is reduced to a mere interlude in a historical process that stretches back to an original time during the emergence of the race and forward to a creative future of new fulfillment.

Indeed, Diop can be said to have constructed a general model of history, stated in geosociological and ethnic terms, within which his particular conception of African development finds its place and meaning. In his book *L'Unité culturelle de l'Afrique noire*, Diop reacts against the evolutionist view of human experience, which, in the hands of Western scholars, almost invariably ascribes a superior position to the White race and to Western forms of cultural expression. Diop proceeds to a vast demarcation of the prehistoric and ancient world between the northern and southern races, using as a basis their different kinship structures. Thus, he associates the patriarchal system with the southern race, arguing that the opposition is the effect of a primitive differentiation between the nomadic life of the former and the sedentary life of the latter. Diop develops this opposition throughout the full range of social institutions and value systems which he sees as characteristic of each race in its original determination. He arrives at the conclusion that the course of human history can be explained by the interaction, often marked by conflict, between the aggressive disposition and pessimistic world outlook of the northern races conditioned by their prolonged nomadism, and the more peaceful inclinations and optimistic approach to the universe of the southern races, due to their much earlier sedentarization—in terms, that is, of the opposition between the divergent historical personalities embodied by the two races.[18]

Few scholars would, I imagine, want to commit themselves to this ethnic conception of history, but it is essential to point out that in its actual exposition in Diop's book, not merely an *opposition* between North and South is postulated, but a *relation*; the manifestations in history of the two races are seen as two distinct currents, two related directions of a single universal historical process. As against the unilateral conception of Hegel and those Western scholars who have derived their philosophy of history from him, Diop proposes an all-embracing perspective from which to view the course of human development: a perspective that throws a new light upon Africa, grasped as an indivisible whole, and upon its contribution to that development. As he says, "Historical science itself cannot shed all the light one might expect it to cast upon the past until it integrates into its synthesis the Black component of humanity, in proportion to the role it has actually played in history."[19] We may conclude, then, that two clear moments emerge in the unfolding of Diop's ideological project. The first consists in the effort to establish a historical and cultural connection between ancient Egypt and Black Africa, in such a way as to give historical depth and resonance to the contemporary African consciousness. The second derives from the will to place the African continent and the Black race firmly within the movement of universal history, to project the vision of a universal history in which Africa is profoundly involved.

The two currents I have distinguished as the *philosophical* and the *historical* within the general movement of cultural nationalism among French-speaking African intellectuals can be said to complement each other admirably, despite their divergence on certain points. Their common acceptance of a global reality of African identity, in whatever terms this is defined, and their common insistence upon its distinctive quality, can be said to resolve their divergent points of view within a common vision of African existence. Both Senghor and Diop proceed by attaching a positive value to the objective difference between African and European civilizations at the moment of their historical confrontation; each takes up, in his own way, the ideological gauntlet thrown down by European racism and ethnocentrism.

The differences between them appear, therefore, largely a matter of detail or, more correctly, of *perspective*, affecting areas of emphasis in each writer's effort to give body to his idea of Africa, to think through the vicissitudes of a disturbing history to a fundamental vision of African integrity.

The two currents represented by Senghor and Diop thus bear upon the same African problematic created by the colonial experience. It would be a simplification to say that the reaction against the trend of intellectual and ideological activity which they both represent arose immediately with the passing of the colonial era, but there can be no doubt that it has developed in amplitude largely as a function of the consequent change in attitudes and by direct reference to the new social and political realities of the postcolonial situation in Africa. The workings of the process leading to this development can be seen in the way the objections to Negritude have converged to define a new perspective upon African problems at the present moment.

The objections to Negritude have tended to focus not only on its explicit theoretical terms, but also on what are taken to be the practical political and social implications of the theory. As we have seen, this double trend was established in Albert Franklin's 1956 essay, "La Négritude: Réalité ou Mystification?" whose vigorous criticism anticipated practically all the arguments that were later developed against Senghor's theory by his adversaries.[20] Again, Franklin attacked Sartre's apparent endorsement of the image, offered in Negritude poetry, of the Black man as a nonrational being, disposed to mystic communion with nature rather than to a technical mastery of it. Franklin observed that such an image had no basis in reality and that, even if it did, it would not imply a fixed essence of the African man but was only a reflection of the low state of technical development in traditional African society—a state which had to be transcended, to give way to a scientific and rational approach to the universe.

This argument, which turned out to be the dominant line of attack on Senghor's theory, was given a detailed elaboration by Stanislas Adotévi in *Négritude et Négrologues*, the most comprehensive critique of Negritude so far published. By placing himself on a resolutely sociological plane, Adotévi came to reject what he regarded as Negritude's static conception of African cultural reality, resulting from an abstract schema out of touch with the diversified forms of concrete life in the various African societies.[21] Not only is Senghor's unified conception of African and Black cultural expression called into question, but also the correlation between race and culture on which it is founded, along with the biological underpinnings woven into the structure of his theory. Adotévi specifically attacks this "biologism," which appears to him to be so embedded in the ideological presuppositions of European racism as to be no more than a restatement of them in terms which amount to an acquiescence to their negation of the Black man.

As can be seen from the turn which Adotévi's critique finally takes, the political objection to Negritude is accompanied by a certain radical stance which does duty in the postcolonial context for the political nationalism of an earlier period and generation. It is in this context that Frantz Fanon came to impinge so directly and so decisively on the development of African thought. Fanon's influence has been dominant in the accentuation of radical thought in postcolonial Africa generally, and especially in the radical tone of an opposition to Negritude by which a significant section of the younger generation of French African intellectuals can be recognized.

When one considers the effect of Fanon's thought on the ideological temper of this generation, there is no little irony in the fact that the point of departure for his entire reflection was Negritude—with the important qualification that it was the profound impression made upon him by the particular manifestation of its spirit in Aimé Césaire's work that impelled him to this reflection. In its total and aggressive response to centuries of denigration and humiliation, Césaire's brand of Negritude involves no elaborate theory of Blackness. The intense symbolism of aggression which is the hallmark of Césaire's poetry not only gives expression to this affirmation in an extraordinary burst of poetic energy, but it also offers a peculiar complexity of imagery stemming from a deep structure of consciousness. Césaire's poetic expression thus becomes quite literally an *affect*: it involves a kind of verbal exorcism, a sloughing-off process by which the complex of negative associations through which the Black subject has been forced to perceive himself is overturned and transformed into a mode of mental liberation and, ultimately, self-acceptance.[22]

Césaire's poetry is essential to an understanding of Fanon's development, because the psychological and moral ferment of Césaire's consciousness, as revealed in his poetry, is the hotbed in which Fanon's thought strikes its roots and and from which it issues. It is hardly an exaggeration to say that Césaire provides the essential ground plan for Fanon's reflection, which can be regarded as a transposition into ideological propositions of the psychological processes and wider implications at play in the poet's work. It is indeed the general application of Fanon's understanding of these issues to the situation of the Black man that forms the subject of his first work, *Peau noire, masques blancs*,[23] a reflection upon Black subjectivity as conditioned by the Black man's situation (in the Sartrian sense) in the world. It is thus, in a sense, a phenomenology of Black existence. In striking psychological terms, Fanon investigates the way in which the introjection of social values is disturbed in the case of the Black subject placed within a sociopsychological field dominated by the White paradigm. The conflict between the external fact of his Blackness and his internalization of a highly valorized symbolism of Whiteness creates a distortion of his self-image and installs within him a profound neurosis, with repercussions upon his total mode of being. *Peau noire, masques blancs* contains a diagnosis of the Black condition that is certainly more pertinent to the Afro-American and Caribbean experience than to the African, but it has a general relevance in that Fanon offers a psychological (one might even say *clinical*) explanation for the experience of colonial alienation.

Fanon's active participation in the Algerian revolution widened his vision beyond the horizons of Negritude and provided a theater for the development of his ideas on a broader front. From the evidence of his testimony on the Algerian war of independence in *Sociologie d'une révolution*,[24] the Algerian insurrection was for Fanon as much a political act, founded upon the moral requirements of an oppressed nation, as an occasion for the colonized natives to effect a reconstruction of their collective personality. The demands of the war, as Fanon recounts it, led to a profound inner transformation of the Algerians themselves: in the general mobilization of the physical and psychic energies of an entire people, old values inappropriate to the situation were swept away and new values created, presaging a new social order. The revolution thus took on the significance of an immense process of collective metamorphosis. The pronounced psychological bias of Fanon's account of the Algerian revolution issues directly in the ethics of violence developed in the first chapter of his last book, *Les Damnés de la terre*.[25] It is essential to view his ideas on violence in their proper historical context, as well as in the full perspective of the evolution of his thought. The mechanisms brought to light in Fanon's analysis were first suggested to him by his reading of Césaire's poetry and later confirmed in the live context of the Algerian war. In this sense, he was doing no more than continuing the diagnosis of his first work, establishing a real correspondence between the symbolic projection and the physical exteriorization of the torment in the colonized subject's consciousness. His advocacy of violence against colonial domination appears therefore as a *prescription*, in the full medical sense of the word. His preoccupation with the psychiatric effects of colonial oppression, the distortions it creates within the colonized native, led him to see in the aggressive reaction against this oppression quite simply a therapeutic means of self-re-creation for the colonized subject. Through the violence directed at his oppressor, the colonized subject remakes himself as a full human being, without any limiting qualifications to his human status and quality.

As Sartre has pointed out, Fanon's ethics of violence has a pedigree within Western political thought, for Friedrich Engels, George Sorel, and V. I. Lenin have all meditated upon the significance of violence in politics. But Fanon gives an original dimension to the question. In his view, the value of violence in the revolutionary situation lies not simply in ensuring the effectiveness of political action, not in being the "midwife of history," but in the self-realization of the historical subject himself; it has to do with a vision of man creating his own identity in the effervescence of a progressive movement in history.

In its bearing upon Negritude, such a vision seems fully in accord with Sartre's emphasis upon the revolutionary significance of the movement, at least of the spirit of its poetic expression as exemplified by Césaire. Senghor's subsequent elaboration of the term into a concept of an African being informed by a living coherence of the traditional culture seems to have alienated Fanon. Indeed, Fanon displayed an insensitivity to the cultural thesis of African nationalism that may be imputed not, as might at first be thought, to his West Indian background, but, rather, to his cosmopolitanism. The Algerian experience seems to have confirmed in him what looks like an aversion to traditional cultures, to which he tended to attribute a factitious character, if not a retrograde significance. To Fanon's ingrained lack of sympathy for the cultural positions of Negritude was joined a political and ideological hostility directly related to his radical commitment. Fanon's sojourn in Ghana as *Front de Libération Nationale* (FLN) ambassador may well have strengthened, if not engendered, this commitment. His observation of Kwame Nkrumah's Ghana opened his eyes and his mind to the contradictions inherent in the postcolonial situation, where a national bourgeoisie substituted itself for the departed colonizer without undertaking an overhaul of the social structure to bring about greater social justice. The Ghanaian experience can be said to have inspired his critique of the new ruling class in Africa in a crucial chapter of his last book that displays a remarkable prescience on the subject. The relevant point here, however, is that his dim view of the African bourgeoisie led him to discount both its pre-independence nationalism and the cultural affirmation that went with it. In the postcolonial situation, the cultural theories of the bourgeoisie amounted, for him, to no more than a form of *ideology*, in the pejorative sense often given to the word by Marx: a superstructural mask thrown over the class interests of the elites. Fanon's scant regard for this form of cultural expression emerges clearly from the following comment: "The substantiality of Negro African culture is built around the people's struggle, not songs, poems, or folklore."[26] Later in the same text, Fanon stresses his point with the converse of this statement: "One can hardly desire the spread of African culture unless one contributes concretely to that culture's conditions of existence—that is to say, to the liberation of the continent."[27]

Fanon's cultural ideas are linked to his radical critique of the new African bourgeoisie in such a way as to lead him to proffer a new and different conception of culture in the context of African development—a revolutionary conception, which presents culture as the product of a collective enterprise involving the historical fortunes and destiny of the people. The significance of Fanon's cultural ideas attaches to the vision of a new, revolutionary humanism which he proposes, the mission he assigns to non-Western peoples "to create a new man." But it is easy to understand how his conception of culture and his wider projection into the Third World does away with the traditional problematic of African thought, centered upon the issue of identity. Fanon transcends this issue and clears the path for a new direction of thought.

Fanon's work belongs to an established tradition of intellectual and ideological interest in Black Africa on the part of New World Blacks, an interest which springs from the sense of a common historical predicament and which has created a pattern of reciprocal ideas and attitudes among Black intellectuals on both sides of the Atlantic. His early preoccupation with the racial problem certainly arises from a sentiment of personal involvement, but his individual temperament and the peculiar inclination of his intellectual gifts made him respond to a new configuration of events which gave a new direction to his thinking. The result of Fanon's contribution was to leave the racial problem shorn of sentimentalities, and the cultural issue raised along with it divested of the sublimities with which it had been adorned by his predecessors. The attitude introduced by Fanon into the debate on African problems, especially on the cultural question, amounts to a new realism; and the ideological spirit it has fostered now pervades the writings of that section of the French-speaking African intelligentsia which it is convenient to call the "new philosophers," represented notably by Marcien Towa and Paulin Hountondji.

The progression from the critique of Negritude to a new ideological position is clearly marked in the succession of three short books published by Towa. The first, as we have seen, is his provocative study of Senghor's poetry, *Léopold Sédar Senghor: Negritude ou servitude*.[28] Towa's analytical approach is seriously compromised by his literal reading of a form which works through allusion and suggestion, by his fastening upon immediate denotations and missing the tense harmony of the structure of connotations in the poetic text. This insensitive approach serves an ideological purpose: to discredit the poetry and, along with it, the theory of Negritude, which is assumed to be its sole reference. Towa thus attempts to place both the poetry and the theory in a direct and unilateral correspondence with Senghor's biography and his actual options in the real world. However, apart from the doubtful value of the procedure in literary criticism, Towa's obvious hostility to Senghor leads him into distortions and simplifications which bear no relation either to the deeper meanings of Senghor's poetry or even to the verifiable facts of his political career. There is an obvious forcing of the radical tone in Towa's first book, which largely invalidates his demonstration.

Towa is on a more even keel in his second book, *Essai sur la problématique philosophique dans l'Afrique actuelle*,[29] in which he leaves poetry alone to deal exclusively with ideas; the result is a remarkably coherent work whose argument ends by forcing conviction. This critique of Negritude is directed against what we have called the *philosophical* current of the movement, the effort deriving from the inspiration of Tempels's *Bantu Philosophy* and sustained by recourse to Western anthropology as a means of demonstrating the existence of a distinctively African mode of philosophical thinking. Towa recognizes that the aim of this effort was to rehabilitate the African by a revaluation of his past, but he objects to the claim that it constitutes a philosophical enterprise. The procedure adopted by the adepts of Negritude in its philosophical garb consists (for Towa) in simply enlarging the concept of philosophy itself in order to include African cultural and mental productions within it. Philosophy in this sense becomes coextensive with culture in the ordinary sociological meaning of the word, and African philosophy becomes no more than an unreflective presentation of certain forms of cultural expression associated with traditional Africa and placed in opposition to Western forms and to a more strongly articulated tradition of Western philosophy. For Towa, this procedure is illegitimate from a strict methodological point of view, since it creates a terminological confusion between philosophy in its nature and function, and cultural anthropology or ethnology considered as a discipline; hence, he dubs this current of thought *ethnophilosophy*. He points out the way in which this confusion is fostered by the equivocal character of the procedure:

> Ethnophilosophy objectively discusses beliefs, myths, rituals, and then suddenly transforms itself into a metaphysical profession of faith, without taking the trouble to either refute Western philosophy or present a rational justification for its adherence to African thought.[30]

Beyond this terminological confusion, Towa discerns in the procedure of the ethnophilosophers an insufficient understanding of the objectives of philosophy, an inadequate grasp of its critical function in an open debate upon ideas and values. This leads him to a denunciation of what he regards as the dogmatic implications of appealing to the past to sanction African thought in the present. It is precisely here that the real direction of Towa's argument begins to emerge. The effort to resuscitate a heritage of values and a worldview from the past is, he contends, irrelevant to present African preoccupations and aspirations: "An original African philosophy torn from the dark night of the past could not be, if it ever existed, but the expression of a situation that was itself in the past."[31]

Elsewhere, Towa makes clear the sense he gives to this relation to the world, by linking the cultural question with the problem of Africa's continued political and economic dependence upon Europe, and with the general issue of the material underdevelopment of the continent. His critique of cultural nationalism in a situation of African weakness takes on the radical tone of Fanon:

> Senghorian Negritude and the ethnophilosophy that seeks to extend its influence keep alive the illusion

that Africa could contribute a "spiritual supplement"
to the European soul before European imperialism
has been totally eliminated from Africa.[32]

Towa's echo of Fanon's cultural ideas gives them a new
resonance by sounding them against a background of disillusionment with African independence and of a grim and lucid
appraisal of the African situation: "For it is our deficiencies that
now impose themselves upon our attention, not our endow-
ments and our possibilities."[33] Towa's critique of Negritude and
ethnophilosophy is thus bound up with an ideological and political position determined by a somber awareness of contemporary
realities in Africa, of the incapacity of cultural nationalism to
effect a genuine transformation in the hoped for direction: of
its *irrelevance*, in a word. The presiding idea in Towa's reflection
develops with an implacable logic out of this awareness. The following passage in which it is expressed can be considered the
most significant in the book:

> The desire to be one's self immediately leads to the
> proud re-appropriation of one's past, because the
> essence of self is no more than the culmination of its
> past; however, when the past is examined and scruti-
> nized lucidly, dispassionately, it reveals that contem-
> porary subjugation can be explained by reference to
> the origins of the essence of the self, that is to say, in
> the past of the self and nowhere else.[34]

Nothing can be more explicit than this statement of a new mode
of self-perception. Here Towa is reversing the whole trend of
African intellectual effort in the modern age, breaking with its
entire framework of presuppositions and valuations. From this
negative appraisal of the effort to affirm a specifically African
and spiritual identity, Towa proceeds to a reformulation of the
African problematic in terms that are more directly related to
the requirements of the moment:

> Therefore, as a warrant of our humanity, we propose
> to replace the search for originality and difference

with a search for the avenues and means to power as
the ineluctable condition for the affirmation of our
humanity and our freedom.[35]

Towa's position here implies an entirely new program of
African intellectual activity, one no longer centered upon the
question of African *identity* but upon that of our *potential* in the
modern world. As he puts it more succinctly elsewhere: "What
we need to become, not what we uniquely are, should determine
our questions."[36]

The complementary aspect of Towa's call for a renuncia-
tion of the self as constituted by the African past represents an
opening toward new perspectives of thought and action. If the
spirit of the traditional past is inoperative in the present, and
if it is understood that the immersion of traditional man in
that spirit is responsible for our conquest and domination by
Europe, then we should seek out the secret of the power which
overwhelmed us and ascertain the direction from which it came.
Towa finds this secret in the European practice of rationality, the
key to the scientific and technological progress which enabled
Europe to master the world of nature and dominate the other
populations of the universe:

> Due to its close affinity with science and technol-
> ogy, European philosophy seems to be the source of
> European power; for that reason, it will help us bring
> about the revolution of consciousness that underlies
> the construction of our own power.[37]

Towa assigns then to Western philosophy a practical function, which amounts to its serving as an agent of development
for African people after their experience of colonial domination. He is careful to specify that his argument does not imply
"a journey to Canossa" by African culture, but rather a total
reassessment within radical perspectives of the conditions of
African life, including a critical interrogation of the past. The
advocacy of Western rationalism appears, therefore, as a tactical
move to ensure a firmer hold by the African on the territory of
his total being, but it implies nonetheless a revolution of being

in the same sense in which Fanon had preached it: a total act of self-regeneration.

The fact that Towa is a professor of philosophy is not without interest for an appreciation of his ideas as developed in this essay, for not only does it reflect a professional concern for a rigorous demarcation of the area of his discipline but indeed a passionate faith in the effective significance of philosophy within the context of real life. This becomes even more apparent in his third book, *L'Idée d'une philosophie africaine*,[38] which represents a development of *Léopold Sédar Senghor: Négritude ou servitude* in many regards. The distinguishing theme of this book, however, is an effort to found the philosophical enterprise in Africa upon a tradition of critical thought within the continent itself.

In *L'Idée d'une philosophie africaine*, Towa begins by developing, at greater length than in the earlier essay, his point that philosophy in its essential meaning is a critical activity, that the philosophical enterprise must be conducted as a reasoned mode of discourse rather than by reference to a general system of beliefs, ethical precepts, or symbolic constructions which, whatever their poetic force, do not contain within themselves any principle of verification. In order to oppose philosophy (considered as thought in its engagement with what he calls *the absolute*) to myth and religion, Towa goes back to the distinction between wisdom derived from considered judgment, on the one hand, and received opinion untested by reason, on the other. By proposing anew this classical dichotomy deriving from Plato, Towa stresses the social significance of a philosophy that implies a liberation of minds and, as a consequence, of individuals in their social determinations.

He goes on to argue for a consideration of the rational spirit manifest not only in ancient Egyptian thought—which, following Cheikh Anta Diop, he ascribes to Africa—but also in traditional folktales. The very fact that a major segment of these tales dramatizes social and moral conflicts gives them a critical function within the context of traditional life; hence, they become the mode of expression of an intelligence that constantly calls into question established values and institutions, including religious beliefs. Their philosophical value and status reside, therefore, in their function as a critical interrogation of the natural world and of social facts.

Against this background, Towa considers the general problem of the place and role of philosophy in Africa at the present time. He returns to his earlier preoccupation with philosophy as an agent of development. As he puts the matter, "The possibility for a philosophical renaissance in Africa is tied to its political and economic fate."[39] Thus, projecting in schematic form a philosophy of history that derives its inspiration from Hegel, he relates the processes of thought itself to their objective manifestations and effects upon human life. Consequently, when he affirms that mind is *activity*, it becomes easy to understand his restatement of the correlation between philosophical activity—pure thought—and the logic of science and technological development, as well as his advocacy of Western rationalism as a means of accession to modernity. In this book, as in the earlier work, Towa's preoccupation with the possibility of an African philosophy, with the problem of philosophy itself, is commanded by immediate concerns of a political and ideological order. He says, "Philosophy is essentially a relation between a theory and the demands of social life."[40] In the particular development that he gives to this proposition, it implies a radical calling into question of the present structures in our contemporary societies as determined by the values, options, and practices of the ruling classes.

Towa's thinking is obviously tributary to Fanon's, but it has an originality all its own, for he follows the latter's ideas to their logical limits, thereby giving explicit conceptual form to their implications in an effort to place these ideas on a sound philosophical foundation. The marked ideological orientation of this effort makes for certain theoretical weaknesses, as we shall see. For the moment, it is useful to point out a contradiction between his earlier stand against the methods of the ethnophilosophers and the procedure, adopted in his third book, of attaching a philosophical significance to traditional folktales, simply on the basis of their critical function. It is obvious that such a value can be given to any form of imaginative expression within any culture, so long as it fulfills a similar function, without compelling a recognition of its status as a form of philosophical thinking in the restricted, technical sense suggested by Towa's own definition. It does seem, therefore, that Towa is attempting to attenuate the cutting effect of his earlier position, which, it should be noted in passing, assumes the existence of a distinctive mode of African thought, even if it rejects both the method of its exposition in ethnophilosophy and the relevance of the mode and its exposition to present African concerns. We might say, then, that Towa is attempting to put back with the left hand what he took away earlier with the right, a procedure that can only be justified at the cost of special pleading.

When we turn to Paulin Hountondji, we find a position that is much more uncompromising. His ideas are developed in a series of journal articles, the earliest of which appeared in 1969. Some of these were included in a volume, *Libertés*, published in Cotonou in 1973; a more complete selection was later collected, revised, and placed together in *Sur la "philosophie africaine,"* published in Paris in 1977.[41] Hountondji's work thus predates and overlaps with that of Towa: their ideas coincide on many points, but Hountondji's critique is more comprehensive and his whole manner more emphatic, hence the greater impact his work seems to have made in French-speaking African intellectual circles.

Hountondji's ideas proceed from the same ideological reaction against Negritude as Towa's, from the same standpoint which links ethnophilosophy with the movement of cultural nationalism, of which Negritude is taken to be the theoretical expression. But as his various references to the movement indicate, he refuses to concede any positive significance to the effort to rehabilitate African culture. For Hountondji, the relationship between this movement and the colonial ideology it is intended to combat reveals a peculiar ambiguity, a pathetic correspondence between the terms of African affirmation and the opposite system of ideas or representations proposed by the colonial ideology in its image of Africa. Thus, he observes,

> By desiring at all costs to compare ourselves to Europe…, we are still defining ourselves in relation to it; we make it our primary term of reference and

> ascribe the origin of our civilization's meaning to it.
> The nature of demonstration of this kind is to be
> essentially reversible: its terms can be reversed, trans-
> formed into their opposites, and cultural superiority
> can be transmuted into inferiority or vice versa, in
> the mythological space of a fruitless comparison. [42]

The motivation of ethnophilosophy in its association with
cultural nationalism renders its entire undertaking suspect: it
accounts for the equivocation discernible in its procedures and
formulations and compromises from the outset the very principle
of its mode of discourse. This fundamental weakness affecting
its conceptual framework becomes the object of Hountondji's
critique, since the equivocal character of ethnophilosophy not
only obscures its ideological motivation but has implications for a
proper understanding of the nature and function of philosophy:

> Precisely for that reason, a political critique of eth-
> nophilosophy could not possibly suffice; one must
> also provide a theoretical critique that transcends
> the changing practical effects of this discourse and
> attacks the concepts on which they are based, for
> in the final analysis the ambiguity of these concepts
> explains the reversibility of its effects. [43]

One might say, then, that Hountondji undertakes a "critique of
ethnophilosophical reason" in its conceptual constitution, a critique directed primarily against its manifestations in the work of
the African practitioners of ethnophilosophy, but also intended to
affect the framework of concepts elaborated by Western ethnology and the value systems they imply, both of which seem to him
to have insidiously made their way into the African formulations.

Hountondji's main line of attack proceeds from the categorical stand he takes against the notion of collective philosophy.
His objection to ethnophilosophy concerns what he sees as its
fixed attachment to the reconstruction of African worldviews
and systems of thought whose common character is that they
can be opposed to European ones. The collective philosophy
derived in this way from African forms of cultural expression

is unconscious and unreflective, merely deduced by the outside observer and assumed to be immanent in a culture and to serve both as the underlying principle of the mental processes of all its members and as a normative reference for moral and social life. Hountondji objects to what he considers the *reductionist* penchant of the ethnophilosophers, who throw a veil of uniformity over processes that are in reality diverse and, by so doing, perpetuate the image of African societies as a spontaneous adhesion of all their members to a common system of ideas and norms.

In order to illustrate the unfruitfulness of the dominant perspective of the ethnophilosophers, Hountondji undertakes in the first three essays of *Sur la "philosophie africaine"* a critical exposition of the ideas and methods of Tempels and his African successors. In view of his recognition of the quality and usefulness of Kagame's work, Hountondji's critique is particularly significant, for it illuminates his own conception of philosophy. While conceding that Kagame's approach shows a greater analytical rigor than that of Tempels, whose ideas it is intended to verify and correct, Hountondji objects to the terms of Kagame's formulation of Rwanda ontology and to his general perspective regarding the idea of a collective philosophy. In the departures made by Kagame from Aristotle's scheme, Hountondji discerns a distortion of the Greek philosopher's method, a distortion which produces an equivocal result. Kagame's attempt to derive the categories of Rwanda ontology from the grammatical structure of the language appears to Hountondji to constitute a misrepresentation of Aristotle's method, for the latter's purpose is not so much to explore the structures of the Greek language as to go beyond their factitious character and to found language itself upon a universal and necessary order. It ought to be said at once that this criticism itself demonstrates a misunderstanding of Kagame's purpose, which is, first, to show that Aristotle's categories *cannot* be universal, since they are formulated within a language quite differently structured from Ki-Rwanda; and, second, to demonstrate, from the insight and vantage point afforded by a non-Western language, a different mode of representation of reality which is not simply inherent in the structures of the Rwanda language but explicit in its larger transformations in the oral tradition.[44]

It is on this point that Hountondji's objection finally rests: the fact that Kagame professes to reconstruct a philosophy from the oral traditions which provide him with what he calls "institutionalized documents." For Hountondji, such a method is illegitimate not only because, by employing it, Kagame subscribes to a myth of collective philosophy, but especially because these institutionalized documents themselves are by their nature anything but philosophical texts. By drawing upon them, Kagame commits a "confusion of genres"; he projects upon them a philosophical significance which they do not and cannot have. The combination in Kagame's work of analytical scruple and the recourse to the oral tradition for his demonstration results in something of a paradox for Hountondji:

> This same scientific rigor prohibits one from arbitrarily projecting a philosophical discourse behind the products of language, which are themselves presented as anything but philosophy.[45]

Again, it is evident here that Hountondji's idea of a philosophical text does not correspond to Kagame's, whose specialized knowledge of the very elaborate forms of Rwanda literature permits him to draw out of them a mode of thought that employs an imaginative key to represent the world and express a human apprehension of it.[46]

The divergence of view between Kagame and Hountondji on the proper status of oral tradition in African philosophy points to a more fundamental disagreement about the nature of philosophy itself. On the basis of Hountondji's critique of Kagame, it becomes evident that the former is at pains to hold ethnophilosophy to a rigorous conception of the discipline, if it is to qualify as philosophy. For Hountondji the assumptions and formulations of ethnophilosophy are, in effect, contrary to the spirit of philosophy, which entails a conscious and explicit mode of discourse:

> No more than any other philosophy, African philosophy could hardly be a collective vision of the world. It cannot exist as philosophy except in the form of

a confrontation between individual thoughts, a discussion, a debate.[47]

This requirement excludes any possibility of considering a reconstruction of African systems of thought as philosophy, of creating a distinctive African philosophy merely by the repetitive recall of an unconscious and implicit collective worldview, without submitting the elements of this worldview to critical appraisal. Hountondji maintains that it is not a *vision* of the world that makes for philosophy, but its *description*, its mode of presentation; not the content, but the form of discourse. At best, philosophy can bear an African label by virtue only of the existence of a body of explicit texts produced by Africans who are conscious of working within a regional tradition and of being at the same time engaged in a discussion which maintains an essential connection to the international philosophical community.

In a sense, the on-going discussion about African phililosophy contributes to the constitution of African philosophy considered from this point of view. Hountondji even remarks that African philosophy already exists in this sense, and he includes within it the work of the African ethnophilosophers whom he criticizes. In his view, they are in reality doing no more than providing an individual interpretation of what they take to be an African vision of the world, with each interpretation producing different and often conflicting results. "Incontestably philosophical, their only weakness was to work out mythically, under the guise of a collective philosophy, the philosophical form of their own discourse."[48]

Hountondji seems to be moving here toward a formal definition of *philosophy*. However, in the most substantial essay of his collection, "La Philosophie et ses révolutions," he attempts to validate his conception of philosophy as a particular form of debate by affirming that philosophy is not a system in the sense of a closed structure of ideas—however coherent or grandiose that structure may be, as in the case of Hegel—but is instead, by its very nature, a perpetual movement, a chain of responses from one individual philosopher to another across the ages, a progression in which the future direction of the philosophical enterprise cannot be determined, since it must keep open the perspectives of human thought. This observation leads him to affirm that, structurally, in its substance, philosophy is *historical*, drawing its life from the evolution of a continuing debate regulated by a single preoccupation with verification, on which point philosophy shares a common nature with science. Here are his words on the question:

> A philosophical or mathematical work can only be understood as a moment in a larger debate that sustains it and passes beyond it: it always refers to previous positions, either to refute them or to confirm and embellish them. It has no sense except in relation to that history—in relation to the terms of a debate which continually evolves and in which the only constant is an unvarying reference to the same object, to the same realm of experience, the definition of which is, moreover, determined during the course of that evolution. In short, scientific literature is historical through and through.[49]

It is surprising that, in expressing this point of view, Hountondji does not seem to have perceived its limitation. Even if we are to believe that history constitutes the essence of philosophy, rather than serving simply as a contingent factor of its incarnation in Europe, there remains a difficulty. For when we roll back its process, by a kind of regressive method, we inevitably arrive at some point of departure in its evolution, and there we are left to wonder how this point, without an antecedent, can assume the character of philosophy. This difficulty is bypassed in Hountondji's discussion by his assimilation of philosophy to science, in contradistinction to mental projections of the imaginative kind. As we have seen in his critique of Kagame, Hountondji does not consider that the material with which ethnophilosophy operates—its sources and texts as provided by the oral tradition—belongs in the category of philosophical literature. The mere fact that they can and do frequently serve as vehicles of thought is not sufficient to class them within that category. The reason he adduces for his rejection is that philosophy forms part of scientific literature. As he says, "It shares the same life and evolves according to the same rhythm as mathematics, physics, chemistry, and linguistics."[50]

Whatever one may think of this large claim for philosophy, it soon becomes plain that Hountondji is not using a metaphor, that his assimilation of philosophy to science is in fact a synonymy. For him, philosophy is in fact a second-order science in its empirical practice, nothing other than the form of its reflection: "Philosophical practice, or that particular form of theoretical practice that is commonly called philosophy, is inseparable from that other form of theoretical practice commonly called science."[51]

The influence of Louis Althusser becomes apparent in the terminology and the turn of mind it suggests. In the immediate context of Hountondji's essay, it leads to his observation that no serious and meaningful philosophical enterprise can be undertaken in Africa without a comprehensive effort of scientific research and activity. "That which Africa needs first of all is not philosophy, but rather science," he declares.[52] And as part of the implication of his assimilation of philosophy to science, fundamental to all his thinking, is his restriction of the meaning of philosophy to theoretical analysis, which has as its corollary the exclusion of metaphysics and all kinds of pure speculation. It is important again to quote him fully on this:

> That sort of philosophy, that sort of theoretical research rigorously constructed on the basis of science, leaves us miles away from the concerns around which the myth of a so-called traditional African "philosophy" crystallized and evolved. It leaves us far from metaphysical problems about the origin of the world, the sense of life, the meaning of death, man's destiny, the reality of the after-life, the existence of God, mythology, and everything else in which philosophical musings habitually take delight.[53]

The statement here represents a frontal attack upon ethnophilosophy commencing from the principles of philosophy. It is not only a normative definition of the proper domain of philosophy—a definition which is, at the very least, controversial—but, more significantly, a vehement call for the application of a rigorous scientific method in African philosophy. Certainly a note of impatience often emerges in Hountondji's writing—which might be considered the emotional overtone of his intellectual reaction to the formulations of ethnophilosophy. His inclusion of Kagame within the trend he is reacting against appears to reveal his lack of a sense for proper discrimination, and it unquestionably does an injustice to the quality of the Rwanda priest's work, although it ought perhaps to be seen as an attempt to deal with the movement as a whole by attacking an exceptional case which, by its very quality, endorses a general trend to facile critique.

Marcien Towa and Paulin Hountondji meet on the common ground of not only their opposition to ethnophilosophy but also their radical commitment to modernization in Africa. Both see ethnophilosophy as an expression of cultural nationalism that is no longer relevant to the African situation and actually constitutes a fruitless diversion from urgent tasks. Again, the pronounced ideological hue of the work of the new philosophers raises a number of issues from which a lively controversy has ensued. It will not be possible here to describe the details of this controversy,[54] but only to remark upon some of the implications and effects of the countermovement they represent.

To start with, the rather peremptory tone of both Towa and Hountondji makes it difficult to discern in their work a concern for the necessary discriminations required in a debate of this kind. It is evident that Towa's attack on ethnophilosophy, motivated by a disaffection toward Senghor, has a passionate character that necessarily affects all arguments *ad hominem*; it is significant that in Towa's last book he displays what amounts to an ambiguous attitude in relation to his earlier position on the question of tradition. Moreover, in their insistence upon the need for Africa to adopt a modern scientific spirit, both Towa and Hountondji are flogging a dead horse; the point itself has never been in doubt among the adepts of cultural nationalism. They take for dogma what is rather a general premise of ethnophilosophy: the possibility of deriving a valid alternative view of human life and experience from the traditional background, what Willie Abraham (who is attacked by Hountondji) calls a *paradigm*. It is true, of course, that reference to tradition and the past eventually acquired a moral value with Senghor, and that Cheikh Anta Diop gave it a didactic significance; nonetheless, it is obvious that the essential aim is to restore to the African a sense of the historical initiative from which colonial ideology diverted him.

Particularly in this regard, the new philosophers lay themselves open to serious criticism. The implication of their position is to leave African thought and effort with no possible perspective other than a Western one. Their linkage of Western ideas and values with modernity and development does not entail an assessment of the inadequacies of Western civilization in all its ramifications: political, social, economic, cultural, and spiritual. It is not made clear in their writings why the rejection of the African past should not imply, as well, an assessment of the Western model in its objective and practical significance, a consideration of why there ought to be a retreat from judgment in regard to this model. Their position seems therefore to be *partial*, in both senses of the word, leading to a disquieting restriction of thought and implying a limitation of the African's sense of creativity.

One is, of course, aware that this result is far from the intention of either writer, but it is evident from the terms and processes of their thinking, especially in the case of Hountondji, that their position arises from an inflexible adherence to conventional Western canons. Hountondji's ideas on language, for example, are limited by a strictly Western conception of speech acts, and even then they lag behind the contemporary findings of linguistics; as a result, he advances views that are actually quite inaccurate. Similarly, in his latest book, Towa focuses upon the present significance of European thought, but in presenting its history he omits important details about the actual process of its development. It seems, then, that both these representatives of the new generation of French-speaking African intellectuals have been so impressed by Western achievement that they feel obliged to offer it as a model for African development.

But for all their theoretical limitations, the strength of these authors' passion is not in doubt. They are moved to take a position against the prevailing spirit of cultural nationalism by their commitment to a progressive vision of Africa. As against the noble idea of the past, which animates cultural nationalism, they are struck by the picture of Africa's present weakness. The disillusionment occasioned by present experience induces in them an acute sense of realism, which runs counter to the romanticism of their elders. They are the counterparts, in the domain of thought, to the new breed of African fiction writers, who are also disinclined to accept a complacent view of Africa. What the Ouologuems, the Kouroumas, and the Fantourés are dramatizing in their novels, Towa and Hountondji are expressing with a relentless logic as explicit, clear ideas. We may discern in the phenomenon they represent—an opposition to earlier movements, ideas, and attitudes—something of a conflict of generations.

However, the more meaningful interpretation is to read this dispute as the conflict between a resolutely unsentimental awareness of African difference (and of the real disadvantages it entails in the modern world) and a nostalgic attachment to that difference: a conflict reminiscent of the one between the modernists and the Slavophiles in prerevolutionary Russia.

It ought to be stressed, however, that the position of the new philosophers carries with it absolutely no hint of an inferiority complex in relation to Europe; there is no suggestion of self-contempt in their work. If anything, it reflects a new self-confidence capable of sustaining a critical examination of the African background. There is an irony here, for the new philosophers owe their new confidence to the effort of their predecessors, against whom they have now turned; the confidence they evince is indisputably an inheritance from their elders. If the younger generation of African intellectuals is able to feel unperturbed by the image of the African and the Black race presented by the colonial ideology, if that image no longer wounds their self-awareness, it is surely because the intellectual and ideological battles have already been fought for them. As a result of those battles, African independence has become a reality; their problem is no longer to justify that reality but to determine what to do with it.

Finally, it is undeniable that the debate initiated by these thinkers has renewed the whole movement of African intellectual activity and given a new sense of urgency to ideological preoccupations in the contemporary context. Cultural nationalism was essentially retrospective in character, even if it involved a vision of the future; the current trend, in contrast, is markedly prospective in nature. Negritude was and remains a limiting concept in the sense that it seeks to circumscribe an area of African being so as to mark it off from others, to define the frontiers of African identity and expression. The ambition of the new generation of French-speaking African intellectuals is precisely to extend those frontiers.

Notes

1. For a full discussion, see Shlomo Avineri, *The Social and Political Thought of Karl Marx* (1968).

2. See Robert July, *The Origins of Modern African Thought* (1968).

3. The point emerges clearly from several studies, notably D. Kimble, *A Political History of Ghana* (1963); and July, op. cit.

4. See my essay, "Faith and Exile: Cheikh Hamidou Kane and the Theme of Alienation," in *The African Experience in Literature and Ideology* (1980).

5. For a general account of the relationship between anthropology and colonial ideology, see Gerard Leclerc, *Anthropologie et colonialisme* (1972).

6. Senghor made the acquaintance of Blyden's work only in 1961, as he admits in his preface to Hollis Lynch, ed., *Selected Letters of Edward Wilmot Blyden* (Millwood, NY: K. T. O, 1978); however, the progression of ideas suggested here is real, inscribed in the logic of the development of African thought from the mid-nineteenth to the mid-twentieth century.

7. Jean-Paul Sartre, "Orphée noir," in *Situations III* (1948); English translation by Samuel Allen, *Black Orpheus* (1962).

8. The title of a well-known book by Ruth Benedict.

9. Léopold Sédar Senghor, "L'Esprit de la civilisation ou les lois de la culture négro-africaine," in *Présence Africaine*, 8-10 (1956), p. 56 ff.

10. Léopold Sédar Senghor, *Les Fondements de l'africannité* (1967).

11. Placide Tempels, *La Philosophie bantoue* (1949).

12. Alexis Kagame, *La Philosphie bantu-rwandaise de l'être* (1956).

13. Alexis Kagame, *La Philosophie Bantu comparee* (1976), p. 56.

14. For a selection of representative works exemplifying this current, see the list of references in Paulin Hountondji, *Sur "la philosophie africaine"* (1977).

15. Cheikh Anta Diop, *Nation nègres et culture* (1955; 3ed., 1979). References are to the later edition.

16. Cheikh Anta Diop, *Antériorité des civilisations nègres: Mythe ou réalité* (Paris: Presence Africaine, 1967); Cheik Anta Diop, *Parenteé génétique de l'égyptien pharaonique et des langues négro-africaines* (Dakar: Nouvelles Editions Africaines, 1979).

17. Diop, *Nations nègres*, p. 212.

18. Cheikh Anta Diop, *L'Unité culturelle de l'Afrique noire* (1959).

19. Diop, *Antériorité*, p. 11. See also Lansina Keita, "Two Philosophies of African History: Hegel and Diop," in *Présence Africaine*, 91 (1974), pp. 41-49.

20. Albert Franklin, "La Négritude: Réalité ou Mystification," in *Présence Africaine*, 14 (1952), pp. 287-303.

21. See "The Négritude Debate," Chapter Four above, for a more extensive discussion of Adotévi as critique.

22. For a fuller discussion, see Irele, *Les Origines de la Négritude à la Martinique: Sociologie de l'oeuvre poétique d'Aimé Césaire* (Unpublished doctoral thesis, University of Paris, 1966).

23. Frantz Fanon, *Peau noire, masques blancs* (Paris: Seuil, 1952).

24. Frantz Fanon, *Sociologie d'une révolution* (Paris: Maspero, 1966). First published in 1959 under the title *L'An V de la révolution algérienne*.

25. Frantz Fanon, *Les Damnés de la terre.* (Paris: Maspero, 1975).

26. Fanon, *Damnés*, p. 164.

27. Ibid., p. 165.

28. Marcien Towa, *Léopold Sédar Senghor: Négritude ou servitude?* (Yaoundxé: C. L. E, 1971).

29. Marcien Towa, *Essai sur la problématique philosophique dans l'Afrique actuelle* (Yaounde: C. L. E., 1971).

30. Ibid., p. 31.

31. Ibid., p. 35.

32. Ibid., pp. 51-52.

33. Ibid., p. 39.

34. Ibid., p. 41.

35. Ibid., p. 53.

36. Ibid., p. 56.

37. Ibid., p. 68.

38. Marcien Towa, *L'Idée d'une philosophie africaine* (Yaoundé: C. L. E, 1979).

39. Ibid., p. 53.

40. Ibid., p. 112.

41. Paulin Hountondji, *Libertés* (Cotonou: Editions Renaissance, 1977); and *Sur la «philosophie africaine"* (Paris: Maspero, 1977).

42. Hountondji, *Libertés*, p. 36.

43. Hountondji, *Sur «la philosophie africaine,"* p. 241.

44. Kagame's approach to the question has been confirmed by the eminent French linguist Emile Benveniste, in his essay "Catégories de pensée et catégories de langue," in *Problèmes de linguistique générale* (Paris: Gallimard, 1966), p. 63-74.

45. Houtoundji, p. 30.

46. See Alexis Kagame, *La Poésie dynastique au Rwanda* (Brussels: Institut Royal Colonial Belge, 1951); and Andre Coupez and Thomas Kamanzi, eds., *Littérature de cour au Rwanda* (Oxford: Oxford University Press, 1970).

47. Houtoundji, p. 48.

48. Ibid., p. 22.

49. Ibid., 100.

50. Ibid., p. 99.

51. Ibid., p. 124.

52. Ibid., p. 124.

53. Ibid.

54. Hountondji's position has been challenged notably by Niamey Koffie, "L'Impensé de Towa et d'Hountondji," in Claude Summer, ed., *Philosophie africaine* (Addis-Ababa: N. P., 1980); and Olabiyi Yai, "Théorie et pratique en philosophie africaine: Misère de la philosophie speculative," *Présence Africaine*, 108 (1978), pp. 65-91.

CHAPTER SIX
ESSENTIAL LANDSCAPE:
IMAGE AND SYMBOL IN THE
POETRY OF AIMÉ CÉSAIRE
❦

The most striking characteristic of Aimé Césaire's poetry is undoubtedly the dominance of the theme of social commitment. The explicit orientation of Césaire's poetry is dictated by his direct, individual response to a historical and social situation and his vigorous espousal of a collective cause. This public theme is so prominent, and the poet's public voice so insistent, that there seems little room in the work for the expression of a private vision of life in its widest human significance. One might suppose that the poet's imagination, in its engagement with the actualities of a lived situation, thus suffered some restriction in its deployment upon experience, such that the resultant expression would have an interest for us only in the limited sense related to the historical and social circumstances of its inspiration.

But if, in its primary movement, as attested by its overt themes and references, Césaire's poetry conveys the impression of being somewhat conditioned by his intense preoccupation with the objective factors of the collective situation in which history has plunged him, the very texture of the work provides an indication of a range and quality of expression that go beyond the requirements of the voicing of a social concern. The evident complexity of the poetry suggests at once a structure of experience that derives its significance not merely from its connection to an objective sphere of existence, but also, and more importantly, from a deeper poetic contemplation of the implications of the human condition and its profound association with the life of the universe in which we have our complete being. Thus, while Césaire's poetic consciousness is focused upon a collective experience in its quest for a social and moral significance, that quest assumes a further dimension by being placed within a spiritual and metaphysical perspective that provides its ultimate meaning.

We have in Césaire's poetry an imaginative transposition of immediate experience offering the expression of an intense engagement with the concrete realities of existence; the social inspiration of the poetry thus provides a constant reference for an evolving drama of consciousness. At the same time, poetic creation becomes for Césaire the medium of a psychological and spiritual adventure that transcends the sociopolitical, offering a privileged mode that culminates in a visionary apprehension of the world. And it is within the poetic language by which this drama is given expression that the poet's experience finds its coherence and its true direction. In other words, it is at the level of the imagery and symbolism proposed by the poetry that the true import of its themes as dictated by the lived experience of the poet is able to emerge in all its fullness.

The social inspiration of Césaire's poetry determines, then, a first level of his imagery related to his immediate concerns, defining an emotional content for its explicit allusions and meanings, and thus establishes what one might call an external framework of its organization. At the same time, the images are given such a forceful charge within this context that they reach down in their resonance to the deeper layer of the poet's fundamental intuitions. There is thus, as it were, a double articulation of Césaire's universe determined by his poetry's double mode of significance. This manifests itself as an initial polarization of the imagery, corresponding to the two opposed directions of the poet's adventure: on the one hand, a tragic apprehension of the world; on the other, a new awareness envisaged as a renewal of the self and of the world.

Césaire's tragic vision finds expression in a cluster of images whose character can be described as *pathetic*, and which represent the nocturnal aspect of his poetic universe. They register a veritable existential malaise, deriving from the poet's experience of a degraded temporal state. The biblical image of *abîme* (abyss) establishes the fundamental theme of an original fall,[1] around which are developed variations such as *ruines, éboulis* (scree), *affaissement* (subsidence, prostration). These images not only designate an immediate experience but also provide a comprehensive perspective for the poet's awareness of the temporal, historical frame of his existence. It is within this perspective that the experience of slavery assumes for Césaire—as for so many other Caribbean poets—a primary significance, as a factor of their collective destiny. In Césaire's poetry, the fact of slavery is given particular focus as the foundation of the poet's historical being, the source of his degraded condition arising from his mode of insertion in time. The numerous direct allusions to slavery in such images as *fouet* (whip), *corde* (rope), and *chaîne* constitute a subsidiary leit-motif to the theme of original fall evoked above. We have in these images not merely an allusion to a somber past but the signs of a lingering presence of the past of slavery in the poet's awareness of the world, the resounding echo in his mind of a past which has remained immediate to his consciousness. The memory of slavery thus comes to determine a phobia of an almost organic character, rendered palpable in his evocations of the experience, as in the following extract:

> *Que de sang dans ma mémoire!*
> *Dans ma mémoire sont les lagunes.*
> *Elles sont couvertes de têtes de*
> *morts. Elles ne sont pas couvertes*
> *de nénuphars...*
> *Ma mémoire est entourée de sang.*
> *Ma mémoire a sa ceinture de cadavres.*

> [So much blood in my memory!
> In my memory there are lagoons.
> They are covered with death-heads. They are
> Not covered with water lilies...

My memory is ringed round in blood
My memory has its hedge of cadavers.] [2]

We have in this poetry, then, something of a psychological experience of time at the root of a structure of complexes brought to light by the series of images which reflect the poet's consciousness of his historical situation. Perhaps the most prominent of these complexes is that of claustrophobia, which presents itself as an intense form of the poet's sense of frustration. In such images as *carcan* (iron collar), *barres* (iron bars), *caveçons* (cavesson, nose band to control a horse), and the like, the idea of constraint is associated with that of confinement, and is further intensified through the imagery of animal domestication in such terms as *baillon* (gag), *muselage* (muzzle), *harnais* (harness), and *trémail* (shackle)—terms that the poet applies to his condition to signify his sense of degradation. The physical and moral effect communicated by these images thus explains the poet's anguished desire for space and movement:

> *La mer sans sape sans poste d'écoute*
> *sans pare-éclats*
>
> *Sans boyaux excoriés de lunes rompues*
> *sur les genoux de fer de la nuit.*
>
> [The sea without sap trench, without listening post
> without light shields
>
> Without peeling guts of moons broken on the iron
> knees of night.] [3]

But it is especially in the series of physiological images that we witness the effects of the poet's existential discomfort; in this respect, the pathetic aspect of his imagery assumes here the character of a pathological obsession. Césaire's poetry contains a catalogue of maladies and afflictions whose significance is none other than to express his profound disaffection for the world as proffered, to provide a graphic representation of the *mal de vivre* which darkens his vision. But the very elaboration of these negative images associated with the body also betrays a more definite phenomenon, the complex of the Black subject disturbed in his relationship with his own body, the sense of a discontinuity between himself and his environment, of a separation from his own essential being.[4]

These various complexes are projected in the poetry through a series of nature images dominated by the idea of impotence, of an organic sterility. The symbolic representation of the natural world in a state of desolation corresponds to a certain morose state of the poet's imagination associated with the season of winter and a general frigid condition of the universe. In this symbolic scheme, which suggests a decrease of vitality—a lowering of the physical and spiritual being—the image of the bare leafless tree (*l'arbre dévêtu*) constitutes a central reference for a cluster of vegetal imagery through which the poet's complex of sterility is conveyed. This group of images has a special importance for grasping the symmetry of Césaire's imagery, for the poet's negative evocation of the natural world through vegetal images suggests something more than a pathetic fallacy; it indicates, rather, a fundamental attachment of the poet to the vegetal as a manifestation of creation, which, as we shall see, emerges more fully in the positive context of his celebration of the universe. At all events, it is this attachment that determines in the poetry a tropical fear of drought. Indeed, the dominant physical sensation in the category of pathetic images in Césaire's poetry is undoubtedly that of thirst. The absence of water clearly symbolizes for him the absence of life: the aridity of the steppe, and the static and menacing monotony of the desert, thus represent for him the absolute misfortune, that is, the cessation of life.

The ultimate reference for all of these negative images employed by Césaire to designate his existential condition is the image of *night*. Unlike Senghor, for whom the atmosphere of night, because of its association with the African environment, symbolizes the protective presence of the ancestors and of beneficial spirits and thus inspires a mood of meditation, Césaire gives a negative value to the image of night.[5] The poet has a horror of all that is unclear, indeterminate, and half-toned.

Fog and mist are thus assimilated to night, which represents the blind condition of spiritual alienation:

> Nuit stigmate fourchu
> nuit buisson télégraphique planté
> dans l'océan pour minutieuses
> amours de cétacés
> nuit fermée.

> [Night cloven stigmatic
> Night telegraph thicket stuck in the ocean
> For painstaking lovemaking of cetaceans
> Night shut tight.] [6]

The image of night thus gathers up the various elements of the poet's perception of his historical situation. It provides a global representation of his existential predicament, of a negative determination which provokes his anguish but also inspires a forceful reaction.

All of these images contain, with their pathetic quality, a primarily descriptive value: they denote the world as encountered by the poet and thus mark a passive state of his consciousness prior to the movement of his imagination toward an active grasp of the world. For Césaire, such action proceeds from the sovereign exercise of will. And, given the particular context of his poetry, it is understandable that Césaire should confront the world with a strategy of provocation. The polemical stance of the poet is thus expressed through the elaboration in his work of a symbolism of *aggression*. All in the human world or the natural environment that possesses a power of destruction comes therefore to be invoked in a ferment of combative images that issue from the poet's enraged consciousness.

The most obvious indication of this aspect of Césaire's poetry is the frequent reference to instruments of war: *couteau* (knife), *flèche* (arrow), *balle* (bullet), and *fusée* (rocket) chart the development from early times to the industrial age of the offensive weapons which humanity has employed in battle. But it is especially in the natural world that the poet finds the most appropriate weapons for his combat, along with privileged allies:

Vois dans la forêt sans sommeil
les amis ont poussé patients.

[See in the ever wakeful forest
friends have patiently sprouted.] [7]

The baleful species of the vegetal realm provide him with a panoply of poisons: *datura, aconit* (wolf's bane) and *mancenillier* (manchineel), the most frequently evoked, have a special significance in that they are drawn from the poet's Caribbean background and are thus familiar to him in every sense of the word. These and other images of the same series indicate a scheme of the poet's imagination centered upon the theme of toxicity, which reaches a paroxysm in the following extract:

Plantes parasites, plantes vénéneuses,
plantes brûlantes, plantes cannibales,
plantes incendiaires, vraies plantes,
filez vos courbes imprévues à grosses gouttes.

[Parasite plants, poison plants
Burning plants, cannibal plants
Flaming plants, true plants
Spin your heedless waves of abundant drops.] [8]

But the ideal medium of the expression of revolt in Césaire's poetry is the animal imagery that plays such a key role in its polemical scheme. In this respect, Césaire's poetry presents itself as a veritable bestiary in which a remarkable range of animals and birds feature as images of destruction. The aggressive potential of the animal genre is represented here not so much in external terms as through functional images; beyond the general note of negation of the human which the animal introduces, the poet insists on its power to *harm*. Thus terms such as *griffes* (claws), *crocs* (fangs), *becs* (beaks), and *serres* (fangs) belong to the same order of reference as variations on the same theme of mutilation. With *chardons*, the thorny plant is animalized and endowed with even greater force, so that this image comes to participate in the same series. The multiple implications of the symbolism of aggression in Césaire's poetry find a single comprehensive reference in the image of the *fleur vampire*: at once plant, animal, and bird. Not only does this mythical creature designate the totality of space in the natural world, it also symbolizes in its elemental force the "operative power of negation" that the poet assumes in his offensive.

The animal imagery in the polemical scheme of Césaire's poetry serves as a counterpoise to the theme of domestication observed above. The evocations of animal force create an atmosphere of impulsive movement which contradicts the immobilism of a condition passively endured. Such deliberately provocative notations as *meute* (pack) or *rut* (heat derived from animal excitement) have no other function than to give vent to the poet's pent-up passion induced by his sense of frustration and to denote his aspiration toward a recovery of his full powers—physical and moral—of what he calls "*la fougue de chair vive*" ("the fire of living flesh")—in other words, to an expansion of being. No extract gives a better idea of this dream of muscular exertion in Césaire's poetry than this beginning of a poem founded in its entire thematic development upon the archetypal image of force, the horse:

> *Et voici par mon ouïe tramée*
> *de crissements et de fusées*
> *syncoper des laideurs rèches*
> *les cent pur-sangs*
> *hénnissant du soleil parmi*
> *la stagnation.*

> [And by my gills conspired
> in a gnashing of teeth
> the screech of rockets
> and harsh ugliness
> behold the hundred thoroughbreds
> neighing with the lust of the sun
> in the midst of stagnation.][9]

To all this agitation in the animal realm, the earth responds in profound sympathy. There is a telluric scheme in the symbolism of Césaire's poetry, whose prominence is first announced by its association with the theme of *revolt*. Its most manifest function is to give forceful expression to the poet's intense feeling for the dynamic potential of the elements. Thus, to immobility, Césaire opposes the vibrant tremor of seismic phenomena, the brusque eruption of volcanoes—often a clear reference to Mont Pélé, of his native Martinique—the blind fury of avalanches and the agitated toss of ocean waves. The various images that Césaire employs to designate the tremendous energies contained in the world of nature assume a heroic significance in direct relation to his poetic offensive on the world:

> *C'est moi qui chante d'une voix*
> *prise encore dans le balbutiement*
> *des éléments.*

> [I am the one who sings with a voice
> still held in the stutter
> of the elements.][10]

Together, Césaire's polemical images compose an apocalyptic vision which corresponds to his refusal of the world as given. In this vision, the image of fire constitutes a key element of his dream of universal demolition. Although this image has other specific connotations—especially the erotic suggestions apparent in several texts—it is its value in the "applied" symbolism of Césaire's poetry that is the most prominent.[11] In effect, fire is the polemical image par excellence, given its eminently destructive potential. This image thus determines what one might call an *incendiary theme* of the poet's imagination—"*ma parole puissance du feu*" ("my word, power of fire") he declares—which counters his revulsion for the cold and static universe of his initial apprehension of the world:

> *ma haine singulière dérivant les*
> *icebergs dans l'haleine des vraies*
> *flammes.*

> [My singular hatred breaking off

Icebergs in the breath of true flames.][12]

This extract enables us to appreciate the conjunction between explicit theme and poetic image in Césaire's imagination, for it demonstrates clearly the way in which the idea of revolt and the attitude it determines imply the elaboration of countervalues projected in image and symbol. The fact, too, that Césaire's apocalyptic vision is centered upon the element of fire enables us to understand the profound meaning of this revolt, for fire is the perfect image of a burning desire for renewal:

> *un oiseau sans peur jette son cri*
> *de flamme jeune*
> *dans le ventre chaud de la nuit.*

> [A fearless bird shoots its cry
> of young flame
> into the hot belly of night.] [13]

The image of fire thus dramatizes the action of the poet clearing a path toward his essential being. The enlivening flame is also a purifying fire, a tempering element which restores the poet to his original force:

> *Et la mer pouilleuse d'îles craquant aux doigts de rose*
> *lance-flammes et mon corps intact de foudroyé.*

> [And the sea lice-ridden with islands cracking under
> rosy fingers
> Flame throwers, and my body delivered whole from
> the thunderbolt.] [14]

The revolt signified by the image of fire leads to, in a word: *metamorphosis*. This points us to what can be considered the most significant theme in the poetry of Césaire: *becoming*, a theme which also translates into an obsession with a durable existence. There is no paradox here, for Césaire conceives of his destiny as a process of constant self-renewal, and his imaginative quest for survival reveals itself as an aspiration toward eternal values.

These concerns fixate around images drawn from the realm of the mineral, images which suggest a movement of descent, a withdrawal into an intimate sphere of the self, as well as a quest for the incorruptible. Both meanings add up to the idea of progression as being *rooted*, as it were, in a connection with the inner secret principle of life. The evocation of this principle determines in Césaire's poetry a whole constellation of telluric and agrolunar images, which animate a strongly formulated theme of regeneration.

Indeed, the recurrence of images expressive of the natural phenomenon of germination is a notable feature of Césaire's poetry; it forms perhaps the most dominant scheme in the structure of his symbolism. These images evoke a universe of fecundity set against the sterile world of his pathetic imagination. Thus the leading images of *pollen* and *oeuf* (egg) drawn from, respectively, the vegetal realm and the animal, with their variants—*germe, bourgeon* (bud), *grain,* and *anthèse* (bloom) for the former, and *larves* and *ovaires* for the latter—constitute a cluster which carries the suggestion of a promise of life. This in turn explains the poet's attachment to the feminine principle, an attachment which is revealed by his sexual symbolism.

It has often been remarked that Césaire gives a large place to sexual imagery in his poetry, but the idea of femininity which governs this imagery derives less from an erotic concern than from its obvious association with fertility.[15] The image of *woman* denotes for Césaire—as it does for Senghor—the principle of life. Woman represents here a source of vitality, and the forceful value attached by Césaire to this image is nowhere more clearly demonstrated than in the poem "Batéké," an evocation of an African woman assimilated to the very idea of liberation:

> *de tes yeux à marées*
> *de ton sexe de crocus*
> *de ton sexe à serpents nocturnes de*
> *fleuves et de cases...*
> *je profère au creux ligneux de la vague infantile*
> *de tes seins le jet du grand mapou*
> *né de ton sexe où pend le fruit fragile de la*
> *liberté.*

[with your eyes of tides
your genitals of saffron
your genitals of night serpents
of rivers and huts...
I cast out to the woody trough of the young wave
of your breasts the great gush born of your genitals
from which dangles the fragile fruit
of freedom.]¹⁶

The assimilation of the image of woman with that of the earth in Césaire's poetry—especially in his evocations of Africa as the mother continent—extends the significance of his sexual symbolism, for it endows with a cosmic dimension the poet's telluric vision, founded as this is upon a veritable pansexualism: "*terre grand sexe levé vers le soleil*" ("earth mighty sex offered to the sun").¹⁷ As the feminine term of the primordial couple, the earth comes to assume a maternal significance for the whole of creation. Césaire's sexual symbolism thus brings together images of the intimate life in which fertility and infancy are firmly associated. Taken together with the mineral imagery whose connotations we have seen, these images suggest an obsession on the part of the poet with an inner experience, his desire for a close and intimate sphere of existence. At a certain level of meaning, the image of the island has a similar symbolic association, but the poet's evocations of his island origins display a certain ambivalence, since they are often shot through with his sentiment of exile and incompleteness—"*toute île est veuve, toute île appelle*" ("every island is a widow, every island beckons")—but this very ambivalence leads us to the ultimate meaning of his images of the intimate life, for they represent not so much a state of repose as that of being in its phase of gestation:

Je m'ébroue en une mouvance d'images
de souvenirs néritiques de possibles
en suspension, de tendances-larves,
d'obscurs devenirs.

[I snort in a simmer of images of neritic remem-
brances
of poised possibilities,
of larvae emerging
of obscure stirrings.] [18]

The direct association of Césaire's telluric imagery with the
theme of metamorphosis emerges even more clearly in these
powerful lines:

à petits pas de pluie de chenilles
à petits pas de gorgée de lait
a petits pas de roulements à billes
a petits pas de secousse sismique
les ignames dans le sol marchent à grands
pas de trouées d'étoiles.

[with little steps of caterpillars
with little steps of gulps of milk
with little steps of rolling balls
with little steps of earth tremors
yams in the soil are moving with giant strides
of star-studded breaches in the clouds.] [19]

It becomes apparent, then, that the telluric vision, with all its
implications in this poetry, proceeds from the poet's intuition
of a movement of life in the universe more essential than the
discernible flux of the historical process. It is this intuition that
conditions his address to the African peasant and forbear:

Paysan frappe le sol de ta daba
dans le sol il y a une hâte que la syllabe
de l'événement ne dénoue pas.

[Peasant strike the earth with your daba
in the earth, there is a haste that the syllable of event
cannot unravel.] [20]

Césaire's preoccupation with this essential life finds its supreme
expression in the image of water. The universal association of

this element with the vital processes of fecundation and germination confers on it a value as the maternal symbol *par excellence*; it thus forms a fundamental part of the telluric scheme in Césaire's imagery. It represents here, at a first level of significance, the positive term to which the poet's imagination converts after its initial apprehension of a sterile and negative universe. In this immediate sense, water features as a polemical image, especially in Césaire's evocations of the sea in which he endows the element with the active force of his determination:

> ô houle annonciatrice sans nombre
> sans poussière de toute parole vineuse
> houle et ma poitrine salée des anses des
> anciens jours et la jeune couleur.

> [O sea swell, herald without number
> full-bodied word without spot
> sea swell and my breast briny from the coves
> of ancient days and fresh complexion.][21]

The sense of movement which the image of water in its dynamic representations also denotes confers on it a further value as the expression of a prophetic vision:

> viennent les ovaires de l'eau où le futur
> agite ses petites têtes.

> [Let the ovaries come forth from the water where the future
> shakes its little heads.][22]

As can be seen, the image of water is central to Césaire's symbolic scheme as it is made to carry the weight of meanings proposed by the poetry. Its symbolic significance resides principally in its quality as lustral element, as an agent of regeneration. As such, it denotes one of the essential values in the poet's imagination, his dream of a transformation of the self, of an accession to a higher level of consciousness and to a second and purer state of being:

Et j'entends l'eau qui monte
la nouvelle, l'intouchée, l'éternelle
vers l'air renouvelé.

[And I the hear water rising
new, untouched, eternal
towards the renewed air.][23]

In its progression from a sombre encounter with the world, with a negative historical experience crystallized in an individual consciousness, and transposed into poetic terms, toward a brighter apprehension of life and of the universe, Césaire's adventure assumes the character of a formidable thrust toward a state and sense of absolute liberation. As we have seen, this involves the elaboration through polemical images of new values intended to counter those implied by an unacceptable reality. It also registers the poet's cultivation of an ideal vision of the world, the celebration of life in its most organic, most essential manifestations.

There is no clearer expression of this aspect of Césaire's poetry than his vegetal symbolism, organized around the central image of the tree, through which this celebration is most notably sustained. There is an obvious sense in which this image has an appeal for a poet like Césaire, for whom the aspiration toward a sense of rootedness is a major preoccupation, forming one of his most prominent explicit themes. But this image acquires a secondary and more intense value in its association with the telluric scheme of the work's symbolic structure. The tree participates in the hidden life of the earth itself, draws sustenance from its depths, so that its growth becomes a manifestation of those inner forces which circulate in the world to maintain the entire realm of creation in perpetual youth:

mais la toujours jeune forêt lance sa
sève, toujours, dépêchant à la plus fine
liane, à la mousse, à la mouche bleue,
à l'incertaine luciole, leur dû irréprochable.

[But the ever youthful forest releases its sap
always, sending forth to the most tender creeper

> to the moss
> to the blue buds
> to the hesitant glowworm
> their rightful share.][24]

There is a pastoral ideal of a singular kind involved here, an intense valorization of nature: the green vegetation is not only an indication of abundance but also an assurance of a universal vitality. The image of the tree has, however, an additional value in that, while it designates a rootedness and a connectedness with the organic life of the earth, it also signifies an upward reach of creation into light. This image therefore also proposes a vertical perspective for the poet's imagination, determines an ascensional scheme associated with an elevation of both body and soul. The tree links the subterranean with the celestial realm and thus symbolizes the totality of space within which all being is located. The upright majesty of the tree in full bloom thus represents Césaire's poetic ideal in its most forceful expression, the ideal of a progression toward a total possession of and harmony with the universe:

> *en terre il est replanté*
> *le ciel pousse*
> *il contre-pousse*
>
> *arbre mon arbre*
> *bel arbre immense.*
>
> [In the earth replanted
> the sky rises
> pushes back
>
> tree, my own tree
> beautiful, immense.][25]

As the integrative image of Césaire's vegetal symbolism, the tree corresponds to the messianic aspect of his poetry.[26] It combines associations of primal vigor with his sense of a historical and spiritual necessity which informs the internal logic of his poetic themes. It also signifies the illumination of his consciousness, a theme reinforced by images of light which recur throughout the work: such ardent notations as *rosace* [rosette], *été* [summer], *jour*, [day], and *midi* [noon, a symbol of revolution] form a veritable cluster of images which can be said to define a luminous ground of the poet's imagination. Beyond their polemical import, they extend the ascensional theme of Césaire's symbolism, a theme which finds its culmination in the symbol of the sun.

As the ultimate promoter of all life, the sun occupies a significant place in Césaire's poetic universe, a universe which presents itself as a vitalist cosmogony. We thus have a constant evocation in his poetry of a dynamic correlation between man and nature, which is most often channeled through the association of blood and sun, as in these characteristic lines:

> *Sang! Sang! tout notre sang ému par*
> *le coeur mâle du soleil.*

> [Blood! Blood!
> All our blood fired by the manly heart of the sun.][27]

The sun represents for Césaire an intensity both of life in its universal manifestation and of the poet's immediate relation to that life itself. Its symbolic expression in his poetry confers on his poetic universe as shaped by the structure of his imagery its full meaning as the representation of a total experience. It completes the significant configuration of his imagery and symbolism, a configuration whose references embrace the various realms of existence and of being within a unified vision of the world. And it is precisely this total apprehension that Césaire celebrates in these famous lines of *Cahier d'un retour au pays natal* in which he first affirmed his Negritude:

> *ma négritude n'est pas une taie d'eau morte*
> *sur l'oeil mort de la terre...*
> *elle plonge dans la chair rouge du sol*
> *elle plonge dans la chair ardente du ciel*

> [my Negritude is not a speck of dead water
> on the dead eye of the earth

> it plunges into the red flesh of the earth
> it plunges into the burning flesh of the sky.][28]

Césaire has written of the poet that his power finds its accomplishment only in the elemental.[29] For him, poetry is not merely a simple projection of the poet's states of mind upon the phenomena of the real world or a figurative expression of his aspirations but, rather, an essential enterprise, a mode of communication with the world. The vision which sustains his poetry is rooted in an animist conception of the universe, so that its lyrical expression becomes something far more than mere evocations, but indeed an invocation of the forces which inhabit the universe. The function of poetry is not therefore simply to designate reality, but to reveal the multiple dimensions of that reality and to call forth the profound life of the world configured in that reality. Nature thus features in poetry based on such a conception as part of "an essential landscape"[30] and the poetry itself becomes a ritual celebration of a cosmic order which regulates human destiny.

As several commentators have remarked, Césaire's use of poetry answers to this conception of poetry as a mode of experience and of knowledge which issues from a mythical consciousness of the integral nature of the universe. His poetic experience is one of a "cosmic passion"—the expression is Walt Whitman's—which responds to the very pulsations of life in the world: in other words, of a "participation" in the exact sense which Lévy-Bruhl gave to the term. Indeed, it is evident that the presiding idea in his practice of poetry is to restore to the form its original character as magical chant, hence his aspiration to a mystic order of expression in these lines:

> *Je retrouverais le secret de grandes*
> *communications et de grandes combustions.*
> *Je dirais orage, je dirais fleuve, je dirais*
> *tornade, je dirais feuille. Je dirais arbre.*
> *Je serais mouillé de toutes les pluies,*
> *humecté de toutes les rosées.*

> [I would recover the secret

of great communications and of great combustions
I would say storm, say river, say tornado, say leaf.
I would say tree.
I would be made wet by all rains
moistened by all the dews.][31]

It is with regard to this mystical aspect of Césaire's poetry that his African vision intervenes to provide a foundation for his enterprise. For the effort to restore to poetry its sacred character is mediated in his work by his identification with the mother continent. In the structure of apprehension proposed by the collective myths of African cultures and societies, the poet's quest for a new mode of experience finds its paradigm and justification. Césaire's aspiration to a sense of belonging which colors his African sentiment thus comes to coincide with his poetic quest for knowledge:

> Vierges d'Ogoué, gratifiez-moi
> d'une étoile dite nouvelle.

> [Virgins of Ogwe,
> Grant me a star newly dedicated.][32]

Césaire's surrealist background is of some importance here, since this metaphysical aspect of his expression derives in part from the influence of the school of André Breton.[33] But this influence leads back, in his case, to an awareness of ancestral origins. The point is that, while his vision arises from his effort to realize in art the immanence of the supranatural in the manifested world, this effort also has personal significance for him as the recovery of a millennial heritage to which he lays claim. It links him to an established tradition of spirituality in which, along with other forms of ritual practices, poetry has a function as an epiphany of the sacred. From this point of view, the African tradition stands behind all of Césaire's imagery and his symbolism. It enables him to articulate a poetic mystique which, while remaining individual, maintains a live connection with a collective sensibility. In other words, the spirituality of Africa serves as a transcendental reference for his poetic universe:

L'Afrique parlait en une
langue sacrée
où le même mot signifiait
couteau des pluies sang de taureau
nerf et tendon du dieu caché
lichen profond lâcher d'oiseau.

[Africa spoke in a sacred language
Wherein the same word meant
Knife of raindrops bull's blood
Nerve and sinew of the hidden god
Deep moss
Release of bird.][34]

The poetic significance of Césaire's Negritude emerges in a singular light from these considerations. Poetry not only serves him as a means of confrontation with history, but also as an expressive channel for the recovery of his original self. It becomes a mode both of triumph over the vicissitudes of a painful experience and of access to a plenitude of being through the exploration of an elemental universe. In other words, the poet's quest for survival also becomes a quest for a more intense experience of the self and of the world:

Je veux un soleil plus brillant
et de plus pures étoiles.

[I desire a brighter sun
And purer stars.][35]

What emerges, then, from a consideration of the structure of imagery and symbolism in the poetry of Aimé Césaire is a movement of the poet's consciousness that marks the peripeteia of a destiny in the making, a progression that finds its accomplishment in an exultant vision.

NOTES

1. For the analysis of Césaire's poetic images, I have relied on the following two studies of universal symbols: Gilbert Durand, *Structures anthropologiques de l'imaginaire* (1963), and Mircea Eliade, *Traité d'histoire des religions* (1962 ed.).

2. *Cahier d'un retour au pays natal* (1956), p. 57-58.

3. "Débris," *Les Armes miraculeuses* (1946), p. 58.

4. For a theoretical discussion of this observation, see Frantz Fanon, *Peau noire masque blancs* (1952), especially chapter VII, pp. 203-214.

5. Senghor's evocation of the atmosphere of night is best represented in the poem "Nuit de Sine" in the volume *Chants d'Ombre* (1948).

6. "Autre horizon," in *Cadastre* (1961), p. 62.

7. "A la mémoire d'un syndicaliste noir," in *Ferrements* (1960), p. 72.

8. *Et Les Chiens se taisaient* (1956), p. 121.

9. "Les Pur-Sang," in *Les Armes miraculeuses*, p. 10.

10. "Aux Écluses du vide," in *Cadastre*, p. 47.

11. For the erotic significance of the image of fire, see Gaston Bahelard, *Psychamalyse du feu*.

12. "Survie," in *Les Armes miraculeuses*, pp. 37-38.

13. *Et Les Chiens se taisaient*, p. 15.

14. "Soleil Serpent," in *Les Armes miraculeuses*, p. 25.

15. Sartre was the first critic to point out the dominance of sexual symbolism in Black poetry – see "Orphée noir", *Situations III*. Paris: Gallimard, 1949, pp. 265-69.

16. "Batéké," in *Les Armes miraculeuases*. p. 33-34.

17. *Cahier*, p. 41.

18. "Les Pur-Sang," in *Armes*, p. 17.

19. "Tam-Tam II," op. cit., p. 69.

20. "A l'Afrique," in *Cadastre*, p. 39.

21. "Visitation," in *Armes*, p. 31.

22. *Cahier*, p. 69.

23. "Les Pur-Sang," *Armes*, p. 11.

24. *La Tragédie du roi Christophe* (1963), p. 145.

25. "Naissance," in *Cadastre*, p. 88. It is interesting to note that Frank Kermode brings out a similar scheme in his discussion of the tree symbol in the poetry of Yeats – see *Romantic Image*, London, Fontana Books, 1971, pp. 97 et seq.

26. For the messianic significance of the tree symbol, see Durand, pp. 365-70.

27. *Cahier*, p. 71.

28. Ibid.

29. "Sa puissance ne triomphe que dans l'élémentaire." Aimé Césaire, quoted by Edouard Glissant, "Aimé Césaire et la découverte du monde," in *Lettres Nouvelles* (Paris), January 1956.

30. A line from "Les Pur-Sang," *Armes*, p. 11.

31. *Cahier*, ed. cit., p. 40. For the notion of 'participation' as developed by Levy-Bruhl, see his *La Mentalité primitive*, Paris, 1921.

32. 'Galanterie de l'histoire', *Soleil Cou Coupé* (1948), p. 41.

33. For a fuller discussion of the metaphysical aspect of surrealism, see Jules Monnerot, *La poésie moderne et le sacré* (1945), and Ferdinand Alquié, *Philosophie du surréalisme* (1955).

34. 'Addis-Abbéba 1963', *Présence Africaine*, 3e trimestre, 1963, p. 175. This poem has been retitled "Ethiopie" and is now included in the section *Noria*, pp. 295-98 of *Poésies*, (1976).

35. 'Les Pur-Sang', *Armes*, ed. cit., p. 17.

CHAPTER SEVEN
IN SEARCH OF CAMARA LAYE
❦

Ever since the publication in 1954 of *Le Regard du roi* (*The Radiance of the King*), barely a year after the appearance of *L'Enfant noir* (*The African Child*), there have been misgivings about Laye's authorship of the book. The remarkable difference between his first two novels gave rise to doubts that Laye could have accomplished within a year the impressive development that the second book appeared to have registered. Lilyan Kesteloot in particular is known to have openly expressed the view that Laye was incapable of writing *Le Regard du roi*, and her repeated pronouncements on the subject, in print and otherwise, have fueled the suspicion that has been gaining ground since the mid-seventies, to the effect that not only was Laye *not* the sole author of the second novel, but that in fact the book was entirely the work of someone else to whom he had merely lent his name for publication.[1]

While this case has been simmering, as it were, over the years, the Francophone literary world has been rocked by the affair of Yambo Ouologuem, who was accused of large-scale plagiarism in the composition of his prize-winning novel *Le Devoir de violence* (*Bound to Violence*), a charge that Calixthe Beyala has also had to contend with more recently with respect to her string of highly successful and controversial novels. It is thus not surprising that attention should have been focused anew on the case of Camara Laye, which Adele King has examined at considerable length in a book entitled *Rereading Camara Laye*, in which she undertakes a comprehensive review of what might well be called *l'affaire Laye*.[2] According to King, this is not just a case of plagiarism and large-scale borrowing, but something far more serious: a case of outright literary fraud, consisting in a claim by Laye to the authorship of works not of his own creation. On this point, King's conclusion is unequivocal:

> After nine years, many letters and interviews and research in available files, I now feel confident that Laye was helped in the composition and writing of *L'Enfant noir* and was given a manuscript of *Le Regard du roi* to which he contributed little.[3]

Adele King's indictment of Laye—for this is what her book amounts to—can be summed up quite simply. From both internal evidence related to textual coherence and cultural references, as well as from the external circumstances of Laye's encounters during his years in Paris as she has been able to reconstruct these in her investigations, King concludes that Laye could not have written the first two novels attributed to him. It is of interest to note here that King's examination brackets *Le Regard du roi* with *L'Enfant noir*, both of which she now concludes must be attributed in varying degrees to two characters complicit in the fraud: one a Belgian, Francis Soulié, a renegade intellectual involved, like Paul de Man, in Nazi and anti-Semite propaganda in Brussels during the Second World War; and the other a Frenchman, Robert Poulet, an editor at Plon, Laye's Paris publisher. Between them, King asserts, these two men played a preponderant role in the manufacture of what she now considers Laye's false literary career. Two other characters, both female, are mentioned as having at some time or the other had a hand in the composition of his first book: Aude Joncourt and Marie Hélène Lefaucheux, both shadowy figures whose fleeting appearance thickens the plot, so to speak, of the complex narrative that Adele King develops in her account of Laye's authorial adventure.

It needs to be said at the outset that, despite the assertive tone of her book, the case King endeavors to make against Laye remains unproven, and must be considered ultimately unconvincing. It is true that she uncovers some interesting and even disquieting facts related to Laye's literary career and the various individuals involved with it. However, it is far from certain that the evidence that she marshals over some 200 pages of her book—admittedly, an impressive work of scholarly research and investigative zeal—justifies the certainties that she offers. She admits that she has no definitive proof (the "smoking gun" as she calls it), and it is noteworthy that she has to rely on conjectures and hearsay in order to fill in the gaps in her account.

Indeed, a disturbing feature of the book is the way it abounds in statements and assertions that are far from illuminating, such as the following which occurs in a note tucked away at the end of the book: "Laye told a Nigerian student of my husband's at Ahmadu Bello University who was studying French in Dakar in 1974, that a white woman had written L'Enfant noir."[4] We are not told who this student was and under what circumstances what would have been a major confession by Laye was obtained by him or her. What is more, the statement is contradicted in another passage where King quotes from a letter to her by Kesteloot, in which we learn that Laye himself had mentioned "an unknown novelist," presumably Robert Poulet, as having helped him to write the first book. (Be it noted, in passing, the vagueness of the description, not so much expressed in Laye's words as attributed to him by Kesteloot, and dutifully quoted by King). In a second letter, Kesteloot adds to the confusion by suggesting that Poulet had also written Le Regard du roi, an allegation to which she returns in a 1982 article in Notes Africaines, in which, writing after Laye's death, Kesteloot publicly casts doubt on Laye's authorship of the novel. The section of the article quoted by King is symptomatic of the simplicities that have gone into the charge against Laye:

> Then a very fine novel, Le Regard du roi, appeared under his name, with a style and subject matter quite different [from L'Enfant noir]. The clear reference to Kafka, the mystical quest, were very little in the thoughts of the Laye we had known, the sophisti-

cated expression, as well as the reference to Mossi
culture, coming from a region that Laye hardly knew,
were elements that divided critics on the authenticity of the book. For us, a conversation with him on
the subject convinced us that he had loaned his name
to support the work of a French friend."[5]

It is legitimate to probe the validity of these assertions. Assuming that Laye's second novel marked a change of style and subject
matter (the extent of which is open to dispute), why should
this fact, a normal development in any literary career, be held
against him? It is not clear either why the reference to Kafka is
interpreted as evidence, *a priori*, of skullduggery rather than the
mark of an influence—a point to which we shall return. And on
the question of authenticity, one might ask whether the Frenchman who is alleged to have written the novel would have a better
acquaintance with Mossi culture than Laye. Kesteloot's article
provides no answer to any of these questions. Finally, Kesteloot
departs altogether from the textual scrutiny with which she
begins and proceeds to an *ex cathedra* judgment in which she
assumes the Olympian posture of an infallible authority. The
gratuitous character of the last statement in the passage cannot
but strike one as breathtaking, but what is interesting is that the
"French friend" is identified in another letter to King, in which
Poulet is finally brought out of the shadows and is specifically
named by Kesteloot as having written and then offered the
second novel to Laye, in circumstances that must appear to us
as extraordinary and even bizarre, especially in the light of the
explanation that Kesteloot offers for Poulet's motivation:

> But why would Poulet, who was already publishing
> at this time, have made this curious deal? Perhaps
> a taste for a challenge. "Can my novel be taken as
> written by a black man?"... With a real person such
> as Camara Laye, this white man would have no risk
> of being found out. And also he would be helping a
> pleasant young black man, who needed the money
> and was a bit naïve.[6]

Kesteloot's explanation is, to say the least, disingenuous. We should add to this the glaring inconsistencies between her various statements—with Poulet's status as a writer seen to fluctuate and the direction of the flow of generosity between him and Laye reversed from one statement to another. All this lends an arbitrary air and even a tendentious character to Kesteloot's interventions.

It has been necessary to enter into these rather trivial matters because King's reliance on the kind of evidence we have been reviewing undermines the credibility of her work. More important, the effect of her declarations is to offer a simplified view of Laye's insertion within the literary, cultural, and intellectual universe that the French colonial system created around the cluster of educated Africans from whom the early Francophone writers were drawn. In other words, the circumstances of Laye's career suggest a much more complex situation than King appears willing to admit. In order to begin to place this situation in proper perspective, it is instructive to consider the case of Bakary Diallo, whose work *Force-Bonté*, an autobiographical novel first published in 1926 and one of the earliest literary works to be attributed to a French-speaking African, for the light it throws on the general question of textual ownership in Francophone Africa and its bearing on the particular case of Camara Laye.[7]

Adele King mentions Diallo's autobiography in her book, merely in passing and without going into any detail, yet this is the clearest example of a work whose text in French, as we have it, could not possibly have been created by the person whose name is advertised as its author. In fact, the evidence for this observation comes directly from the book, and principally from Bakary Diallo himself, who states at many points in the book that he was illiterate. Thus he avows: *"Mais je comprends à peine le français; je ne sais ni lire ni écrire"* ["But I hardly understand French. I can neither read nor write"].[8] Earlier, one of his friends, a certain Demba, is reported as saying to him: *"Je regrette que tu ne saches pas lire et écrire"* ["I'm sorry that you can't read or write"].[9] It is indeed significant that a good part of the narrative is devoted to Diallo's efforts to learn French and to read and write.

The question that immediately arises is: how then did *Force-Bonté* get to be written? The nearest we get to an answer is the prefatory note (*avertissement*) by Diallo's publisher, Jean Richard Bloch, in which he informs us that he received the manuscript from *Mlle.* Lucie Cousturier, who happened to have died shortly afterwards. Bloch seems to have no doubt about Cousturier's part in the creation of the work, for he counts *Force-Bonté* among her three publications, and even calls it, strangely enough, her *"testament spirituel"* ["spiritual testament"]. Of the man who forms the subject of the book and whose voice it ostensibly projects, Bloch has only this to say: *"Bakary Diallo n'est pas un noir de convention. Il n'est même pas instruit"* ["Bakary Diallo is not your conventional African. He is not even educated"].[10] It seems safe therefore to conclude that the text as we have it is indeed the work of Lucie Cousturier. It is important, however, to observe that, although at no time does Bakary Diallo identify her as the author of the book, in the literal sense of the word, there is no suggestion of guile or deception on his part. He seems to have considered her a kind of public letter writer, albeit an elevated one, who by reason of her privileged position as a Frenchwoman was in a position to set down for him the story of his experience as a *tirailleur sénégalais*.

At least two points arise from an examination of *Force-Bonté*, having to do with the nature of the experience recounted in the book and its literary and ideological significance, points which must affect any effort of interpretation of the work. In the first place, there can be no doubt that it is truly Bakary Diallo's lived experience that the book records. Furthermore, there are numerous indications that Diallo was an active agent in the construction of the text. It is of more than passing interest to observe the occasional occurrence of *petit nègre* in the book. We can be certain that Cousturier was not acquainted with this pidgin, which served as a sort of lingua franca among the French colonial soldiers, so that it is legitimate to speculate that Diallo either dictated parts of the book to her in *petit nègre*, or even began the work himself in this idiom, so that the fragments in *petit nègre* may well represent retentions from his original manuscript.

Here we are obviously in the realm of pure speculation. What is certain is that the narrative is not only marked by a specificity of detail that reflects Diallo's consciousness of himself as singular individual, it also bears the imprint of a distinct cultural sensibility, attested by the many expressions and proverbs in Peul—accompanied by translations and explanations in French—with which the text is interspersed. The latter part of the book is remarkable for the series of songs and proverbs that give an extended development to this character, imparting to the narrative a quality of expression that lifts it beyond the often banal quality of the episodes that mark Bakary Diallo's account of his experience as a colonial soldier.[11] This dimension of the work is strikingly exemplified by the grandiose image which occurs in a report by Diallo of his encounter with one of his French commanders:

En partant, mon capitaine Coste me tape doucement sur la joue droite et me quitte aussi silencieusement qu'il était venu. Dans son silence je comprends mille choses nobles, comme je comprends le grand soleil, qui sans bruit éclaire l'univers entier.

[On his way out, Captain Coste tapped me gently on the right cheek and left as silently as he had arrived. In his silence, I understood a thousand noble things, as I understand the sun which silently illuminates the whole universe.] [12]

Thus, a remarkable aspect of the book is the way Diallo's voice comes through the French text. It thus becomes obvious that, at the level of content and, at least in part, that of form, the book originated with him. Even if the actual text as we have it in French is not of his own making, it is evident that the ordering of events and the very texture of the narrative proceed in large part from his directing will. We might conclude then that, although *Force-Bonté* exemplifies what Alain Ricard calls "supervised literature," Bakary Diallo was far from being "a man of straw" as regards the production of the text; rather, he emerges as an engaged participant in the reformulation in the French language of his own story, as it issues from his original conception of it in Peul, his maternal language.[13]

This observation prompts a consideration of the impulse behind Diallo's work. In his preface to the 1985 reprint of the book, Mohammadou Kane reserves some harsh comments for Diallo, for what Kane takes to be his blind devotion to the French and his insensitiveness to the colonial problem. But Kane also observes that Diallo was the first to turn to the biographical genre in Francophone Africa and to invest it with significance as a form of testimony to the colonial experience.[14] This observation affords an insight into Diallo's motivation in the retelling of his experience, for on closer inspection the book appears to be something else than the naïve eulogy of French colonialism it has generally been taken to be. When it is realized that the latter part of the book has to do with his odyssey as he seeks proper medical attention after suffering severe injuries at the front during the First World War, it becomes clear that his real intention in telling his story was to make public his mistreatment by the French military authorities. It is this objective that is dissimulated by the excessive and even self-abasing terms of Diallo's hymn of praise for the French. In short, Diallo's book is in fact a deeply subversive work, an element that is deemphasized by *Mlle.* Cousturier's reconstruction, but which gradually emerges as central to his narrative.[15]

We are led, then, to the conclusion, that Lucie Cousturier functioned for Diallo as an *amanuensis*, helping to give textual form, in the language of the colonial master, to his account of service to France and his subsequent disillusionment with the French administration. Given the profuseness of Diallo's protestations of loyalty in the book, we may perhaps read his story as the expression of unrequited love, a reading that the note of bitterness that dominates the latter part of the book seems to suggest, lending it at least an ambiguous character. Whatever the value of this interpretation, it complicates the task of assessment of the book's authorship, which must take account not only of the text as material fact, but also of its emergence, as *intention*, from a particular consciousness, modified in its reconstruction by Cousturier. The question that remains is whether these considerations can be invoked either to establish or to deny Diallo's right to be considered the author of a book he obviously did not *write*, but which so fully embodies a narrative of his own conception, with a deeply personal meaning for him as an individual subject to the multiple pressures of the colonial system. It is in the light of this conundrum that, it seems to me, we need to consider the case of Camara Laye.

We might begin by observing that, like Diallo's *Force-Bonté*, Laye's *L'Enfant noir* is a testimony of an individual experience in the specific context of French colonial domination. King now reads the work as a text that betrays a spirit of collaboration with French colonialism. But this is to overlook the ideological implication of the book at the time it was published, for implicit in Laye's story of a happy childhood in Africa, and the sense of loss at separation from his native environment which the book registers, is a refutation of the thesis of a *mission civilisatrice* of the French colonial enterprise in Africa. To be sure, the counterthesis is not overtly made, but lurks as it were within the images and evocations that make for the atmosphere of the book, colored as these are by the intense nostalgia that pervades the text from beginning to end. In other words, Laye's autobiography bears a polemical import in the historic circumstances of its writing. It is this ideological implication that Mongo Beti entirely missed in his celebrated review of the book published under his real name, Alexandre Biyidi.[16]

Adele King goes even further than Beti to argue that Laye's book was actively promoted by certain colonial officers and that, for this reason, we are justified in the presumption that it had in fact been crafted within the Ministry of Colonies, this with the sole aim of serving French colonial interests. King constantly harps upon the connection between Francophone texts and the French literary establishment, in order to suggest that Laye's literary career was fabricated as part of a vast colonialist design by the French, but it is not clear what this has to do with the matter. The fact is that the details she offers of the circumstances of the alleged fabrication of Laye's first novel and the individuals involved in it are muddled: there are at least three people, including Poulet, whom she holds responsible for the operation. But if her allegation is true, the fact would lend an ironic twist to Laye's case, compounding the ideological significance of his

193

work, with Laye's African child made to serve, quite incongru-
ously, as proof of the benefits of French colonization. In any case,
the zeal of colonial officers cannot serve as evidence of literary
fraud, for the most that can be granted to King's argument was
that Laye himself came to serve for these colonial officers as an
emblem of French benevolence and as a showcase of the French
assimilation policy. We may also add— considering the role that
literature had begun to play at this time in the emergence of an
African consciousness—that, as the saying goes, these officers
would have been unwittingly sawing the branch on which they
perched. Whatever the case, the assertion that the book was
written for Laye does not appear to me to be warranted by the
facts adduced by King, which on this particular point are at best
vague and speculative, like so much else of the book.

Nonetheless, despite the reservations that we are entitled to
entertain about the validity of the evidence that King offers, it
is essential to attend to the argument that informs her book,
for, notwithstanding her claims about the purely literary objective of her book, its very appearance must be considered to have
tarnished the memory of Camara Laye, and to be damaging
not only for his reputation but also for the status of African literature. King's argument comprises two main points. The first
amounts to nothing less than a disparagement of Laye, who is
deemed by King as not having been educated enough in French
to have developed into the accomplished writer to which the
novels attributed to him testify. We may restate this argument
as a question of linguistic and literary competence. The second
point concerns the content of the novels—what King views as
their fundamental inauthenticity as regards cultural references
and anthropological details.

On the question of competence, King's argument rests on
the assumption that Laye's education did not go much further
than the elementary level, from which she concludes that he was
incapable of writing French at the level demonstrated in the first
two novels. There are two possible objections to this argument.
The first and obvious one is that there is nothing in *L'Enfant
noir* that was beyond the competence of an educated African of
Laye's generation. (The case of *Le Regard du roi* is somewhat dif-

ferent, and I shall come to that in due course.) The very simplicity of the style reflects the viewpoint of the child that Laye seeks to capture in the work. We need to consider in this respect the high standard of education dispensed by the elementary schools both in France and in the colonies during this period, a standard that was a legacy of the Third Republic, sustained by the dedication of the humble school teacher, the *instituteur*, who came to be held in veneration and represented something of an icon in French cultural life.

It is revealing of the tenacity of King's purpose that she attempts to turn the very simplicity of *L'Enfant noir* against Laye when she remarks that the episode of the snake with which the book begins provides evidence of what she calls a "European sense of literary form."[17] We are not told how the episode in question serves to illustrate this uniquely European sense, nor indeed what this sense consists of, except that the passage in Laye reads for her like a reminiscence of Joyce's *Portrait of the Artist as a Young Man*. King draws the parallel to make the point that since Laye could not have known Joyce's work, he was unlikely to echo Joyce unaided, to exhibit in his own writing the Joycean trait that she discerns in the opening chapter of Laye's autobiography. But one might retort that Joyce was not a household name in France in the 1950s, so it is difficult to see how the stylistic trait she makes so much of could have been imported into Laye's work by a French writer who is alleged to have shaped the book on his behalf.

Here, it is pertinent to remark on Adele King's curious skepticism about the scrupulous use of the imperfect subjunctive in Laye's book, which she takes as evidence that the novel was essentially the work of Robert Poulet, who is known to have served as his copy editor at Plon. But there is hardly any mystery here. Given the formal nature of French, a strict observance of grammatical norms formed part of training in the language, with the rules governing *concordance des temps* and the appropriate forms of the subjunctive forming an essential part of the normative system of French grammar.[18] The occurrence of the imperfect subjunctive in Laye's book can thus be seen as no more than a sign that Poulet, who edited Laye's manuscript, corrected the text so as to make it conform to the accepted norm of literary French, what Roland Barthes was later to denounce as the stylized idiom or *écriture* of the French bourgeois novel. Like any other conscientious editor, Poulet was doing no more than what seemed to him to be within his professional obligations.

But an imperfect mastery of the French subjunctive in its full structural range is hardly a sufficient indication of Laye's lack of linguistic competence or of a sense of style. Although King goes into considerable detail to uncover the background of Francis Soulié, and to a lesser extent that of Robert Poulet, there is very little mention in her book of the actual conditions of Laye's formal education. But we know that, before going to Paris, Laye attended the technical school in Conakry, which offered at least two complementary years of formal education beyond the elementary level, an education that would have been analogous to that received by many of the early Francophone African elite at teacher training institutions in the French African colonies, notably at the *Ecole Normale William Ponty* at Gorée. Laye belonged to this generation of Francophone Africans whose education did not extend to the secondary level as dispensed at the *lycée*, but who were well equipped to write French in a register that was more than adequate to create valuable works. This generation comprised individuals such as Ahmadou Diagne, whose novel *Les trois volontés de Malic*, published in 1921, is generally regarded as the first novel by a Francophone African writer; Abdoulaye Sadji, the author of *Mirages de Paris* and *Nini, la mulâtresse*, both of whom in a curious way anticipate Cheikh Hamidou Kane's classic novel, *L'Aventure ambigüe*; Paul Hazoumé, who achieved a respectable reputation with his historical novel, *Doguicimi*; Bernard Dadié whose work in various genres is central to Negritude expression; and, most striking of all, Amadou Hampaté Bâ, who by his death in 1991 had left an abundant and impressive body of accomplished work. For this generation of African writers, the classics of French literature as taught in the schools—in particular seventeenth-century drama and the nineteenth-century novels of Flaubert, Stendhal, and Balzac—served not only as models of the language, but as a global and enduring reference of imaginative life and creation.

It is to this cultural legacy of French colonization that Cheik Hamidou Kane testified when, in answer to a question about his mastery of French, he declared:

> *C'est peut-être la marque que les écrivains classiques que je lisais ont laissée en moi. C'est aussi un espèce de tribut que je dois rendre aux gens qui m'ont enseigné cette langue, mes instituteurs sénégalais et français ainsi que les professeurs.*

> [It is perhaps the mark imprinted in me by the classical writers that I read. It is also a kind of tribute that I owe to those who taught me the language, my Senegalese and French school teachers, as well as my university professors.][19]

Laye could not but have benefited from this highly valuable education—in a way in which Bakary Diallo did not—acquiring in the process a language whose qualities were manifested in the literary texts to which he was exposed.

Adele King is on firmer ground when she points to the linguistic and stylistic evidence of another hand than Laye's at work in *Le Regard du roi*, to which she devotes her entire fourth chapter. Her meticulous analysis demonstrates the point, largely through the recondite vocabulary and unusual turns of phrase that turn up in the text. But unless one is determined to press the argument that the novel was entirely the work of Soulié, as King maintains, it is possible to take the view that these were interpolations that are not even properly integrated into the text, one that Laye had elaborated in accordance with his own design and in a language within his own expressive compass. Indeed, what is striking here is the incongruity of many of these phrases and expressions, which bear hardly a relation to the cultural setting, narrative development, and symbolic significance of the novel.

The disconnect between language and thematic reference in several passages of the book has long been a source of malaise for many readers of the novel; for King, it represents the mark of its fundamental inauthenticity. The lack of correspondence between certain cultural references in *Le Regard du roi* and ascertainable facts in the anthropological literature on Laye's background serves for King as definitive proof that the novel was written by a European who had at best only a secondary or vicarious acquaintance, derived from books, with African culture. It is here that King specifically fingers Francis Soulié, who, we are informed, had dabbled during his youth in exotic writing, and was later to benefit from his relations with Laye to foist his imaginings and his obsessions on an unsuspecting world.

But, as Kenneth Harrow has pointed out in his review of King's book, hers is an essentialist approach that reduces the work of literature to the worldly attributes of the writer. It is also an approach that misses an important condition of imaginative creation, the artistic freedom it entails. For we might ask: should an African novel be no more than an ethnographic document that is required to be true to life in every detail? And was Laye thus constrained to an exclusive reproduction of his indigenous culture? King's critique relies moreover on generalizations about Africa that are sometimes worrisome, as for example when she observes that Laye depicts a scene in which girls are adorned with flowers in their hair, a scene which for her is inconceivable in a West African setting.[20] Even if this observation is true, must we discount the possibility of an expanded experience from his encounter with other cultures that enabled Laye to incorporate in his novels images that derived from realms of experience beyond his immediate world? In other words, to give freer rein to his imagination than is permitted by a literal and reductive conception of imaginative expression?

In King's rereading of Le Regard du roi, the cultural question centers on the nature of the spirituality that is reflected in the novel and its connection to the mystic tradition of Sufist sects in West Africa. This is an element of the novel that has been discussed at length in several studies, most notably by Christopher Miller and Kenneth Harrow.[21] But the relevance of an ethnographic reading of Laye's novel has never been obvious, least of all as regards his affiliation to Sufism. Apart from what one gathers from Louis Brenner of the exclusive character and esoteric preoccupations of Sufist sects in West Africa, Laye was taken too soon out of his community to have assimilated any of the tenets of this branch of Islam, sufficiently at any rate for these to have entered into the structure of his creative faculty.[22] What remained with him, however, was a general disposition to the supernatural and the mystical to which he sought to give elaboration in *Le Regard du roi*. It is of course in this connection that Kafka came to exert a peculiar fascination for him.

No part of King's book conveys so much her disparagement of Laye as her discussion of the influence of Kafka, admittedly a vexed question but which King treats with a prosecuting attitude, in keeping with the general spirit of her book. Her conviction that *Le Regard du roi* is entirely the work of Soulié conditions the dim view she presents of any serious encounter with the work of Kafka on the part of Laye, whom she is not far from casting as an outright impostor. She insists on concrete evidence, impossible in any case to verify, that Laye actually read Kafka, despite her own report of an interview she conducted with him in which he acknowledged Kafka's influence on his work.[23] For King, everything in *Le Regard du roi* that recalls Kafka could only have been the work of Soulié, even down to the presence of beggars in the novel. It is astonishing that on this point, she overlooks the fact that, as a Muslim, Laye was only too conversant with beggars to whom his religion enjoined the giving of alms, an article of faith that serves as the thematic foundation of Aminata Sow Fall's remarkable novel *La Grèves des Bàttu*.

King's reluctance to give credence to Laye's declaration is symptomatic of the relentless determination with which she prosecutes her case against him, for her refusal flies in the face of what we know has been the powerful presence of Kafka in all areas of modern awareness and the pervasive influence he has consequently exerted on successive generations of writers, not only in the West but universally.[24] As is well known, the religious interpretation of Kafka's work propagated by his friend and biographer, Max Brod, was the dominant one in the critical reception of Kafka until fairly recently, and a major factor in the estimation of his work by the cultivated public. Its appeal therefore to a writer of Laye's temperament and background can easily be understood. It is apparent from the interview with Adele King alluded to above that Laye perceived a congruence between the presiding mode of Kafka's work, with its nonrational vision of the world precluding a strict realism of fictional representation, on the one hand, and, on the other, the modes of the indigenous narrative tradition in his own culture, and in African societies in general, modes predicated on the interpenetration of the everyday world and a transcendent universe of mystical entities, on the existential continuity between a visible and an invisible realm of event and experience. As I have remarked elsewhere, Laye's was an imagination attuned by his indigenous antecedents to the supernatural, over and beyond the traces in his work of collective belief systems and cultural practices.[25] It is true that he did not share Kafka's anguished apprehension of the world. But it is perfectly plausible to surmise that in Le Regard du roi, with its enactment of a quest for fulfillment, Laye undertook a rewriting of Kafka from a less dejected, perhaps even an affirmative point of view that nonetheless explored the affinities in vision and narrative discourse between the modernist allegories of Kafka, and the otherworldly orientation of the folktales with which he was familiar, despite the divergent sources of their inspiration.

Perhaps the most troubling aspect of King's book is the assumption that underlies her reinterpretation of Laye, that the subjects of imaginative literature are either taken straight from immediate experience or derive from the writer's reading; she appears in fact to privilege the latter over the former. This leads to the curious reasoning that informs her challenge of Brenda Bertrand's interpretation of some of the rituals that occur in Laye's second novel:

> Laye never showed any detailed knowledge of such rituals in his interviews. Even if we were to accept Bertrand's reading, it would not establish that Laye wrote the book. It could be that Soulié, who studied African culture, had found such rituals in his reading.[26]

It seems easier for King to accept that Soulié would derive a closer knowledge of African ritual from anthropological literature than Laye, whose father, as we learn from L'Enfant noir, was a goldsmith, with all that this implies of ritual obligations within the culture. In the same work, Laye introduces us in one of the high points of the narrative to the initiation process he underwent. But considerations of this order do not seem to count with King. So insistent is she to give all the credit for *Le Regard du roi* to Soulié that she offers an interpretation of the novel as a function of his pathetic past and an expression of its imprint upon his psyche:

> *Le Regard du roi* may be read as Soulié's desired escape from European culture. Clarence's dismissal by his fellow European may be an expression of the bitterness Soulié felt for the harshness of the Belgian court's judgment against him. Clarence's acceptance by the king is Soulié's hope for redemption. Perhaps the children that Clarence sired express a desire for descendants, which Soulié could attain only indirectly, through adopting an African.[27]

One may be permitted to treat this as fantasy rather than serious literary analysis.

Elsewhere, King contests Toni Morrison's observation that the narrative development in *The Radiance of the King* represents a reversal of European representations of Africa, on the ground that Laye could not have read the works of the particular authors, mainly English speaking, cited by Morrison to illustrate her point. It does not occur to King that Laye did not need to have read any literature at all, least of all these particular authors, in order to form a precise idea of the negative image of Africa in the Western mind and to react against this image, almost instinctively, in his own work. Besides, he was likely to have encountered this image as purveyed by the French exotic literature—associated in the French context with the work of Pierre Loti and the corpus of the *roman colonial*. Similarly, a reference by Laye to Lautréamont triggers from King a roster of writers, including Leiris, whom King speculates may have been brought to Laye's attention by Soulié or any of his French mentors, although she is openly skeptical about his capacity to understand any of this literature.

How much Laye read and absorbed we cannot tell, and the importance of this for his work and career is hard to judge, except insofar as it provides an indication of Laye's endeavor to expand his education in a way that would advance him beyond what he may have felt was his limited literary and cultural horizon, in comparison with his French acquaintances. In other words, Laye aspired to become an acknowledged writer in the mainstream of French and European modernism. It is reasonable to suppose that, in this quest for a certain level of cultivation and of status, Poulet and Soulié served as mentors for Laye, each at different times taking the author under his wing. Everything that King reports of his relations with both men suggests that they saw in him a kind of African/Black Pygmalion, whose talent required to be carefully nurtured. The question is whether they played a role that went further than this, whether by ghosting whole works for Laye they went beyond the role of benefactors and *amanuensis* that, as we have seen, Lucie Cousturier had played for Diallo.

The question becomes urgent at this time, since, as King reports, Laye acknowledged editorial help from Poulet, without ever admitting that his books were written for him. Why then are we still being urged to believe that Laye did not write them? It is indeed surprising that in more than fifty years, no one has ever come forward to claim authorship of the novels attributed to him. Here, the central puzzle about this affair, one that King and Kesteloot fail to address, is: why would a European intellectual want to ghost a novel for a totally unknown African? For unless we are to accept Kesteloot's naïve explanation of a generous disposition on his part, it is difficult to believe that Poulet— or for that matter, Soulié—would have gone to the trouble of writing a long and complex novel only to hand it over to another person, White or Black, totally unrelated to him, and allow that person to take lifelong credit for it.

As already noted, King does indeed provide linguistic and stylistic evidence of outside intervention in the redaction of *Le Regard du roi*, but, as I have argued, there is no reason to consider the results of this intervention as other than interpolations. The notion too that the novel represented a radical break from Laye's earlier work is exaggerated, for characteristic traits were carried over from the first novel to the second, traits which recur in *Dramouss*.[28] A stylistic continuity can thus be discerned in all his work, enough to justify the view that Laye produced at least an initial framework on his own for his three novels. All that King's investigations indicate is that his French mentors intervened in his work, presumably to tidy up his texts and, in the case of *Le Regard du roi*, in an endeavor to expand its scope; in this case, we are in fact entitled to the view that these interventions were not altogether beneficial. Here, one might cite the example of Ezra Pound's emendations to the original manuscript of T. S. Eliot's *The Waste Land*, as revealed in the facsimile edition published by Eliot's wife after his death, emendations that were so extensive as to have sparked doubts about the wisdom of Pound's interference. But this has not occasioned denial to Eliot of the authorship of the poem; indeed, Eliot himself was so little troubled by this collaboration that he paid fulsome tribute to Pound, whom he acknowledged as *"il miglior fabbro"* ["the best craftsman"]. Nonetheless, the example raises the question of textual ownership, as to how much intervention is acceptable to justify ascription of a work to a particular or sole author.

This question leads further into the terrain of disputed authorship that has so often formed part of the background to literary history. We only need to mention the controversy that still surrounds the case of Mikhail Shokolov, who is suspected of having stolen the manuscript of *Quiet Flows the Don* and published it under his name, to be reminded of the relevance of this question to our present discussion. But the most celebrated case of all concerns Shakespeare, whose work has been attributed by certain skeptical critics to the Earl of Oxford, on the ground that the erudition and sophistication demonstrated in his plays are incompatible with the level of formal education that Shakespeare—who we may observe, avowed he had little Latin and no Greek—is presumed to have received. The doubt is especially acute as regards the Sonnets, which, in their complexity evince what Helen Vendler calls "an intense lyric energy."[29] But we know that education in the schools in Shakespeare's times was so extensive that it enabled boys to take degrees at Oxford and Cambridge at ages between sixteen and eighteen. Furthermore, Shakespeare was well known in his own time as both actor and playwright, as attested by tributes paid to his genius by Ben Jonson, who would have had a right to be considered the greatest playwright in English had Shakespeare not lived. But the best sign of his recognition is the fact that folios began to be gathered soon after his death, thus laying the foundation early for the scholarship devoted to his work.[30]

King concludes her book by proposing that *L'Enfant noir* and *Le Regard du roi* be considered as European contributions to African literature. The idea of two classics of African literature being written by Europeans—one a French literary editor, and the other some obscure Belgian—is an intriguing and even seductive one, but it is inadmissible without the solid evidence that is required to ground it. Nothing in King's book prevents us from accepting the common sense proposition that the originating consciousness of all the works attributed to him was indeed Laye's own, that he was responsible in large part for their composition, and that they emerged ultimately from his creative efforts.

But it seems to me that the real issue here has less to do with validating Laye's claim to authorship of these works than with his conscious effort, in *Le Regard du roi*, to appropriate a Western model, leading to the derivative quality of his reworking of Kafka, an effort that Soyinka famously deplored.[31] For it is open to question whether Laye's second novel achieves the meditative depth we associate with Kafka's work and that was inherent in the material that went into its composition. An African Kafka seemed an oddity, which is the figure that, unfortunately, Laye presented.[32] But his relative failure need not imply that African writers cannot draw productively on the universal heritage of literature to give form to their imaginings. The remarks of the Beninois critic Nouréini Tidjani-Serpos appear to me especially pertinent to the point:

> *En effet, inscrire son action créatrice dans les coordon-*
> *nées esthétiques, politiques, philosophiques d'une école de*
> *pensée née ailleurs ne met nullement en cause l'origina-*
> *lité des écrivains si les instruments conceptuels emprun-*

tés sont repensés et adaptés aux aspirations exprimées
sur la base des besoins ressentis de manière endogène.

[To situate one's creative activity within the aesthetic, political and philosophical framework of a
school of thought conceived elsewhere does not
in any way call into question the originality of the
writers, as long as the conceptual tools borrowed are
rethought and adapted to aspirations that are given
expression according to the requisites of an endogenous impulse.][33]

As they touch on the relationship between Western models and
African works, these remarks go to the heart of the problematic of African literature written in European languages. With
respect to the Francophone writers with which we have been
concerned, this issue revolves in the first place around their relationship to the French language as an institutional phenomenon:
not only to French as an expressive medium and to the literary
tradition it sustains, but also to the protocols of authorship that
obtain as a function of the structure of social and economic life
within which, in the modern world, literary works are created,
disseminated, and evaluated. It has come to be assumed within
this structure of life that the individual author takes entire
responsibility, in a deeply moral sense, for the work that is published under his or her name. It is in this sense that the cases of
Camara Laye, Yambo Ouologuem, Calixthe Beyala, and others
can be said to merit the sustained attention they have received.

In order to place their situation in perspective, we need to
invoke the notion of textual authority which was prevalent in
the premodern age, by which certain works were invested with
status as master texts to which reference could be freely made, in
order to give special weight to one's own discourse. This is strikingly illustrated by St. Augustine's *Confessions*, which is threaded
through and held together with quotations and allusions from
both Christian scripture and pagan texts.[34] Moreover, the habit
of allusion was often linked with the art of imitation, considered
not only as a form of literary exercise but as having a value *per se.*
The point here is that until the advent of modernity and its valu-

ation of individual genius, textual ownership was not an issue that counted in the institutional context of literary and artistic creation.[35] We know that in the African oral tradition, the proverbs and stories represented a common fund from which all creative effort derived not only its fundamental impulse but also its material, which the oral artist was free to develop according to the dynamics of the performance event. Such material thus formed part of a collective cultural capital and imaginative resource. And it is this condition, arising from their oral mode of existence, that enabled Birago Diop to adapt the tales of Amadou Koumba to his own expressive needs in his transposition of the tales into the literate mode in the French language, and thus to attach his own name to them permanently.[36]

What we witness here, then, is the ambiguous status of the written text in the African context. This situation is complicated by the derivation of African literature in the European languages from the metropolitan corpus, governed by the conventions of literary production and authorship that this relationship determines. It is this ambiguity that haunts the work of the Francophone writers we have been discussing, and which is thrown into special relief by the cases of Bakary Diallo and Camara Laye, despite the differences between them.

Finally, it seems to me proper in the light of my remarks, to offer a reflection arising from my personal encounter with Laye in Dakar two days before his death in 1980, an encounter that I reported in the obituary I wrote in the London weekly *West Africa*. King refers to this article without much comment. It is however important to restate here the impressions I took away from this meeting. I recall having been struck by the similarity between Laye's speech patterns and his writing style: the short, hesitant phrases and repetitions that are a hallmark of his texts, a fact that settled for me once and for all the question of the provenance of the novels that bear his name. An important detail from this meeting, which King mentions but does not expand upon, concerns Laye's declaration to me that he had decided to abandon French and to write henceforth only in Malinké. We can deduce from this that he had become demoralized by the rumors swirling around his work and was determined to prove himself by writing in a different language than French. He may well have come to the awareness too, like Ngugi wa Thiong'o, of the need to address his immediate audience in a language and idiom common to author and public. But the collective consideration seems to me less important than a personal creative drive, a profound desire on Laye's part to finally bring his expression in line with his vision.

Notes

1. References will be provided below of Kesteloot's published observations, as quoted by Adele King.

2. Adele King, *Rereading Camara Laye* (2002).

3. King, p. 4.

4. King, p. 177.

5. King, pp. 62-63.

6. King, p. 66.

7. Bakary Diallo. *Force-Bonté*, Nouvelle édition, Préface de Mohammadou Kane (Dakar: Les Nouvelles Editions Africaines, 1985).

8. Ibid., p. 85.

9. Ibid., p. 50.

10. Ibid., p. 1.

11. Ibid., p. 127.

12. Ibid., p. 87.

13. 2004: 185. Alain Ricard is careful to distinguish between Diallo and Laye in his discussion of the sponsorship of Francophone African texts (191). To complete the picture of literary competence by the first generation of writers, it is imperative to cite the case of Ousmane Sembene, who, despite his patchy education, went on to write a series of successful novels, including *Les bouts de bois*, considered today a classic of socialist realism. Further afield, we have the case of the South African writer Sol Plaatje, who wrote of his experience in this passage:

> "We have often read books, written by well-known scholars, who disavow, on behalf of their works, any claim to literary perfection. How much more necessary then, that a South African native workingman, who has never received any secondary training, should in attempting authorship disclaim on behalf of his work, any title to literary merit."

But perhaps the best example that disproves the idea that lack of formal education can be an obstacle to a successful literary career is that of Richard Wright, who received hardly any formal education at all, yet went on to become one of the major figures in American and indeed modern literature. No one, as far as I know, has ever disputed his authorship of the masterpiece *Native Son* or any of the other books attributed to him.

14. Kane, in Diallo, pp. iii-xix. Kane was almost certainly thinking of works such as Bernard Dadié's *Climbé*, Aké Loba's *Kocoumbo, l'étudiant noir* and Laye's *L'Enfant noir*, perhaps also, for its autobiographical significance, Cheikh Hamidou Kane's *L'Aventure ambigüe*.

15. In its depiction of the French military's lack of regard for the *tirailleurs sénégalais* whose service and sacrifice was crucial to the French war effort during the two world wars, Diallo's book lays bare the roots of the tragic drama at Tyaroye, to which Senghor devoted one of his most moving poems. The martyrdom of the black soldiers at Tyraoye was later celebrated by Keita Fodeba's *Aube Africaine*, and by Ousmane Sembene in his cinematic retelling of the event.

16. Alexandre Biyidi, (Mongo Beti). "Afrique noire, littérature rose." (Review of *L'enfant noir*). *Présence Africaine*, First series, No. 1955, 133-40. The quotation of Beti that serves as the epigraph to King's book suggests an unfortunate shallowness of judgment on his part.

17. King (2004), p. 51.

18. Maurice Grevisse's *Le bon usage*, long the "Bible" of French grammar, is a comprehensive codification of these rules.

19. Little, J.P. *Cheikh Hamidou Kane: L'Aventure ambiguë*. (2000), p. 44.

20. The danger of this kind of generalization is illustrated by Jack Goody's assertion, in *Love and Food*, that Africa is the only continent that lacks an aesthetic appreciation of flowers, yet a common name for women in Lesotho is Palesa, which means, precisely, flower. In his classic work, *Facing Mount Kenya*, Jomo Kenyatta states that the entrance to the hut where Gikuyu girls prepare for initiation are decorated with "sacred flowers." (134). Shane Doyle (2003) offers a more extended refutation of Goody's assertions in her exposition of the coded message of flowers employed by the precolonial Bunyoro elite for the transmission of messages that span an extended range of emotions.

21. Miller, Christopher. *Theories of Africans: Francophone Literature and Anthropology in Africa*, (1990); Harrow, Kenneth W., *The Marabout and the Muse: New Approaches to Islam in African Literature*, (1996).

22. Brenner, Louis. *West African Sufi: The Religious Heritage and Spiritual Search of Cerno Bokar Salif Taal.* London: C. Hurst and Company, 1984.

23. King, p. 40.

24. See Ritchie Robertson (Introduction to Wagenbach, 2004: x-xi) for a roster of authors influenced by Kafka, among whom the South African, J. M. Coetzee, whose *Life and Times of Mr K* won him his first Booker prize. It is interesting to note that in *Hyènes*, the masterpiece of the Senegalese cineaste Djibril Mambéty, the final scene is a conscious recall of the execution scene in Kafka's *The Trial*, although the film is a reworking of Dürenmatt's *Der Besuch der alte Dame*.

25. Irele, Abiola, "Camara Laye: An Imagination Attuned to the Spiritual," *West Africa*, London, April 7, 1980. 617-18.

26. King, p. 56.

27. King, p. 62.

28. To buttress her case against Laye, King points to the obvious weakness of *Dramouss*, written after his return to Africa, as proof that he was unable on his own to meet the standard of the two earlier novels. This overlooks the fact that Laye was already a sick man and in exile when he wrote the book. In any case, a decline in Laye's powers does not prove that he did not write the earlier books. One could argue that the many "wooden" passages in Beti's *Perpétue* and the incoherence of *Remember Ruben* "prove"

that he could not have written *Le pauvre Christ de Bomba* and *Mission terminée.*

29. Helen Vendler, 1997, p. x.

30. There is of course room for debate as to how much of the early works is his own (see Vickers, 2004), but as any student of Shakespeare is aware, his distinctive idiom emerges with his later plays: the histories, the tragedies and the late romances.

31. Soyinka, Wole. *Myth, Literature, and the African World,* (1990).

32. This may have provoked Sartre, in what may have been an allusion to Laye, to question the value of a Kafkaesque novel against the reality of a child in the Third World dying of hunger. (personal recollection)

33. Tidjani-Serpos 2004, p. 90. One direction of the relationship between metropolitan and colonial literature is suggested by Françoise Lionnet's examination of the intertextual relation between Condé's *La Migration des coeurs* and Charlotte Brontë's *Wuthering Heights.* Lionnet charts the many links in Condé's work, from the point of view of content and allusion, between historical events across the continents—links that suggest a continuity of experience across borders, attenuating the sharp division between center and periphery—and, from the point of view of narrative convention, between "metropolitan" and colonized writers that Condé consciously evokes, and whose authority she invokes to give resonance to her own fiction. The complex web of connections in historic and textual terms that Lionnet uncovers in *La Migration des coeurs* thus leads her to the conclusion that Condé's novel is "a site of convergence" ("Narrating the Americas").

34. The numerous references by St. Augustine to consecrated texts are carefully tracked by Henry Chadwick in his translation of the *Confessions.* There is a sense in which Eliot may be said to have revived the practice of allusion in his *The Waste Land,* although in his case, he takes care to identify his references. Yambo Ouologuem is reported to have invoked this precedent in his own defense against the charge of plagiarism, by declaring that, like Eliot, he had provided references for the texts he had quoted in *Le Devoir de violence,* but that these references were removed by the house editor at Seuil. It is of interest to observe that in the volume of poems entitled *Lagon, Lagunes* published by Gallimard., Sylvie Kandé, following Eliot's example, offers deliberate

quotations of her sources and recalls past masters of her poetic inspiration, features that weave a dense intertextual network through the volume.

35. Händel's habit of borrowing from other musicians is well attested. Interestingly enough, Mozart came in turn to borrow from Händel; the tune of the "Kyrie Eleison" and the "cum sancto spiritu" passage in his Requiem is a direct quotation from Händel's *Messiah*, an edition of which, as is well known, Mozart prepared. The public status of creative works in the Arab and Muslim literary tradition well into the mid nineteenth century is remarked upon by Beverly Mack and Jean Boyd, in their study of the writings of Nana Asma'u, the daughter of Osman dan Fodio, "Authorship was not owned by the individual, nor was personal credit expected for such authorship" (Mack and Boyd, 2000: 10). The emergence of the notion of intellectual property and the legal and ethical problems it has stirred up are discussed by Paul K. Saint-Amour. See also the contributions by various writers to the special number of *New Literary History* on "Anonymity," especially Lisa Samuels, "Relinquish Intellectual Property" (pp. 357-74).

36. Birago Diop's reclaiming of Amadou Koumba's tales forces comparison with Hampaté Bâ's appropriation of Wangrin's discourse in *L'Etrange destin de Wangrin*, supposedly dictated to him in Bambara, but written in French, in the third person as Wangrin's life narrative, and as such, attributed to Hampaté Bâ as his original work. Hampaté Bâ's work raises a number of questions such as the following: has he merely reworked the story told him in Bambara into French? Is Wangrin an invention, or is there indeed a real person behind this character, as claimed in the Postface, originally written for the English translation and now reproduced in the second edition of the French text?

ADDENDUM
PHILOSOPHY AND THE
POSTCOLONIAL CONDITION
IN AFRICA
❦

A review of *The Struggle for Meaning* By Paulin Houn-
tondji. Trans. John Conteh-Morgan. Foreword by Anthony
Kwame Appiah. Athens: Ohio UP, 2002. xiv + 308 pp.
ISBN 0-889680-225-6.

Paulin Hountondji is acknowledged as one of the most
prominent figures in the debate on African philosophy,
a debate that has been, unquestionably, the central theme of
African intellectual expression in the post-independence era.
He came to attention with the publication in 1976 of *Sur "la
philosophie africaine,"* a collection of essays spanning some ten
years which had appeared in various journals and in which he
developed a systematic critique of "ethnophilosophy," a term that
he employed to designate the efforts by several scholars, beginning with Placide Tempels in *Bantu Philosophy* (1949), to derive
philosophical content and meaning from the belief systems of
various African peoples. The English translation of Hountondji's
collection, published in 1983 under the title *African Philosophy:
Myth or Reality*, was widely acclaimed and won the Herskovits
award of the African Studies Association the following year. It

was reissued in 1996 in a second edition, with a new preface by the author.

The present book, which represents a sequel and a complement to the 1976 collection, needs to be placed in its institutional context in order to understand its structure and to appreciate its significance. It belongs to a category of French academic texts without a parallel in the English-speaking world: a book-long essay written to supplement previously published works, with a view to the award of the higher State doctorate degree (*Doctorat d'Etat*). This category of works emerged in the early seventies as a result of reforms to the French educational system introduced after the events of May 1968. Previously, the State doctorate degree was awarded on the basis of a massive thesis that took years—indeed the best part of the candidate's professional life—to prepare. This degree was the sole determinant for entry into the upper levels of the French academic establishment and for advancement within it; in fact, French academics could not take credit for work they published before they had obtained the state doctorate degree with a standard thesis. With the post-1968 reform, the absurdity of the prevailing system was finally recognized and eliminated, so that it became possible to submit one's published writings for consideration toward the award of the *Doctorat d'Etat*.

An important condition was, however, attached to the new procedure. The candidate now had the obligation to write a substantial essay reviewing his or her own previous research and publications, thus placing them in a comprehensive intellectual perspective. This exercise necessarily entailed an account of the candidate's academic career and development, as a background to the review that was required of his or her work. In the case of the Marxist philosopher Louis Althusser, who was one of the first to take advantage of the new procedure, the essay he wrote took the form of an intellectual autobiography and a statement of his philosophical positions: indeed, the essay was published under the title *Positions* (1976). Hountondji's book under review here was written to satisfy the same conditions for the award of the new State doctorate in France as Althusser's. It bears another relation to this work, however, for Althusser was one of Hountondji's teachers at the prestigious Ecole Normale Supérieure (ENS), at the rue d'Ulm, in Paris. It was as a scholarship student at this institution (practically a graduate college, something like All Souls College at Oxford) that he prepared for and obtained the highly competitive degree of *Agrégation* in Philosophy. It is worth noting that another of his teachers at ENS was Jacques Derrida, the originator of the literary-cum-philosophical movement known as "Deconstruction." The impact upon his own development and his work of these two towering figures of intellectual life in France—as indeed in the Western world generally—is reflected in the present work: a point to which we shall return.

Hountondji wrote a master's thesis on the German philosopher Edmund Husserl, followed by a dissertation on the same philosopher for the *Doctorat de Troisième Cycle* (roughly equivalent to the Anglo-American PhD), a degree that was considered at the time as no more than a half-way house to the State doctorate. He taught thereafter at the University of Besançon in France and Lovanium University in The Congo Democratic Republic (formerly Zaire) before returning to his native country of Benin in 1972 to take up a position as Professor of Philosophy at the newly founded national university. An outspoken critic of the military regime that ruled Benin for two decades, Hountondji came into public prominence as one of the architects of his country's return to a democratic regime in 1992. These facts which mark the principal stages of Hountondji's career are recalled in his new book entitled *Combats pour le sens* in the original French edition published in 1997. It is now offered in an excellent English translation that negotiates with aplomb the terminological difficulties with which its early chapters—devoted as these are to an extended discussion of Husserl's philosophy—fairly bristle; moreover, the translation captures at the same time the lively quality of Hountondji's prose.[1]

In his foreword to Hountondji's book, Kwame Anthony Appiah rightly stresses the historic significance of the recall in its early pages of the exhilarating intellectual atmosphere in France in the 1960s and early '70s within which his advanced training in philosophy took place. Hountondji's evocation of its leading figures and his review of the theoretical issues upon which their activity was focused conveys a vivid sense of the extraordinary energy, the charged intensity, that characterized this period of French intellectual history. It is obvious that his own work derives its essential impulse from the dominant intellectual currents in France in this period, in relation to which he was centrally placed by reason of his education at the ENS, in a privileged moment of his adventure as an ex-colonial/postcolonial intellectual. Thus, true to the genre described above, Hountondji offers in this book an absorbing narrative of his intellectual development, beginning with his early education in Dahomey/Benin, moving on to his years in Paris and his encounter at ENS with the great philosophical movements in postwar France, in the shaping of which the influence of modern German philosophy has played such a determining role—a fact that explains his choice of Edmund Husserl for his thesis and his dissertation. He takes the narrative beyond the French years to the brief period he spent in Zaire, where he witnessed at first hand the Mobutu dictatorship, in all its venality and repressive brutality, up to his return to Dahomey (as Benin was then called) where, for some two decades, he was also to live the reality of another military dictatorship, whose Marxist rhetoric masked a fatal disconnection from reality and a gross incompetence in the management of national affairs, until its miraculously peaceful supercession following the national conference of 1992. The narrative he presents is an enlightening one: it not only provides the background of personal experience of his intellectual development but also fills in for us the social and political circumstances that account for the expansion of his intellectual horizons and of his philosophical concerns to which the book bears witness.

Hountondji returns here to his earlier critique of ethnophilsophy, but places this critique in the wider perspective of the historical process in Africa, of the conditions that underlie the universe of discourse and thus affect the elaboration of systems of knowledge on the continent. It is pertinent to recall that Hountondji's objections to ethnophilosophy in his earlier work concern the way in which its adherents offer their projections of collective worldviews as instances of a unified African philosophy. As he sees it, their efforts to reconstruct African systems of thought rest on an erroneous conception of philosophy: as an entity implicit in the complex array of images and collective representations generated within the precolonial cultures, whose philosophical content and significance it becomes the vocation of the scholar to elucidate and conceptualize in the language of Western philosophy, hence in a discourse that, according to Hountondji, bears no correspondence to the nature and original intent of the ethnographic material upon which it is founded. Hountondji's career has been devoted largely to an effort to combat ethnophilosophy, and attempts to define a meaning and import for philosophy as a rigorous discipline. The need for clarity on this point is compelled for him by what he sees as the wrong-headed annexation of philosophy by African scholars and intellectuals in an effort to press a loose notion of it into the service of an unreflexive cultural nationalism. What he feared as the ultimately debilitating effect of this gesture on the intellectual endeavor required by the African predicament underlies his insistence upon the character of philosophy as a theoretical activity that serves as the foundation for the form of determinate knowledge that goes by the name of science.

The radical import of Hountondji's critique of ethnophilosophy, coupled with the abrasive tone of his writing, created the impression of a determined onslaught upon what one might call the received wisdom of African cultural nationalism, and provoked, quite predictably, strong reactions in African intellectual circles: reactions that ranged from passionate dissent to outright indignation.[2] While some of these reactions were ideological, Hountondji's view of philosophy, which was so restrictive as to exclude metaphysics from its purview, raised issues not merely of definition but also of the larger implications of philosophy as a discipline and as a form of cultural practice. Thus, the Ghanaian philosopher Kwame Gyekye, in a book that seems to have been conceived as an extended rejoinder to *Myth and Reality*, has objected to the limitations of the purely technical view of philosophy espoused by Hountondji and his denial of a valid epistemological status to the products of the various efforts to reconstruct a collective African philosophy deemed implicit in

the ethnographic material related to the continent. His refutation has taken the form of a rigorous technical analysis of concepts denoted by terms in the Akan language, with a view to
demonstrating the coherence of the categories of thought that
structure the conceptual system that serves as the comprehensive
cultural reference of his exposition. In a deliberate challenge to
Hountondji's objection to the transposition of African systems
of thought into a Western key of discourse, Gykeye interprets
the Akan system by positing parallels between the categories
of thought by which it is structured and those denoted by
concepts available in the western repertoire.[3] In this way, he is
able to discern a pragmatic thrust in the habits of mind of the
Akan people and their formulation of experience, as these come
through in the structure of their language and codified forms
of public discourse; what is more, he insists upon the propo-
sitional import of these forms and their capacity to serve as
channels of genuine philosophical reflection.[4] But it is especially
in his investigation of the moral ideas by which collective life
is regulated within traditional Akan society and their bearing
upon culture that Gyekye's project assumes its full pertinence.
As he says: "The relationship between philosophy and culture
is the pivot on which my thesis regarding the nature of African
philosophy turns" (Gyekye 25). Thus, for him, Akan thought is
not merely a symbolic and imaginative variable of the culture,
but also a reflective and indeed cognitive dimension of an all-
encompassing apprehension of the world.

It has been necessary to consider Gyekye's book at some
length because it contains the most forceful response to Hountondji's critique, all the more compelling as it emanates from an
anglophone African scholar trained in the Anglo-American ana-
lytic tradition. Its careful and detailed argumentation articulates
in a sustained development the various objections to Hountondji's position regarding the possibility of constructing an African
philosophy from traditional sources, a possibility of which his
own work seeks indeed to provide a concrete demonstration.
The pertinence of Gyekye's rejoinder obliged Hountondji, in the
preface to the second edition of *Myth and Reality*, to answer these
objections, which he confronts anew in this new book, offering

in the process important clarifications that reflect a moderation of his earlier rigid stance on the nature of philosophy. He begins by restating his advocacy of a rigorous philosophical practice in Africa, situating it within a personal history of sustained engagement with the work of Husserl, who was committed to a view of philosophical thought and method as a form of scientific endeavor, capable of grasping even the inner truth of things. This latter claim informs Hountondji's lengthy exegesis of Husserl's work, which occupies the first part of his book, an exegesis that for all its subtlety and erudition leaves open the question of the final resting point of Husserl's exploration of mind and experience. For Hountondji's presentation alternates between two interpretations of Husserl, two profiles of the German philosopher that appear to be at first sight incompatible, but which he is at pains to reconcile. He specifically rejects the view that Husserl evolved from a materialist into an idealist philosopher, but the trajectory that he projects takes us from an account of Husserl's early effort to establish the rational basis of philosophical thought and culminates with an image of Husserl concerned with grasping the concrete quality of lived experience, in all its inwardness, as the very source of thought. Indeed, Hountondji celebrates Husserl's phenomenology in his later work as an emancipation from the austere intellectualism of Descartes, with its radical divorce from the immediacies of experience. This is how he sums up the reversal operated by Husserl: "Here, then, the initial perspective is reversed. The point of departure is no longer 'figurative contents' but the emotional and sensual depth of experience (l'épaisseur charnelle et émotionelle du vécu)" (22). This begins to look like a form of vitalism, not so different from Nietzsche's or Bergson's. Such a reading is of course a matter for debate among professional philosophers—a debate that cannot for obvious reasons be pursued here—but one cannot help but speculate that had he continued his investigations of Husserl, Hountondji would have developed greater tolerance, perhaps even sympathy, for Senghor's concept of Negritude than he has displayed in his polemical engagement with the ideas of the great African poet and cultural theorist.

The book further indicates that to the seminal impact of Husserl must be added the direct and immediate influence of Althusser, who, as is well known, conceived of philosophy as the paradigmatic discourse of science, a view that provides the grounding principle of Hountondji's critique of ethnophilosophy. Hountondji's effusive homage to Althusser not only registers the seismic impact of the latter's deployment of Bachelard's notion of "epistemological break"—his positing of a decisive shift from the pronounced Hegelianism of Marx's early work as illustrated by the so-called "1844 manuscripts" to the rigorous analysis of *Capital* conducted in a new and more precise language—in order to open up and revitalize Marxist thought; he also celebrates Althusser's refusal of all forms of dogmatism as inimical to the conduct of philosophical enquiry. The terms of this homage may strike the anglophone reader, however, as too reverent, leaving out of sight some of the more debatable aspects of Althusser's thought and career, exemplified notably by his promotion of Lenin as a serious philosopher, a disposition that must be adduced to his party allegiances.[5]

Matters are somewhat different when we consider the case of Derrida, who is acknowledged by Hountondji as another major influence. In his elaboration of deconstruction as an analytical method, Derrida has most powerfully embodied in our own day, albeit in his own idiosyncratic way, the skeptical tradition in Western intellectual history, with a status comparable in this respect to that of David Hume. Hountondji's critique of ethnophilosopy draws much of its energy from this tradition and owes its peculiar thrust to what Barbara Johnson has called "the deconstructive *questioning* of absolute claims," a gesture that she further associates with a particular state of mind—"skepticism toward existing cultural arrangements, toward the supposed 'universality' or 'impartiality' of existing 'truths'" (Johnson 26, 85). All this is obviously salutary, enabling a piercing insight into the inherent paradoxes of discourse, an insight that Hountondji has extended to the area of African expression. However, in at least one respect having to do with the status of oral speech, the influence of Derrida must be considered problematic. Hountondji's disparagement of the oral tradition—especially with regard to Abbé Kagame's invocation of its authority in his effort to establish a Bantu ontology grounded in language—his denial to oral speech of the capacity for sustained enunciation, reflects an alignment with Derrida's position on language in *De la Grammatologie* (1967), the precedence (in both senses of the word) that Derrida accords to writing as the presiding category of language. This is a position that goes against the very tenets of modern linguistics, the emphasis on oral speech that enabled the effective development of its analytical method. The least that can be said is that Hountondji's citing of the master text of deconstruction to support a devaluation of orality thus harbors a curious misconception of its constitutive function in language and, most of all, its dominance in the manifold expressive schemes to be encountered within his own African background.[6]

To point up the blind spots in Hountondji's assessment of his intellectual antecedents is not to suggest, however, a crippling dependence on the authority of his French masters, but rather to observe the remarkable growth in his awareness, marked by the distance traversed between the publication of *Myth and Reality* and writing of the work under review. Hountondji tells us in the new book that, despite his wholehearted investment in the philosophy of Husserl, he discontinued his investigations because of what he began to feel as the remoteness of his work to African concerns, a decision that, moreover, was facilitated by the general loss of interest in Husserl that has since occurred in French philosophical circles.[7] This presumably freed him for the task he subsequently set himself: to clear the decks, as it were, of African philosophy, a task for which, as his book stresses, his French education provided an indispensable foundation. As his account progresses, however, Hountondji's concerns are seen to expand, to cover an ever-widening range of political and social issues that impart a special urgency to his theoretical preoccupation with the nature of philosophy. The new book thus extends the scope of the earlier work, whose preoccupations are mainly procedural and methodological, into a striking new dimension, embracing substantive issues of values as they impinge upon contemporary African experience.

It is in this perspective that he draws attention to the correlation between, on one hand, the collective view of African philosophy, which posits a conformism of thought in traditional society that precludes the possibility of argument and debate—elements that are constitutive of the very nature of philosophy—and, on the other, the authoritarian trend of African political systems in the postcolonial era, a correlation that enables him to argue for the critical function of philosophy in Africa. His positing of a direct relation between intellectual effort and political agency reflects a deeply rooted Marxist conviction, clearly in evidence in his 1992 essay on "Daily Life in Africa," in which he draws on the Benin experience to articulate the depressed social reality in contemporary Africa.[8] The essay registers the pragmatic orientation that Hountondji's work has progressively taken since the publication in 1976 of his collection of essays, an orientation that is confirmed by the tenor of his new book.

The emphasis that has lately emerged in Hountondji's work on the dynamic relationship between theory and practice manifests itself most directly in his advocacy for the insertion of philosophy into the fabric of African life. As a direct consequence of his early encounter with Husserl, overlaid and reinforced by that of Althusser, his intellectual project has now taken the form of a continuing reflection on science as a cultural phenomenon, and, in the specific African context, on its function as a necessary component of the modernity project in Africa.[9] His thinking on these questions has culminated in his current preoccupation with what he calls "endogenous systems of knowledge" (savoirs endogènes) in Africa, a preoccupation that first surfaced in the collective volume he edited of the proceedings of a conference on the subject due to his initiative (Hountondji, "Démarginsaliser" in Les Savoirs endogènes). He enlarges upon this question in the present book, in a clear-headed consideration of the inadequacy of the institutional support for the scientific culture in Africa and the impoverishment of African intellectual life that this situation entails. He dwells in particular on the multiple disabilities, both theoretical and practical, that arise from the phenomenon he names as the "extraversion" of African knowledge in its present condition: its derivativeness from and subservience

to Western modes of discourse, and consequently to the impera-
tives of Western systems of production. It is the lucid awareness
of this problem that compels Hountondji's reappraisal of the
rationality of traditional systems of thought, and his project for
a re-appropriation of the positive science as well as the functional technologies that they have engendered.

Hountondji makes it clear that the recuperation of an indigenous science does not imply a celebration of a supposed African
genius, but rather an effort bent towards the reintegration of
the positivist insights derived from experience in traditional
cultures, the intuitions and practical wisdom they propose, into
a universal process of knowledge production. This effort necessarily involves in turn a broadening of intellectual horizons and
an expansion of the African mental universe. We are thus made
aware, on the evidence of this book, that Hountondji has come
progressively to adopt a more inclusive notion of philosophy as
science, in which traditional modes of thought and Western conventions are envisaged in a single perspective: that of a universal
rationality. This is not the abstract universalism that Tsenay
Serequeberhan has reproached him with (see *The Hermeneutics
of African Philosophy*), but one grounded in the actualities of the
African situation. And it is the strenuous reflection upon these
realities that gives density to the universalism that, at the very
outset of the book, Hountondji stipulates as at the same time
the condition and direction of an African practice of philosophy.

The Nigerian philosopher Olusegun Oladipo has defined
the responsibility of African philosophers in these terms: "to
establish and clarify the intellectual foundations of their societies." He adds: "They will also help to establish a tradition of
public philosophy, the primary aim of which will be to generate
and propagate the ideas, beliefs, and values that are required to
govern our societies and regulate public conduct" (66). This definition seems to me to sum up the burden of Hountonji's present
work. *The Struggle for Meaning* makes clear that what is at stake
in his theoretical activity and the critical effort it enjoins is the
capacity of Africa to achieve a new mode of integration compat-
ible with the exigencies of the contemporary world, an article of
faith that is advertised by the title of the 1995 doctoral essay of

which this book is an expansion: "Enjeux d'une critique: philoso-phie, anthropologie des savoirs et politiques en Afrique." In other words, for Hountondji, the practice of philosophy is inseparable from the task of reconstruction in Africa, the quest for what he has called "the utopia of another society" ("Daily Life" 364).

What this book reveals, finally, is the *situatedness* of Houn-tondji as philosopher, the way in which his work is inscribed within the framework of an intellectual adventure that perhaps only a francophone African could have gone through. It is inter-esting in this regard to note that the subtitle of the original French edition of the book—*un itinéraire africain*—echoes that chosen for his autobiography, published in 1966, by another prominent French-speaking African intellectual, the Senegalese deputy Lamine Guèye, at whose initiative the French National Assembly passed a law in 1948 that enabled Africans to acquire French citizenship. This was a status that was treasured as the ultimate prize held out by the French policy of assimilation. The seductiveness of this mirage vanished with independence, so that it is no longer a meaningful aspiration for the postcolo-nial cohort of francophone intellectuals to which Hountondji belongs.[10] For while this book offers ample testimony to the intellectual debt he owes to France, it also marks his desire to establish a cultural and intellectual authority that will confirm Africa's autonomy, one that has remained painfully nominal in the political, cultural, and intellectual spheres. The philosophical project outlined in this and his other writings seeks nothing less than to give this nominal autonomy a reality as much in African consciousness as in objective institutional terms.

NOTES

1. The merits of the translation need to be measured against the quandaries and pitfalls that Jonathan Ree points out in his remark-able essay, "The Translation of Philosophy." It is not without inter-est to observe that Rée himself played a significant part in the translation into English of Hountondji's 1976 collection.

2. For a summary of early reactions to Hountondji's critique in something of their full range, see Chapter Four above.

3. T. Carlos Jacques misses the deliberate character of Gyekye's challenge in the long criticism of the Ghanaian philosopher's work that forms a central part of his review of the issues involved in the debate on African philosophy (238-52). He leaves entirely out of account many of the key points in Gyekye's argument. We may mention some of these. The historical circumstances, arising from modern colonialism, of the Western-trained African philosopher imposed an obligation to write in the European languages and therefore to have recourse to the repertoire of concepts embedded in these languages. The implications of this for African philosophy have been examined by Kwasi Wiredu who has devoted considerable attention to the question in several essays (see *Cultural Universals*; see also "Toward Decolonizing African Philosophy and Religion"). Gyekye maintains that the application of Western terms and concepts to the analysis of African thought is not only legitimate, it offers the additional advantage of projecting a comparative perspective upon the entire field of philosophy, enabling an even finer analysis of concepts (see also note 4 below). Finally, despite the inevitable disparities—what Wiredu has called "conceptual roadblocks to intercultural communication"—the various modes by which cultures across the world have formulated human experience are not incommensurable. Wiredu has summed up the import of this for the African philosopher: "Thus, in investigating our traditional philosophies, we will also be responding to elemental promptings to philosophical reflection which are 'interior' to the human condition" (*Cultural Universals* 150).

4. Gyekye may be said to have carried forward Kagame's philosophical initiative begun some thirty years earlier and focused on his native KiRwanda. And as with Kagame before him, Gyekye's analysis of the semantic field and denotative range of Akan words and expressions leads him to observe that the philosophical terms they can be made to yield sometimes present greater conceptual adequacy, as compared to English (180). In a similar way, Wiredu has declared that, in his opinion, the "locative concept of existence" found in the Akan language is "more conducive to sound metaphysics than its rivals" (*Cultural Universals* 142).

5. We might add that Fredric Jameson's critical project in *The Political Unconscious*—his effort to recover a sense of the wholeness of narrative art, of its moral and historical cogency—was undertaken in reaction not only against what he felt was the ethical

blindness of poststructuralist aesthetics but also what he inti-
mates as the hidebound formalism of Althusser's interpretation
of literature, linked to his concept of "mechanical causality" (see
Jameson 23-29 and 55 ff.)

6.   For a sustained critique of Derrida's position on language, see
     Ellis 8-66. It is not without relevance to the question at issue
     to draw attention to the logical impasse that haunts Derrida's
     brand of skepticism, and which has been perceptively articu-
     lated by Philip Lewis: "[D]econstruction comes up against the
     paradoxical relation between its discourse and its theses. While
     the latter typically declare the incapacity of language to ground
     itself, the inaptitude of speech acts to justify their claims to
     make true or consistent statements and so forth, they also make
     such declarations unconditionally; the discourse is informed by
     assumptions about its own expressive adequacy that are not, and
     indeed cannot be, consistent with those theses" (18). As regards
     the question of orality in the African context, it has been left to
     another francophone philosopher, Jean-Godefroy Bidima, to
     provide a corrective view to that of Hountondji, by demonstrat-
     ing, in his essay on *La Palabre*, its function not simply as a mode
     of imaginative and symbolic expression, but also as an effective
     medium of social practice founded upon a clearly articulated
     system of legal procedures and ethical precepts (see Bidima; see
     also Hallen and Sodipo).

7.   A major factor was of course the displacement of Husserl in the
     firmament of French philosophy, whose center of gravity shifted
     in the 1960s from phenomenology to structuralism and its
     various derivatives and applications; interest centered no longer
     on discourse as discovery of meaning, but on the very process of
     signification, internal to the phenomenon of discourse itself. This
     constituted a paradigm shift that found its ultimate validation
     in the fact that both Marxism (in the work of Althusser) and
     psychoanalysis (in that of Lacan), disciplines concerned most
     centrally with history either as a collective force or the unfolding
     of individual existence, came to appropriate the abstract model of
     structuralism for their analysis of lived situations.

8.   As the title suggests, Hountondji's essay derives its inspiration
     from Henri Lefebvre's extensive explorations and critique of the
     contradictions that frame "everyday life" in the modern world.
     Hountondji's essay may be said, incidentally, to have initiated

the theme of the "postcolony" which has since found powerful elaboration in the work of Achille Mbembe (*De la postcolonie*).

9. Jacques, in the article already cited, is not far from qualifying Hountondji's advocacy of a scientific culture in Africa as the manifestation of a naïve delusion. He cites the postmodern distrust of science, reflected in particular by its representation in the work of Michel Foucault and Bruno Latour as an expression of power. But it has become increasingly clear that neither Foucault nor Latour can be considered a fount of wisdom in these matters. In any case, their problematic—which can be deemed a carry-over of Heidegger's wrestling with the question of technology—has no relevance to Africa, the one continent that cannot afford the disabling quietism, that, as Terry Eagleton has pointed out, postmodernism tends to foster. It hardly needs emphasizing that the case for the development of science and its practical corollary in technology rests on the urgent necessity for the amelioration of the appalling conditions of existence on the African continent today, an objective that in its human dimension presents itself as nothing less than a moral imperative. One might add that its attainment crucially involves breaking the cycle of dependence maintained by the tenacious hold of Western powers on African economies, and consequently, on African lives. It is no exaggeration therefore to affirm that science and technology are required in Africa in order to complete the decolonization of the continent.

10. In his very informative sociological account of the situation of the francophone African intellectual in the postcolonial period, *Les intellectuels africains en France*, Abdoulaye Guèye provides valuable insights into the stresses introduced into this situation by the anti-immigrant policy officially pursued by successive French administrations in the wake of independence, a fact that has helped to dissipate all lingering notions of French benevolence.

BIBLIOGRAPHY

Abble, Albert, et al. 1957. *Des Prêtres noirs s'interrogent*, 2nd ed., Paris: Karthala, 2007.

Abraham, Willie E. 1962. *The Mind of Africa*. London: Weidenfeld and Nicolson.

Adelaja, Kola. 1968. *Edward Wilmot Blyden et la naissance de la pensée politique africaine*. These de doctorat de 3ᵉ Cycle, Université de Paris.

Adotévi, Stanislas Spero K. 1972. *Négritude et Négrologues*. Paris: Union Générale d'Éditions.

Albérès, René Marill. 1969. *L'Aventure intellectuelle du XXe siècle: panorama des littératures européennes, 1900-1970*, 4th ed. Paris: Albin Michel.

Althusser, Louis. 1976. *Positions*. Paris: Editions Sociales.

Archer-Straw, Petrine. 2000. *Negrophilia: Avant-Garde Paris and Black Culture in the 1920s*. New York: Thames & Hudson.

Armah, Ayi Kwei. 1967. "African Socialism: Utopian or Scientific." *Présence Africaine* 64: 6-30.

Arnold, A. James. 1981. *Modernism and Négritude. The Poetry and Poetics of Aimé Césaire*. Cambridge, MA: Harvard University Press.

Augustine, Saint, Bishop of Hippo. 1992. Henry Chadwick (trans.). *Confessions*. Oxford: Oxford University Press.

Avineri, Shlomo. 1968. *The Social and Political Thought of Karl Marx*. London: Cambridge University Press.

Bâ, Sylvia Washington. 1973. *The Concept of Négritude in the Poetry of Léopold Sédar Senghor*. Princeton, NJ: Princeton University Press.

Badiane, Mamadou. 2009. *The Changing Face of Afro-Caribbean Cultural Identity: Negrismo and Négritude*. Lanham, MD: Lexington Books.

Bahoken, Jean-Calvin. 1978. *Clairières métaphysiques africaines: Essai sur la philosophie et la religion chez les Bantu du Sud-Cameroun*. Paris: Présence Africaine.

Balandier, Georges. 1953. "Messianismes et nationalismes en Afrique noire." *Cahiers Internationaux de Sociologie* 14: 41-65.

_____. 1957. *Afrique ambigüe*. Paris: Plon.

_____. 1962. "Les mythes politiques de colonisation et de décolonisation en Afrique." *Cahiers Internationaux de Sociologie* 33: 85-96.

_____. 1963. *Sociologie actuelle de l'Afrique noire: dynamique sociale en Afrique centrale*, 2nd ed. Paris: Presses Universitaires de France.

_____. 1966. Robert A. Wagoner (trans.). "The Colonial Situation: A Theoretical Approach (1951)." In Immanuel Wallerstein (ed.), *Social Change: the Colonial Situation*. New York: Wiley, pp. 34-61.

Baldwin, James. 1992. *Nobody Knows My Name*. New York: Vintage.

Barthes, Roland. 1953. *Le Degré zéro de l'écriture: suivi des éléments de sémiologie*. Paris: Éditions du Seuil.

Bastide, Roger. 1950. *Sociologie et Psychanalyse*. Paris: Presses Universitaires de France.

_____. 1958. "Le Mythe de l'Afrique noire et la société de classe multiraciale." *Esprit*. Octobre: 401-413.

_____. 1960. *Les Religions africaines au Brésil: vers une sociologie des interpénétrations de civilisations*. Paris: Presses Universitaires de France.

_____. 1961. "Variations sur la négritude." *Présence Africaine*.36: 7-17.

_____. 1962. "Problèmes de l'entrecroisement des civilisations et de leurs œuvres." In Georges Gurvitch (ed.), *Traité de sociologie*, 2nd ed. Paris: Presses Universitaires de France, pp. 315-330.

Beier, Ulli. 1959. "The Theme of the Ancestors in Senghor's Poetry." *Black Orpheus*. 5(Mai): 15-17.

_____. 1967. ed. *Introduction to African Literature*. London: Longmans.

Bernasconi, ed. 2001. *Race: Blackwell Readings in Continental Philosophy*. Malden, MA.: Blackwell Publishers.

Bergson, Henri. 1959. *Œuvres*: Textes annotés par André Robinet. Introd. par Henri Gouhier.Paris: Presses Universitaires de France.

Bernabé, Jean, Patrick Chamoiseau, Raphaël Constant. 1993. *Eloge de la Créolité*. Paris: Gallimard.

Bidima, Jean Godefroy, 1995. *La Philosophie négro-africaine*. Paris: Presses Universitaires de France. Collection "Que sais-je?"

_____. 1997. *La Palabre: une juridiction de la parole*. Paris: Michalon.

Berrian, Albert H. and Richard A. Long (eds.). 1967. *Négritude: Essays and Studies*. Hampton, VA: Hampton Institute Press.

Béti, Mongo. 1956. *Le Pauvre Christ de Bomba*. Paris: R. Laffont.

Biyaoula, Daniel. 1996. *L'Impasse*. Paris: Présence Africaine.

Biyidi, Alexandre (Mongo Béti). 1955. "Afrique noire, littérature rose." (a review of *L'Enfant noir*). *Présence Africaine* 5: 133-40.

Blyden, Edward Wilmot. 1962. *Christianity, Islam and the Negro Race*. Edinburgh: Edinburgh University Press.

_____. 1978. Hollis Ralph Lynch (ed.). *Selected Letters of Edward Wilmot Blyden*. Millwood, NY: KTO Press.

Bokiba, André-Patient (ed.) 2001. *Le Siècle Senghor*. Paris: L'Harmattan.

Brenner, Louis. 1984. *West African Sufi: The Religious Heritage and Spiritual Search of Cerno Bokar Saalif Taal*. London: C. Hurst.

Breton, André. 1947. "Un Grand Poète noir." [Préface]. In Aimé Césaire, *Cahier d'un retour au pays natal* (Memorandum on my Martinique). Paris: Bordas.

_____. 1948. "Un Grand Poète noir." In Breton, André, *Martinique: Charmeuse de Serpents*. Paris: Sagittaire.

Burns, Alan, Sir. 1948. *Colour Prejudice: with particular reference to the relationship between whites and Negroes*. London: G. Allen and Unwin.

Camille, Roussan. 1956 *Assaut à la nuit*. Paris: Gallimard.

Cendrars, Blaise. 1947. *Anthologie nègre*. Paris: Corrêa.

Césaire, Aimé. 1941. "Présentation." *Tropiques* 1(Avril): 5-6.

Césaire, Aimé. 1946. *Les Armes miraculeuses*. Paris: Gallimard.

_____. 1956a. *Et Les Chiens se taisaient, tragédie*. Paris: Présence Africaine.

_____. 1956b. *Cahier d'un retour au pays natal*. Paris: Présence Africaine.

_____. 1958. *Discours sur le colonialisme*, 3ed. Paris: Présence Africaine. Trans. Joan Pinkham. *Discourse on Colonialism*. New York: Monthly Press Review, 2000.

_____. 1959. "L'Homme de culture et ses responsabilites." *Deuxième Congrès des écrivains et artistes noirs. Présence Africaine* 4-5: 116-22 .

_____. 2001. *Notebook of a Return to the Native Land*. Translated and Edited by Clayton Eshleman and Annette Smith. Middletown: Wesleyan University Press.

_____. 1976. *Œuvres complètes*, 3 Vols. Fort de France: Éditions Désormeuax

_____. 1983. Clayton Eshleman and Annette Smith (trans.), *Aimé Césaire: The Collected Poetry*. Berkeley, CA: University of California Press.

_____. 1994. *La Poésie*. Paris: Seuil.

_____. 2005. *Nègre je suis, nègre je resterai. Entretiens avec Françoise Vergès*. Paris: Albin Michel.

Césaire, Suzanne. 2009 *Le Grand Camouflage*. Paris: Seuil.

Clark-Bekeredemo, John Pepper. 1991 *Collected Plays and Poetry, 1958-1988*. Washington D.C.: Howard University Press.

Conklin, Anne. 1985. *A Mission to Civilize: The Republican Idea of Empire in France and West Africa 1895-1930*. Stanford: Stanford University Press, 1985.

Constant, Isabelle, and Kahiudi Mabana eds. 2009. *Négritude: Legacy and Present Relevance*. Newcastle: Cambridge Scholars Publishing, 2009.

Coulthard, George Robert. 1962. *Race and Colour in Caribbean Literature*. London: Oxford University Press.

Cullen, Countee. 1925. *Color*. New York: Harper and Brothers.

Dadié, Bernard Binlin. 1956. *La Ronde des jours*. Paris: Seghers.

Damas, Léon-Gontran, ed. 1947. *Poètes d'expression française: d'Afrique noire, Madagascar, Réunion, Guadeloupe, Martinique, Indochine, Guyane, 1900-1945*. Paris: Editions du Seuil.

Damas, Léon-Gontran. 1956. *Black Label, poèmes*. Paris: Gallimard.

_____. 1963. *Pigments*. Paris: Présence Africaine.

D'Arboussier, Gabriel. 1949. "Une Dangereuse Mystification, la théorie de la négritude." *Nouvelle Critique* 7: 34-47.

Decraene, Philippe. 1959. *Le Panafricanisme*. Paris: Presse Universitaires de France.

Delafosse, Maurice. 1922. *Les Noirs de l'Afrique*. Paris: Payot. Second Edition, 2008.

Depestre, René. 1967. *Un Arc-en-ciel pour l'Occident chrétien*. Paris: Présence Africaine, 1967), 108, 112 ; in English as *A Rainbow for the Christian West*, trans. Joan Dayan (Amherst: University of Massachusetts Press, 1977).

_____. 1970. "Les Métamorphoses de la négritude en Amérique," *Présence Africaine* 75, 2e trimester (1970): 19-33.

_____. 1970. "Haïti ou la Négritude devoyée," *Afric-Asia*. No. 5/6 (January 1970).

_____. 1980. *Bonjour et Adieu à la négritude*. Paris: Éditions Robert Laffont.

Dia, Hamidou. ed. 2002. *Poètes d'Afrique et des Antilles d'expression française. Anthologie*. Paris: Table Ronde.

_____. 2003. *Poésie africaine et engagement: parcours libre*. Paris:ACORIA

Diagne, Ahmadou Mapaté. 1920. *Les Trois Volontés de Malic*. Paris: Larose.

Diagne, Pathé, 1981. *L'Europhilosophie face à la pensée nègre*. Dakar: Editions Sankoré.

Diagne, Souleymane Bachir. 2007 *Léopold Sédar Senghor: l'Art africain comme philosophie*. Paris: Riveneuve editions.

Diallo, Bakary. 1985. *Force-Bonté, Nouvelle édition*. [Préface de Mohammadou Kane.] Paris: Les Nouvelles Éditions Africaines, Agence de Coóperation Culturelle et Technique.

Diawara, Manthia. 1998. *In Search of Africa*. Cambridge. MA: Harvard UP

Dieng, Aly Amady. 1979. *Hegel, Marx, Engels et les problèmes de l'Afrique noire*. Dakar: Sankoré.

Diop, Alioune. 1947. "Niam n'goura ou les raisons d'être de *Présence Africaine*." *Présence Africaine*. No 1: 8.

_____. 1959. "Discours d'ouverture," Deuxième Congrès des Ecrivains et Artistes Noirs. *Présence Africaine*, No XXIV-XXV.

Diop, Babacar Mbaye, ed, 2009, *Le Destin de la Négritude.* Lervallois-Perret: Editions Lune.

Diop, Cheikh Anta. 1959. *L'Unité culturelle de l'Afrique noire: domaines du patriarcat et du matriarcat dans l'Antiquité classique.* Paris: Présence Africaine.

_____. 1960. *L'Afrique noire précoloniale.* Paris: Présence Africaine.

_____. 1967. *Antériorité des civilisations nègres: Mythe ou réalité.* Paris: Présence Africaine.

_____. 1977. *Parenté génétique de l'égyptien pharaonique et des langues négro-africaines: processus de sémitisation.* Dakar: IFAN-Nouvelles Éditions Africaines.

_____. 1979. *Nations nègres et culture: de l'Antiquité nègre égyptienne aux problèmes culturels de l'Afrique noire d'aujourd'hui,* 3ed. Paris: Présence Africaine.

_____. 1989. *Egypte ancienne et Afrique noire.* Dakar: IFAN.

Diop, David. 1960. *Coups de pilon.* Paris: Présence Africaine

Diop, Madjemout. 1958. *Contribution à l'étude des problèmes politiques en Afrique noire.* Paris: Présence Africaine.

Dollard, John. 1949. *Caste and Class in a Southern Town,* 2ed. New York: Harper.

Doyle, Shane. 2003. "The Language of Flowers: Knowledge, Power, and Ecology in Precolonial Bunyoro." *History in Africa.* 30: 107-116.

Drachler, Jacob (ed.). 1963. Melville Jean Herskovits (pref.). *African Heritage: Intimate Views of the Black Africans from Life, Lore, and Literature.* New York: Crowell-Collier Press.

Du Bois, W. E. B. 1907. *The Souls of Black Folk: Essays and Sketches,* 7ed. Chicago, IL: A. C. McClurg.

_____. 1939. *Black Folk, Then and Now: An Essay in the History and Sociology of the Negro Race.* New York: H. Holt and Company.

_____. 2007 *Dusk of Dawn.* Oxford: Oxford University Press.

Dufrenne, Mickel. 1953. *La Personnalité de base: un concept sociologique.* Paris: Presses Universitaires de France.

Durand, Gilbert Durand. 1963. *Structures anthropologiques de l'imaginaire.* Paris: Presses Universitaires de France.

Durkheim, Emile. 1963. *Sociologie et philosophie.* Paris: Presses Universitaires de France.

Eagleton, Terry. 1996. *The Illusions of Postmodernism.* Oxford: Blackwell.

Eboussi-Boulaga, Fabien. 1970. *La Crise du Muntu.* Paris: Présence Africaine.

Edwards, Brent Hayes, 2003. *The Practice of Diaspora: Literature, Translation and the Rise of Black Internationalism.* Cambridge: Harvard University Press.

Egar, Emmanuel. 2008. *The Crisis of Negritude: A Study of the Black Movement Against Intellectual Oppression in the Early 20th Century.* Boca Raton: BrownWalker Press.

Eliade, Mircea. 1962. *Traité d'histoire des religions.* Paris: Payot.

Eliot, Thomas Stearns. 1948. *Notes towards the Definition of Culture.* London: Faber and Faber.

Ellis, John M. 1989. *Against Deconstruction.* New Jersey: Princeton Univerdity Press.

Eluard, Paul. 1944. *Poésie et vérité 1942.* London: Gallery Editions.

Essien-Udom, Udosen, 1962. *Black Nationalism: A Search for an Identity in America.* Chicago, IL: University of Chicago Press.

Eze, Emmanuel Chukwudi, 1997. *Postcolonial African Philosophy: A Crticial Reader.* Cambridge, MA.: Blackwell Publishers.

_____. 2001. *Achieving Our Humanity: The Idea of the Postracial Future.* New York: Routledge.

Fabre, Michel, 1991. *From Harlem to Paris: Black American Writers in France, 1840-1980.* Urbana: University of Illinois Press.

Fanon, Frantz. 1952 *Peau noire, masques blancs.* Paris: Seuil.Tr Charles Lam Markmann as *Black Skin, White Masks.* New York: Grove Press, 1967.

_____. 1959 "Fondements réciproques de la culture nationale et des luttes de liberation." *Deuxième Congrès des Ecrivains et Artistes Noirs.* Paris: Présence Africaine.

_____. 1961. *Les Damnés de la terre,* 2nd ed. Paris: F. Maspero. Tr Constance Farrington , *The Wretched of the Earth.* Harmondsworth, UK: Penguin. 1968.

_____. 1966. *Sociologie d'une révolution.* Paris: Maspero. Tr Haakon Chevalier, as *A Dying Colonialism.* New York: Grove Press, 1967.

Ferry, Anne. 2002. "Anonymity: The Literary History of a Word." *New Literary History.* 33(2): 193-214.

Franklin, Albert. 1953. "La Négritude: réalité ou mystification? Réflexions sur 'Orphée noir.'" *Présence Africaine.* 14: 287-303.

Fonlon, Bernard. 1978. *La Poésie et le réveil de l'homme noir.* Docotoral dissertation, National University of Ireland, Cork.

Frazier, Edward Franklin. 1949. *The Negro in the United States.* New York: Macmillan Company.

_____. 1957. *Race and Culture Contacts in the Modern World.* Boston, MA: Beacon.

Freyre, Gilberto. 1952. *Maîtres et esclaves: la formation de la société brésilienne.* Paris: Gallimard.

Frindéthié, Martial Kokroa. 2008. *The Black Renaissance in Francophone African and Caribbean Literatures.* Jefferson, N.C.: McFarland & Company.

Frobenius, Léo. 1936. *Histoire de la civilization africaine,* 3ed. Paris: Gallimard.

Garrett, Naomi. 1963. *The Renaissance of Haitian Poetry.* Paris: Présence Africaine.

Garvey, Marcus. 1923. Amy Jacques-Garvey (ed.). *The Philosophy and Opinions of Marcus Garvey*. New York: Universal Publishing House.

Gellner, Ernest. 1965. *Thought and Change*. London: Weidenfeld and Nicholson.

Gilroy, Paul. 1993. *The Black Atlantic: Modernity and Double-Consciousness*. Cambridge, Mass.: Harvard University Press.

Gleason, Judith. 1965. *This Africa: Novels by West Africans in English and French*. Evanston: Northwestern University Press.

Glissant, Edouard. 1956. "Aimé Césaire et la découverte du monde," in *Lettres Nouvelles* (Paris), January 1956.

———. 1981. *Le Discours antillais*. Paris: Seuil, 1981. Tr J. Michael Dash, *Caribbean Discourse: Selected Essays*. Charlottesville: University Press of Virginia. 1989.

Gordon, Lewis, T. Denean Sharpley-Whiting, and Renée T. White, eds. 1994, *Fanon: A Critical Reader*. Oxford: Blackwell Publishers.

Gore, Jeanne-Lydie (ed.). 1973. *Négritude africaine, négritude caraïbe*. Paris: Université de Paris-Nord, Centre d'Etudes Francophones.

Grevisse, Maurice. 1980. *Le Bon Usage: Grammaire française avec des remarques sur la langue française d'aujourd'hui*, 11ed. Paris-Gembloux: Duculot.

Griaule, Marcel. 1948. *Dieu d'eau: Entretiens avec Ogotemmêli*. Paris: Éditions du Chêne.

Gueye, Abdoulaye. 2001. *Les Intellectuels africains en France*. Paris:: L'Harmattan.

Guèye, Lamine. 1966. *Itinéraire africain*. Paris: Présence Africaine.

Guillen, Nicolas. 1947. *El Son Entero: suma poética, 1929-1946*. Buenos Aires: Editorial Pleamar.

_____. 1959 *Elégies et chansons cubaines*. Paris: Éditions Pierre Seghers.

Gusdorf, Georges. 1953. *Mythe et Métaphysique*. Paris: Payot.

Gyekye, Kwame. 1987. *An Essay on African Philosophical Thought: The Akan Conceptual Scheme*. Cambridge: Cambridge University Press. Rev. ed. Philadelphia: Temple UP, 1995.

Hallen, Barry, and Sodipo, J. Olubi. 1997. *Knowledge, Belief, Witchcraft: Analytical Experiments in African Philosophy*. Stanford: Stanford UP, 1997.

Hardy, Georges., 2005. *Une Conquête morale: l'enseignement en AOF. Présentation de J. P. Little*. Paris: L'Harmattan,

Harrow, Kenneth W. (ed.). 1996. *The Marabout and the Muse: New Approaches to Islam in African Literature*. Portsmouth, NH: Heinemann.

_____. 2004. "Rereading Camara Laye." *Research in African Literatures*. 35(3): 170-174.

Hazoumé, Paul. 1956. "L'âme du Dahoméen animiste révlée par sa religion." *Premier Congres des écrivains et artisites noirs*. Présence Africaine. 233-51.

Henriques, Fernando. 1951. "Colour Values in Jamaican Society." *British Journal of Sociology*. 2(2): 115-121.

Herskovits, Melville J. 1941. *The Myth of the Negro Past*. New York: Harper and Bros.

Hodgkin, Thomas Lionel. 1956. *Nationalism in Colonial Africa*. London: Muller.

Hough, Graham Goulden. 1970. *The Romantic Poets*, 3ed. London: Hutchinson.

Hountondji, Paulin. 1976. *Sur la "philosophie africaine".: critique de l'ethnophilosophie*. Paris: Maspero. Rpt. Yaoundé: CLE, 1980. Trans. by Henri Evans and Jonathan Rée as *African Philosophy: Myth and Reality*. Bloomington: Indiana UP, 1983. 2nd ed., with new preface, 1996.

_____. "La Vie quotidienne en Afrique noire: éléments d'une critique." *Albert Tévoèdjré, compagnon d'aventure.* Ed. Albert Ekué and Edmond Jouve. Paris: Berger-Levrault, 1988. Trans. as "Daily Life in Black Africa: Elements for a Critique." *The Surreptitious Speech.* Ed. V. Y. Mudimbe. Chicago: U of Chicago P, 1992. 344-64.

_____. "Démarginaliser." *Les Savoirs endogènes: pistes pour une recherche.* Dakar: CODESRIA, 1994. Trans. by Ayi Kwei Armah as *Endogenous Knowledge: Research Trails.* Dakar: CODESRIA, 1997.

_____. 1997. *Combat pour le sens.* Cotonou: Les Editions du Flamboyant.

_____. 1992. "Daily Life in Black Africa." in V.Y. Mudimbe, ed., *The Surreptitious Speech.* Chicago: Chicago University Press. 344-364.

Hughes, Langston. 1958. *The Langston Hughes Reader.* New York: G. Braziller.

_____ (ed.). 1960. *An African Treasury: articles, essays, stories, poems, by Black Africans.* New York: Crown Publishers.

_____ (ed.) 1963. *Poems from Black Africa.* Bloomington, IN: University of Indiana Press.

_____ and Arna Wendell Bontemps (eds.). 1970. *The Poetry of the Negro, 1746-1970.* Garden City, NY: Doubleday.

Hymans, Jacques Louis. 1971. *Léopold Sédar Senghor: An Intellectual Biography.* Edinburgh, UK: Edinburgh University Press.

Irele, F. Abiola. 1966. *Les Origines de Ie Négritude à la Martinique: Sociologie de l'oeuvre poétique d'Aimé Césaire* (Unpublished doctoral thesis, University of Paris).

_____. 1977. "Négritude: Philosophy of African Being." *Nigeria Magazine.* 122/123: 1-13.

_____. 1980. "Camara Laye: An Imagination Attuned to the Spiritual." *West Africa,* (London). April 7, pp. 617-618.

_____. 1981. *The African Experience in Literature and Ideology.* London: Heinemann.

_____. 2008. *Négritude et Condition Africaine.* Paris: Karthala.

_____. 2009 "The Poetic Legacy of Aimé Césaire." In *French Politics, Culture and Society.* Vol 27, No 3, Winter, 2009. 61-97

Ischinger, Barbara . 1974. "Négritude: Some Dissident Voices," *Issue.* 4, 4: 23-25

Jack, Belinda Elizabeth. 1996. *Francophone Literature: An Introductory Survey.* New York: Oxford University Press.

_____. 1996. *Negritude and Literary Criticism: The History and Theory of "Negro-African" Literature in French.* Westport: Greenwood Press, 1996.

Jacques, T. Carlos. 1995. "Is There an African Philosophy?" *The Centennial Review* 39.2 231-64.

Jahn, Janheinz. 1958. "Poetry in Rumba Rhythm." *Black Orpheus.* 3: 32-36. Rpt in Ulli Beier, 1967, 139-50

_____. 1961. *Muntu: An Outline of the Neo-African Culture.* London: Faber and Faber.

_____. 1968. *Neo-African Literature: A History of Black Writing.* New York: Grove Press.

James, Cyril Lionel Robert. 1980. *The Black Jacobins: Toussaint L'Ouverture and the San Domingo Revolution.* London: Allison and Busby.

Jameson, Fredric. *The Political Unconscious: Narrative as a Socially Symbolic Act.* Ithaca: Cornell UP, 1981.

Johnson, Barbara. 1994. *The Wake of Deconstruction.* Cambridge, MA: Blackwell.

Johnson, Paul. 1993. "Colonialism's Back—and Not a Moment Too Soon." *New York Times Magazine,* April 18, 1993.

Jones, Donna V. 2010. *The Racial Discourses of Life Philosophy: Négritude, Vitalism and Modernity.* New York: Columbia University Press.

Jules-Rosette, Bennetta. *Black Paris: The African Writers' Landscape.* Urbana: University of Illinois Press, 2000.

July, Robert William. 1968. *The Origins of Modern African Thought: Its Development in West Africa During the Nineteenth and Twentieth Centuries.* New York: Frederick A. Praeger.

Kagame, Alexis. 1956. *La Philosophie bantu-rwandaise de l'être.* Brussels, Belgium: Académie Royale des Sciences Coloniales.

_____. 1976. *La Philosophie bantu comparée.* Paris: Présence Africaine.

Kandé, Sylvie. 2000. *Lagon, lagunes: Tableau de mémoire.* Paris: Gallimard.

Kane, Cheikh Hamidou. 1971. *L'Aventure ambigüe.* Paris: Union Générale d'Éditions.

Kane, Mohammadou. 1982. *Roman africain et tradition.* Dakar: Nouvelles Editions Africaines.

Kardiner, Abram. 1946. *The Psychological Frontiers of Society,* 2ed. New York: Columbia University Press.

Kardiner, Abram and Lionel Ovesey. 1951. *The Mark of Oppression: A Psychological Study of the American Negro.* New York: Norton.

Kariuki, Josiah. 1963. *Mau Mau Detainee: the Account by a Kenya African of His Experiences in Detention Camps, 1953-1960.* London: Oxford University Press.

Keita, Lansana. 1974. "Two Philosophies of African History: Hegel and Diop." *Présence Africaine.* 91: 41-49.

Kennedy, Ellen Conroy, ed., 1975. *The Negritude Poets. An Anthology from the French.* New York: Thunder's Mouth Press.

Kenyatta, Jomo. 1962. *Facing Mount Kenya: The Tribal Life of the Gikuyu.* New York: Vintage Books.

Kesteloot, Lilyan. 1963. *Les Écrivains noirs de langue française: naissance d'une littérature.* Brussels: Université libre de Bruxelles, Institut de sociologie. Tr Ellen Conroy Kennedy,

Black Writers in French: A Literary History of Negritude. Washington D.C.: Howard University Press, 1991.

————. 1968. *Négritude et situation coloniale.* Yaundé, Cameroun: Éditions CLÉ.

Kimble, David. 1963. *A Political History of Ghana: The Rise of Gold Coast Nationalism, 1850-1928.* Oxford: Clarendon Press.

King, Adele. 2002. *Rereading Camara Laye.* Lincoln, NE: University of Nebraska Press.

Koffie, Niamey. 1980. "L'impensé de Towa et d'Hountondji." In Claude Sumner (ed.), *Actes du Séminaire sur la philosophie africaine, Addis Abéba, 1-3 décembre 1976.* Addis Ababa: Chamber Printing House for Addis Ababa University.

Kohn, Hans. 1944. *The Idea of Nationalism: A Study in Its Origins and Background.* New York: Macmillan.

Lamming, George. 1994. *The Emigrants.* Ann Arbor, MI: University of Michigan Press.

Lanternari, Vittorio. 1962. *Les Mouvements religieux des peuples opprimés.* Paris: Maspero. Lisa Sergio (trans.). *The Religions of the Oppressed: A Study of Modern Messianic Cults.* New York: Knopf, 1963.

Larrier, Renée. 2000. *Francophone Women Writers of Africa and the Caribbean.* Gainesville University Press of Florida, 2000.

Laye, Camara. 1953. *L'Enfant noir.* Tr James Kirkup. *The Dark Child.* London: Collins, 1955. Renamed *The African Child* in subsequent editions.

————. 1954. *Le Regard du roi, roman.* Paris: Plon. Trans. James Kirkup, *The Radiance of the King.* New York: New York Review Books, 2001.

Leclerc, Gérard. 1972. *Anthropologies et colonialisme: essai sur l'histoire de l'africanisme.* Paris: Fayard.

Legum, Colin. 1962. *Pan-Africanism: A Short Political Guide.* New York: Praeger.

Léro, Etienne. 1979. "Misères d'une poésie," *Légitime Défense*. Paris: Jean Michel Place.

Lévy-Bruhl, Lucien. 1922. *La Mentalité primitive*. Paris: Presses Universitaires de France. Trans. L. Clare, *Primitive Mentality*. New York: AMS Press, 1978.

———. 1949. *Carnets*. Paris: Presses Universitaires de France.

———. 1936. *Morceaux choisis*. Paris: Gallimard.

Lewis, Philip. 1982. "The Post-Structuralist Condition." *Diacritics*. 12: 2-24.

Lewis, Shireen K. 2006. *Race, Culture and Identity: Francophone West African and Caribbean Literature and Theory from Negritude to Creolité*. Lanham: Lexington Books.

Linton, Ralph (ed.). 1940. "The Distinctive Aspects of Acculturation." In *Acculturation in Seven American Indian Tribes*, pp. 501-520. New York: D. Appleton-Century Company.

——— (ed.). 1945. *The Science of Man in the World Crisis*. New York: Columbia University Press.

——— and Irving Hallowell. 1943. "Nativistic Movements." *American Anthropologist*. 45 (2) 230-240

Lionnet, Françoise. 2002. "Narrating the Americas: Transcolonial *Métissage* and Maryse Condé's *La Migration des cœurs*." In Monika Kaup and Debra J. Rosenthal (eds.), *Mixing Race, Mixing Culture: Inter-American Literary Dialogues*, pp. 65-87. Austin, TX: University of Texas Press.

Little, Janet Patricia. 2000. *Cheikh Hamidou Kane, L'Aventure ambiguë*. London: Grant and Cutler.

Lynch, Hollis Ralph. 1967. *Edward Wilmot Blyden: Pan-Negro Patriot, 1832-1912*. London: Oxford University Press.

Mabanckou, Alain. 1998. *Bleu-blanc-rouge: roman*. Paris: Présence Africaine

Malinowski, Bronislaw. 1961. *The Dynamics of Culture Change: An Inquiry into Race Relations in Africa*. New Haven, CT: Yale University Press.

Mannheim, Karl. [1930] 1968. *Ideology and Utopia: an Introduction to the Sociology of Knowledge*. Tr. Louis Wirth and Edward Shils. New York: Harcourt Brace.

Manning, Patrick, 2009. *The African Diaspora: A History Through Culture*. New York: Columbia University Press, 2009.

Mannoni, Octave. 1950. *Psychologie de la colonisation*. Paris: Seuil.

Maran, René. 1921. *Batouala: Véritable roman nègre*. Paris: Albin Michel.

Markovitz, Irving Leonard. 1969. *Léopold Sédar Senghor and the Politics of Négritude*. New York, Atheneum.

Marton, Imre. 1966. "De la Négritude au socialisme africain." *La Pensée*. 130: 3-10.

Masolo, D.A. 1994. *African Philosophy in Search opf Identity*. Bloomington, IN: Indiana University Press.

Mbembe, Achille. 2000. *De la Postcolonie: Essai sur l'imagination politique dans l'Afrique contemporaine*. Paris: Karthala. Trans. as *On The Postcolony: Studies in the History of Society and Culture*. Berkeley: U of California Press, 2001.

McKay, Claude. 1957. *Banjo: A Story Without a Plot*. New York: Harvest Books.

Melone, Thomas. 1962. *De la Négritude dans la littérature négro-africaine*. Paris: Présence Africaine.

Memmi, Albert. 1957. *Portrait du colonisé: précédé du portrait du colonisateur*. Paris: Buchet/Chastel.

Mensah-Sarbah, John. 1968. *Fanti Customary Laws*. London: Frank Cass.

Mezu, Sebastian Okechukwu. 1968. *Léopold Sédar Senghor et la défense et illustration de la civlisation noire*. Paris: M. Didier.

_____. 1972. "Senghor, Gobineau et l'inégalite des races humaines." *Abbia*. 26: 121-141.

Milcent, Ernest and Monique Sordet. 1969. *Léopold Sédar Senghor et la naissance de l'Afrique moderne*. Paris: Seghers.

Miller, Christopher L. 1985. *Blank Darkness: Africanist Discourse in French*. Chicago: Chicago University Press.

_____. 1990. *Theories of Africans: Francophone Literature and Anthropology in Africa*. Chicago: University of Chicago Press.

_____. 2008 *The French Atlantic Triangle: Literature and Culture of the Slave Trade*. Durham: Duke University Press.

Mittelhölzer, Edgar. 1964. *A Morning at the Office*. Harmondsworth, UK: Penguin

Montenegro, José. 1967. *A Négritude: dos mitos às realidades*. Braga, Portugal: Editôra Pax.

Moore, Gerald. 1962. *Seven African Writers*. London: Oxford University Press.

Mortimer, Edward. 1969. *France and the Africans*. London: Faber and Faber

Moudileno, Lydie. 2006 *Parades postcoloniales*. Paris: Karthala

Mphahlele, Ezekiel. 1974. *The African Image*. London: Faber.

Mudimbe, Valentin. 1967. "Physiologie de la Négritude." *Études Congolaises*. 10(5): 1-13.

Mulago, Vincent. 1973. *La Religion traditionelle des Bantu et leur vision du monde*. Kinshasa: Presses Universitaires du Zaire.

Myrdal, Gunnar. 1944. *An American Dilemma: The Negro Problem and Modern Democracy*, 9ed. New York: Harper.

Nadeau, Maurice. 1945. *Histoire du surréalisme*. Paris: Éditions du Seuil.

Nardal, Paulette, Louis Achille, Leo Sajous. 1992. *La Revue du Monde Noir/Review of the Black World: 1931-1932 Collection complète n 1 à 6*. Paris: Jean-Michel Place, 1992.

Nardal, Paulette. *Beyond Negritude: Essays from Women in the City*. Tr and edited by Tracy Sharpley-Whiting. New York: State University Press, 2009.

Ndaw, Alassane. 1983. *La Pensée africaine: recherche sur les fondments de la pensée négro-africaine.* Dakar: Nouvelles Editions Africaines.

Ndengue, Jean-Marie Abanda. 1970. *De la Négritude au négrisme: Essais polyphoniques.* Yaoundé, Cameroon: Éditions CLE.

Ndiaye, Pap. 2008 *La Condition noire: Essai sur une minorité Française.* Paris: Calmann Lévy.

Ngal, Georges. 1994. *Créations et rupture en littératures africaines.* Paris: Harmattan.

Nimrod. 2003. *Tombeau de Léopold Sédar Senghor.* Cognac: Le temps qu'il fait

Njami, Simon. 2006. *C'était Senghor.* Paris: Fayard.

Nkrumah, Kwame. 1964. *Consciencism.* London: Heinemann

Nyerere, Julius Kambarage. 1968. *Ujamaa: Essays on Socialism.* Dar es Salaam: Oxford University Press.

Ogot, Bethwell. 1963. "From Chief to President." *Transition.* 10: 26-30.

Okigbo, Christopher. 1962. *Heavensgate.* Ibadan, Nigeria: Mbari Publications.

Oladipo, Olusegun. 2001. "Knowledge and the African Renaissance." *Philosophia Africana* . 4.1: 61-67.

Olney, James. *Tell Me, Africa: An Approach to African Literature.* Princeton, N.J. Princeton University Press.

Park, Robert Ezra. 1950. *Race and Culture.* Glencoe, IL: Free Press.

Paul, Emmanuel C. 1956. "L'Ethnologie et les cultures noires." *Premier Congès International des Ecrivains et Artistes Noirs.* Paris: Présence Africaine. 8-10: 143-153.

Picon, Gaëtan. 1976. *Panorama de la nouvelle littérature française.* Paris: Gallimard.

Ploncard d'Assac, Jacques. 1965. *Doctrines du nationalisme.* Paris: Editions du Fuseau.

Price-Mars, Jean. 1928. *Ainsi parla l'oncle: Essais d'ethnographie.* Port-au-Prince, Haiti: Imprimerie de Compiègne.

Plaatje, Solomon Tshekisho. 1991. *Native Life in South Africa: Before and Since the European War and the Boer Rebellion.* Athens, OH: Ohio University Press.

Présence Africaine. 1972. *Colloque sur la négritude* Paris: Presence Africaine.

Rabemananjara, Jacques. 1956. "L'Europe et nous." *Premier Congès International des Ecrivains et Artistes Noirs.* Paris: Présence Africaine, 8-10: 20-28.

Ree, Jonathan. 2001. "The Translation of Philosophy." *New Literary History* 32.2: 223-57.

Reed, John. 1963. "Between Two Worlds." *Makerere Journal,* Kampala. 7.

Reinhardt, Catherine. 2007. *Claims to Memory: Beyond Slavery and Emancipation in the French Caribbean.* New York: Berghahm Books.

Reza-Villarello Rosa María. 1975. *Negritud y colonialismo cultural en Africa.* Mexico: Facultad de Ciencias Políticas y Sociales, Universidad Nacional Autónoma de México.

Ricard, Alain. 2004. Naomi Morgan (trans.). *The Languages and Literatures of Africa: The Sands of Babel.* Oxford: James Currey.

Rosello, Mireille. 1992. *Littérature et identité créole.* Paris: Karthala

Roumain, Jacques. 1945. *Bois-d'ébène.* Port-au-Prince, Haiti: Imprimeries H. Deschamps.

Said, Edward. 1979. *Orientalism.* New York: Vintage Books.

———. 1994. *Culture and Imperialism.* New York: Knopf.

Saint-Amour, Paul K. 2003. *The Copywrights: Intellectual Property and the Literary Imagination.* Ithaca, NY: Cornell University Press.

Sartre, Jean Paul. 1947. *Situations I.* Paris: Gallimard.

———. 1948. *Qu'est-ce que la littérature?* Paris: Gallimard.

_____. 1949. "Orphée noir." *Situations III*, pp. 229-230. Paris: Gallimard. Trans. Samuel Allen (trans.). *Black Orpheus*. Paris: Présence Africaine, 1963.

Scharfman, Ronnie Leah, 1980. *Engagement and the Language of the Subject in the Poetry of Aimé Césaire*. Gainesville: University of Florida Press.

Senghor, Léopold Sédar. 1945. "Défense de l'Afrique noire." *Esprit*. July.

_____. 1948a. *Anthologie de la nouvelle poésie nègre et malgache de langue française*. Paris: Presses Universitaires de France.

_____. 1948b. *Hosties noires*. Paris: Éditions du Seuil.

_____. 1956a. *Ethiopiques: Poèmes*. Paris: Éditions du Seuil.

_____. 1956b. "L'Esprit de la civilisation ou les lois de la culture négro-africaine." *Présence Africaine*. 8/10: 51-65.

_____. 1962a. "De la Négritude: Psychologie du Négro-africain." *Diogène*. 37: 3-16.

_____. 1962b. *Pierre Teilhard de Chardin et la politique africaine*. Paris: Éditions du Seuil.

_____. 1964a. "*Liberté 1: Négritude et humanisme*." Paris: Seuil.

_____. 1964b. On African Socialism. New York: Praeger.

_____. 1964b. John Reed and Clive Wake (trans.). *Selected Poems*. London: Oxford University Press.

_____. 1967. *Les Fondements de l'Africannité: ou, négritude et arabité*. Paris: Présence Africaine.

_____. 1971. *Liberté 2: Nation et voie africaine du Socialisme*. Paris: Seuil

_____. 1985. *Poèmes*. Paris: Seuil

_____. 1977. *Liberté 3: Négritude et Civilisation de l'Universel*. Paris: Seuil.

_____. 1983. *Liberté IV: Socialisme et Planification*. Paris: Seuil.

_____. 1993. *Liberté V: Le Dialogue des cultures*. Paris: Seuil.

_____. 1976[1965]. John Reed and Clive Wake (trans.). *Prose and Poetry*. London: Heinemann Educational.

_____. 1986. "The Revolution of 1889 and Leo Frobenius." in Isaac Mowoe and Richard Bjornson, eds., *Africa and the West: The Legacies of Empire*. New York: Greenwood Press.

_____. 1991. *The Collected Poetry of Léopold Sédar Senghor*. Translated with an Introduction by Melvin Dixon. Charlottesville: University of Virginia Press.

Serequeberhan, Tsenay. 1994. *The Hermeneutics of African Philosophy: Horizon and Discourse*. New York: Routledge.

Sharpley-Whiting, Denean T. 2002. *Negritude Women*. Minneapolis: University of Minnesota Press.

Sow, Alpha I., Ola Balogun, and Honorat Aguessy. 1977. "Prolégomènes." *Introduction à la culture africaine: aspects généraux*. Paris: Union Générale d'Editions.

Soyinka, Wole. 1963. *The Lion and the Jewel*. London, Oxford University Press.

_____. 1976. *Myth, Literature and the African World*. Cambridge: Cambridge University Press.

_____. 1988. *Art, Dialogue and Outrage*. Ibadan: New Horn Press.

_____. 1999. *The Burden of Memory: The Muse of Forgiveness*. New York: Oxford University Press.

Stonequist, Everett V. 1937. *The Marginal Man: A Study in Personality and Culture Conflict*. New York: C. Scribner's Sons.

Stovall, Tyler. 1996. *Paris Noir: African Americans in the City of Light*. Boston: Houghton Mifflin Company

Taoua, Phyllis. 2002. *Forms of Protest: Anti-Colonialism and Avant-Gardes in Africa the Caribbean, and France*. Portsmouth: Heinemann.

Taylor, John Vernon. 1963. *The Primal Vision: Christian Presence Amid African Religion*. London: SCM Press.

Tchikaya U Tamsi, 1978. *Le Mauvais Sang,* suivi de *Feu de brousse* et *A triche-coeur.* Paris: L'Harmattan.

Tempels, Placide. 1949. A. Rubbens (Trans.). *La Philosophie bantoue.* Paris: Présence Africaine.

_____. 1952. *Bantu Philosophy.* Tr Colin King. Paris: Présence Africaine.

Tévoédjré, Albert. 1958. *L'Afrique révoltée.* Paris: Présence Africaine.

Thomas, Louis-Vincent. 1963. "Une Idéologie moderne: la Négritude." *Revue des Psychologie des Peuples.* 3ᵉ Trimestre, 1963. 246-72.

Thompson, Vncent Bakpetu. 1974. *Africa and Unity: The Evolution of Pan-Africanism.* London: Longman.

Tidjani-Serpos, Nouréini. 2004. "Création littéraire et imitation." *Archéologie du savoir négro-africain.* Paris: AFRIDIC.

Towa, Marcien. 1971a. *Essai sur la problématique philosophique dans l'Afrique actuelle.* Yaoundé, Cameroon: Editions CLE.

_____. 1971b. *Léopold Sédar Senghor: Négritude ou Servitude.* Yaoundé, Cameroon: Editions CLE.

_____. 1979. *L'Idée d'une philosophie négro-africaine.* Yaoundé, Cameroon: Editions CLE.

Van Niekerk, Barend van Dyk. 1970. *The African Image in the Work of Léopold Sédar Senghor.* Cape Town, South Africa: A. A. Balkema.

Vendler, Helen Hennessy. 1997. *The Art of Shakespeare's Sonnets.* Cambridge, MA: Belknap Press of Harvard University Press.

Vickers, Brian. 2002. *Shakespeare, Co-Author: A Historical Study of Five Collaborative Plays.* New York: Oxford University Press.

Wagenbach, Klaus. 2003. Ewald Osers (trans.). *Kafka.* Cambridge, MA: Harvard University Press.

Wagley, Charles and Marvin Harris. 1958. *Minorities in the New World: Six Case Studies*. New York: Columbia University Press.

Wagner, Jean. 1963. *Les Poètes nègres des États-Unis: le sentiment racial et religieux dans la poésie de P. L. Dunbar á L. Hughes (1890-1940)*. Paris: Librairie Istra.

Wilder, Gary. 2005. *The French Imperial Nation-State: Negritude and Colonial Humanism Between the Two World Wars*. Chicago: The University of Chicago Press.

Williams, Eric Eustace. 1966[1944]. *Capitalism and Slavery*. New York: Capricorn Books.

Wiredu, Kwasi. 1980. *Philosophy and an African Culture* . Cambridge: Cambridge University Press.

_____. "Toward Decolonizing African Philosophy and Religion." *African Studies Review*. http://web.africa.ufl.edu/asq/v1/4/3.htm.

_____. 1996. *Cultural Universals and Particulars: An African Perspective*. Bloomington: Indiana University Press.

Wright, Richard. 1940. *Native Son*, 4ed. New York: Harper.

_____. 1954. *Black Power: A Record of Reactions in a Land of Pathos*. New York: Harper.

_____. 1956. "Tradition and Industrialization: The Plight of the Tragic Elite in Africa." *Présence Africaine*. 8-10: 347-360.

Yai, Olabiyi Babalola. 1978. "Théorie et pratique en philosophie africaine: Misère de la philosophie spéculative." *Présence Africaine*. 108: 65-91.

INDEX

❦